The China Development Model

Also by Dominique de Rambures

LES SYSTEMES DE PAIEMENT

LES TRANSFERTS DES MIGRANTS

CHINE, LE GRAND ECART

PAYMENT SYSTEMS (*with Alec Nacamuli*)

The China Development Model

Between the State and the Market

Dominique de Rambures

palgrave
macmillan

Softcover reprint of the hardcover 1st edition 2015 978-1-137-46548-1

First published 2015 by
PALGRAVE MACMILLAN

Palgrave Macmillan in the UK is an imprint of Macmillan Publishers Limited, registered in England, company number 785998, of Houndmills, Basingstoke, Hampshire RG21 6XS.

Palgrave Macmillan in the US is a division of St Martin's Press LLC, 175 Fifth Avenue, New York, NY 10010.

Palgrave Macmillan is the global academic imprint of the above companies and has companies and representatives throughout the world.

Palgrave® and Macmillan® are registered trademarks in the United States, the United Kingdom, Europe and other countries.

ISBN 978-1-349-49955-7 ISBN 978-1-137-46549-8 (eBook)
DOI 10.1057/9781137465498

This book is printed on paper suitable for recycling and made from fully managed and sustained forest sources. Logging, pulping and manufacturing processes are expected to conform to the environmental regulations of the country of origin.

A catalogue record for this book is available from the British Library.

A catalog record for this book is available from the Library of Congress.

Typeset by MPS Limited, Chennai, India.

Contents

List of Tables, Figures and Boxes

Tables

Figure

Boxes

List of Abbreviations and Acronyms

ABC	Agricultural Bank of China
ACFTU	All-China Federation of Trade Unions
AMC	assets management company
BOC	Bank of China
BOCOM	Bank of Communications
CBRC	China Banking Regulatory Committee
CCB	China Construction Bank
CCP	Chinese Communist Party
CDB	China Development Bank
CIC	China Investment Corporation
CIT	communication and information technology
CITIC	China International Trust and Investment Corporation
ETF	Exchange Traded Fund
EU	European Union
FDI	foreign direct investment
FPLG	Financial Leading Group of the Party
GDP	gross domestic product
GIC	Government Investment Company
GNP	gross national product
HKMA	Hong Kong Monetary Authority
HSBC	Hong Kong and Shanghai Banking Corporation
HST	high-speed train
ICBC	Industrial and Commercial Bank of China
ICBC	Industrial and Commercial Bank of China
IPO	initial public offering
ITC	information and telecommunication
NAFTA	North America Free Trade Agreement
NBFI	non-banking financial institution

NBS	National Bureau of Statistics
NDRC	National Development and Reform Commission
NFSS	National Fund of Social Security
NSSF	National Social Security Fund
NGO	non-governmental organization
NLA	National Liberation Army
PBOC	People's Bank of China
PNA	People's National Assembly
PPP	purchasing power parity
PRC	People's Republic of China
PX	paraxylen
R&D	research and development
RCC	rural credit cooperative
SAFE	State Agency of Foreign Exchange
SASAC	State-owned Assets Supervision and Administration Commission
SEA	Special Economic Area
SEZ	Special Economic Zone
SMCI	Stock Market Index
SOB	state-owned banks
SOE	state-owned enterprise
SSE	Shanghai Stock Exchange
TPP	Trans-Pacific Partnership
TVE	township and village enterprise
UK	United Kingdom
USA	United States of America
WHO	World Health Organization
WMP	wealth management product
WTO	World Trade Organization

Introduction

A Barbarian who knows the rites is Chinese. A Chinese who doesn't know their rites is a Barbarian.
(Chinese saying)

According to Tocqueville, who had been through several revolutions, 'the most dangerous time for a government is the time when it starts reforming itself'. Over the last 30 years, China has been reforming its economy at breakneck speed; nonetheless, nothing has changed in its institutional framework. It is hard to believe that the communist regime has not changed at all while everything else has changed so dramatically. In China, as in every other country, a period of reformation is a crucial time. Confucius' answer when a student asked him what he would do should he be in charge of the government is well-known: 'I would start by checking names.' Obviously, Confucius (Kong Fu zi) did not intend to rewrite the dictionary but to make sure that words fit with what they are supposed to mean. His close follower Mencius (Meng zi) used to say: 'If words communicate the truth, that's enough' and 'I hate the things which are not what they are supposed to be.' (XV-41). Not all members of the Chinese Communist Party are devout Confucian, but they know the power of words.

China is no more a market (*shi*) economy *per se*, than it is a democracy (*min zhu*). Moreover, there is no indication that China is moving in that direction. The few features of formal democracy and market economy are not designed to build up a market economy or a pluralistic democracy. Rather, they are there to improve the performances of the Chinese economy and strengthen governmental power. China has all the predicates of a pluralist democracy and a free market. A dozen political parties are authorized along with the Chinese Communist

Party (CCP) within the so-called 'National Front'. Some members of the government even come from one of these parties (though only in marginal positions); the number of members of these non-communist parties is far beyond the imagination of any Western political party. The 1982 Constitution guarantees freedom of speech, freedom of meeting and freedom of religion. Furthermore, 1985 legislation states that low-level officials of the State and the Party should be elected with a further directive stating that the number of candidates should be greater than the number of *positions to be filled*! This is not enough to make a fully fledged democracy. China has implemented such market instruments as 'privatization' of state-owned banks and companies, free prices, liberalization of interest rates and deregulation of the stock market. However, it is not enough to make a fully fledged market economy. Actual market instruments are only tools at the disposal of the Party-State to improve the performance of the Chinese economy. 'The State intervenes in the market and the companies are steered by the market' (Zhao Zi yang); 'The market is within the Plan as a bird in its cage' (Chen Yun).

Party members are experts in manipulating such fetish words as 'real democracy', 'market economy', 'socialism with Chinese characteristics', 'law and order', and so on. When one talks about 'democracy' to the average citizen, the response is: 'fight against corruption, against inequalities, limitation of local officials' power ...' They do not expect to participate in the decision making process but, rather, to be heard. When one talks about 'democracy' to a Party member, the answer is 'decentralization', as though transferring certain responsibilities to lower levels would be a form of democracy. Far from being a sign of democracy, 'decentralization' sounds to most of the Chinese to be the sign of an increased source of corruption of local Party members. Thanks to the Emperor yesterday, the Party today, the 'Centre' is expected to be a shield against the wrongdoings of local officials, whether they are Mandarins or Party members.

The ideas of political reform in the 1980s – when Deng Xiaoping needed the support of the intellectuals and the reformists – appear to have been short-lived. The links between Deng and the reformists had already broken down long before the June 1989 Tien An Men Square events. Deng did not hesitate to sacrifice his closest associates: Hu Yaobang, the former General Secretary was forced to resign in 1987, Zhao Zi Yang, a former Prime Minister then General Secretary (Hu's successor) in 1989. Deng was not a Liberal (neither in the European nor the American sense); neither was he a supporter of a free market or free enterprise, or a Democrat. In fact, he was a devout Communist who dedicated his whole life to the Party, served Mao faithfully and gave a hand to the witch hunt whenever necessary. He was demoted twice by Mao, twice recalled but was not physically eliminated like Liu Shaoqi (the former President) because he always turned out to be useful at the right time. On several occasions, Deng made the point that a pluralistic regime of checks and balances, powers and counter-powers, was not suited to govern China or implement the policy of reform and opening-up.

Today, the Communist regime is no longer 'communist' *stricto senso*: the government rule is still Communist, but the ideology is not. Lacking any ideology at all, the CCP is delegitimized. The only ideology which may link the Party and the People is a mix of 'economic growth' and 'fussy nationalism'. The transition period is no more intermediary but it is becoming a sort of 'continuous revolution', as it used to be in Marxist *doxia*. If the mechanics are broken down or merely slowing, the whole system collapses; the more the market is 'privatized', the more the Party tightens its grip over society.

The notion that economic reform naturally leads to political reform as well, or that capitalism is leading to democracy, is not confirmed by history. Democracy is not, and has never been, the final goal of the reform policy. Market instruments and democratic rituals are made to reinforce the Party's influence. The marketization and the monetarization of the economy provide fresh opportunities for Party officials to extend their power and wealth. The top leadership is now hereditary. The 'Princelings' (*taizi*), the sons of the former Party veterans, have monopolized government appointments. Mao's grand-daughter, Kong Dong-mei, is now a very successful real estate investor. To a brilliant student, the Party University is the *voie royale* (royal road) to a successful career, similar to the imperial examinations for the Mandarins. The local party leaders become rich by purchasing farmers' lands at knockdown prices and reselling it at market price to a real estate dealer or an industrial investor once the building permit has been granted.

But it is increasingly difficult for the Party to recruit local members because the positions are not sufficiently well-paid. Local officials stay in office long enough to build up a network of connections (*guanxi*) which could be profitable once they move on to the private sector. The heads of all state-owned companies (SOEs) are Party members. The owner of a successful private company must join the Party. The résumé of an ambitious Party member, a candidate chasing top positions, must include the management of a province and/or the management of a large SOE. A new class of technocrats has been formed that includes high-ranking bureaucrats involved in business or administration. They are tightly knit and highly dependent on economic growth and party privileges.

Private companies, whether individual, small/medium-sized or hi-tech start-ups are not 'free', since they are heavily dependent on local party members. Foreign companies contribute to the increasingly deteriorating environment: corruption, nepotism, destruction of natural resources, a lack of labour regulations, no labour contract, wages paid late – or not at all. JP Morgan is being prosecuted by the SEC, the US Stock Exchange supervisor, because they hired family members of Chinese leaders. The stealing of foreign patents is common practice. If they bring the case before a court, foreign companies are often condemned for stealing their own patents which, in the meantime, have become 'Chinese'. In such an event, good connections are more helpful than a fair trial. Most appellants send a claim directly to the highest echelons of the Party through a memorandum. This is a very ancient practice which dates back to imperial times when a subject was allowed to report the wrongdoings of a local Mandarin directly to the Emperor himself. Today, the Party deals with more cases than the courts.

Nonetheless, the Chinese growth model has so far proved to be a success story. Performance is astounding: an average growth rate of 7 per cent over the last 30 years, 10 per cent + over the last 10 years, 7.8 (7.5 %) per cent in 2013 after a double-dip crisis. From the Western point of view, there are ample reasons why the Chinese model should not be workable ... but it works nonetheless. The CCP managed not only to produce economic growth, but also to maintain a stable political and social environment. According to an IMF report, China has contributed over 50 per cent to the world growth rate over the past five years. Poverty, famines, epidemics and illiteracy have disappeared. Recurring droughts and floods have been brought under control. A middle class of 300–400 million people has emerged, equivalent to the entire population of the European Union (EU) – twice as many as the United States of America (USA). A potential market of up to 1,370 million people is hardly touched by marketization and mass consumption. China has now returned to the narrow circle of the Great Powers. China has more scientists than the USA or the EU. Chinese companies are buying back crisis-stricken companies from the West at low market prices.

To know where China is going, we must first establish from whence she has come. China missed the Industrial Revolution: a number of researchers have tried to explore the actual reasons for this. Perhaps it would be more sensible to ask why it was Great Britain that had an Industrial Revolution and not China. Some may say that the Chinese system reached a kind of perfection which made reforms unappealing, if not dangerous. The purpose of this work was not to sort out such a critical issue but, rather, to act as a reminder of the tragic events of the last two centuries, which nearly destroyed China several times. The two Opium Wars (1840 and 1859); the Taiping Revolution (1854–70); the first Japanese war and the disastrous Treaty of Shimonoseki (1894–95); the Hundred Days Reform (1898); the Boxer Rebellion (1900); the fall of the Empire and the birth of the Republic (1911–12), the dictatorship of General Yuan Shekai (1912–16), the reign of the War Lords (1917–27); the invasion and occupation of Manchuria by the Japanese Imperial Army of Kwantung (1931); World War II (1937–45), which started three years before the Western democracies; the Civil War (1947–49); the 'anti-rightist' campaign; the Hundred Flowers movement (1956); the Great Leap Forward (1958–60); the Cultural Revolution (1966–76).

Climatic events – flood, drought and famine – also impacted China. In 1855, the Yellow River (*Huang He*) changed its course, resulting in the deaths of millions of people when the river mouth moved from north to south of the Shandong peninsula; it moved back again in 1948. But the main reason is institutional: China benefited from all necessary natural and human resources but it did not build up institutions indispensable to the stimulation of economic growth to go beyond the take-off point.

In order to quantify the (positive or negative) 'externalities' which decrease or increase transaction costs, one must reflect on the institutional context and the historical legacy. Production costs are dependent on technical factors, but transaction costs are dependent on institutional factors. Spreading corruption, lack of the Rule of Law, lack of patent protection and informal credit, and so on, may increase or decrease the cost of transaction or reinforce (or decelerate) the rate of growth. When an illegal payment is made, it may be positive if it makes the completion of the transaction easier, or negative if the transaction becomes more expansive or lengthier.

According to the great historian Sima Qian (126–85 BC), author of the *Shi ji* (*Historical Memoirs*), China's history is just a set of recurrent cycles of unity and disunity, somewhat similar to Arnold Toynbee's 12 volumes of *Study of History*, but with a major proviso: every time a dynasty collapsed, a new one was born so that China's history kept repeating itself over the centuries. A new dynasty was born, grew and collapsed. After a period of chaos, a strong man reunited the country through iron and blood. A new dynasty was born and the set of dynastical cycles resumes its course. As the new Emperor was either a foreign Barbarian (Mongol, Manchu, Jurchen ...), or an uneducated Chinese general or a soldier of fortune, he needed the support of the literati established all over the country to rule over such a large territory and such a numerous people.

In 1820, China accounted for 35 per cent of the world's GNP while the USA hardly reached 4 per cent. In 1945, it was the opposite. The USA accounted for 30 per cent of the world's GDP and China only 2 per cent. Today, China is the second-largest economy in terms of GDP (27 per cent). A new cycle started 30 years ago. But Chinese growth is backed by a wide and still-virgin market, while the US market is credit-addicted and almost saturated. For example, the car market penetration ratio amounts to 98 per cent of the US market and 3 per cent of the Chinese market. Quite often, the Chaos Cycle is not necessarily a lost century. When the central state is weaker, the country seems to be released from her social straightjacket and free to explore new avenues. Between the fall of the Empire (1911) and the victory of the Communist armies (1949), China had experienced a blossoming 50 years in the fields of science, literature, foreign influence, technological progress and industrial ventures. Generally speaking, in spite of a stable (not to say frozen) institutional context, the Chinese have managed to demonstrate a remarkable capacity for adaptation and recovery.

To produce the very specific context which allowed the rebirth of the Chinese economy, both Mao and Deng Xiaoping were needed – the bloody tyrant who destroyed the Old World, and the reformist who built up a New World out of the ashes of the Old. As with the Roman Empire, the first signs that a declining dynasty has reached its zenith are visible when the Centre is no longer able to run such a large country; it is forced to release its tight grip over the bureaucratic system and the armies standing on the borders – armies composed of experienced Barbarian fighters headed by foreign generals.

Throughout China's history, the relationship between the Centre and the Country has been the key to Chinese politics. The CCP is the first political party to design a system strong enough to resolve the contradiction: a decentralized bureaucracy combined with a centralized one-party system. This is the reason why there was – and there will be – no 'demaotization' process. Mao's statues are still standing on every avenue and at every crossroads, the same canonical statue of a forever-young Mao in a long coat, right hand raised. His picture can still be seen attached to taxi drivers' keys and in houses, shops or offices, as a protective *shen* (*daimon*). His birth place, Shaonan in Hunan, is a site of massive pilgrimage. Mao used to compare himself to the first Emperor, Qin Shi Huangdi (259–10 BC). A bloody and uneducated tyrant who presided over the burning of books along with their authors! He turned farmers into slaves, changed the writing system (*heresy*) to make it more convenient, unified the system of weights and measures, and spread the use of a single currency.

China's Empire lasted over 50 centuries, with each new dynasty becoming embedded in the institutions inherited from its predecessor. After the fall of the Qing dynasty, a foreign (*mandchu*) dynasty, the usual period of chaos lasted 50 years (1911–49) until the country was reunited and a new dynasty emerged. In just one century, China experienced all existing forms of governance; the enlightened autocracy during the late Empire; the British model of constitutional monarchy during the last few years of the Empire; an American style of republic (1911–27); a Nationalist, Fascist type regime (1927–49) and the present popular democracy (1949). For years, it was widely agreed that the key ingredient for economic take-off was the importance of natural resources (e.g. coal mining in Great Britain). Now, human resources are more important, more 'profitable' for Chinese society as a whole rather than raw materials. This follows the Asian tigers – Japan in the 1960s, Korea in the 1970s. It is now China's turn.

Many times throughout the centuries, China has been invaded and every time she recovered because China has never been a colony. She never inherited an artificial foreign model of governance. 'The main point of making a modern state was to resist foreign domination by using some of the foreigners' own technologies of dominance, both material and societal.'[1] Pragmatic, open-minded, cured from past ideological constraints, her new leaders have carefully studied what has been achieved in foreign countries. This is particularly true among her neighbouring 'Asian tigers' (Japan, Korea, Taiwan, Singapore), from whom China's leaders picked up what could best serve Chinese interests. Nothing escaped from the wave of reforms – nothing but the Party itself.

Chinese 'hubris' is opposed to Western 'autism'. As a sort of specular effect, Westerners have repeatedly tried to bring China back into a European-driven history. From the eighteenth century onwards, Europe has built up a particular idea of China. For the then European elite, China is by nature and by definition the 'Other'. For Leibnitz, due to the ideogram writing system, the Chinese language was the best candidate to become the global universal language. Everyone can understand the Chinese ideogram even if they do not speak Chinese. For Voltaire, the Chinese Emperor epitomized the ideal of the wise king. This ideal dated as far back as Plato, a model of the 'enlightened despot' of his time: consider also Frederic II, Joseph II, Catherine II. For the Jesuits, Confucianism was close to the Christian faith. When they came to translate the Bible, as there is no 'God' in Chinese thought, they used the character *Tien* which means 'Heaven', rather than 'God'. Western intellectuals expected the Far East to remedy the sins of their time. In the second half of the nineteenth century, it was the turn of the Chinese to search out what was missing from their own backward country from their Western counterparts. In the 'Hundred Days Reform' (1898), the young Emperor Guangxu and a group of reformists tried to transfer Western techniques to China en masse, something similar to the Meiji Revolution. The attempt was brutally crushed by the Dowager Empress Ci Xi, supported by General Yuan Shekai, who would later become the president of the Republic in 1912. Chinese intellectuals sought to create a mix of 'Western technology' and 'Eastern wisdom'. Intellectuals debated whether China should follow the Western path, or work out a path of its own ('with Chinese characteristics'). China is asking questions to which we cannot provide an answer because we do not possess the words and concepts required to express it.

The present situation is more or less a reminder of the crisis of the 1930's, when the capitalist model of democratic countries was near exhaustion and a number of countries, as a result, were experiencing alternative models such as fascism or communism. This crisis led to a world war and the death of 50 million people. The mechanics which led to World War II are the same as they are today – the race to access to raw materials.

In Chinese, the translation of the word 'economy' is '*Jing shi*', a character made of two ancient signs, *shi* (*shi*) *ji* (*min*) , meaning 'put [the world] in order and help [the people]'. This is the state's responsibility. In Greek, 'economy' translates to '*oikonomia*' which is 'the management (*nomos*) of the household (*oikos*)' (i.e. the statist system on one hand, and the liberal system on the other). In China, 'freedom' is translated to '*zi you*', which means: 'to be oneself', a definition which would undoubtedly suit a Stoic from the Hellenistic world. It would not, however, suit a classical thinker like Aristotle, for whom 'freedom' is the privilege of a City-State citizen, who can (and must) participate in the decision making process of the City. In China, liberty is 'what Man is made of when he is born' (Mencius). A man becomes a man when he manages to keep control of his passions thanks to education under the teachings of a Master. As words can sometimes be misleading, we must extend our study from China's 'growth' model to her 'development' model.

1
What is the Socialist Market Economy?

The truth is not pleasant. Pleasant words are not the truth.
(Lao seu)

For any sensible mind, the term 'socialist market economy' is an oxymoron the two adjectives conflict. This definition appeared relatively late – in 1992, during the 14th National Congress of the Communist Party of China – as the policy of reform and opening that began in 1978. Up to this point, one spoke of a 'commodity economy' to avoid using the words 'market economy', which were taboo. The 'market economy' was discovered before the word was used. The policy of 'reform and opening' was meant to be a transition, but a transition to what? Towards socialism, or towards capitalism? It took Poland three years to complete what China has not yet achieved in thirty. The word 'transition' is the only stable part of the policy of reform – a sort of new 'perpetual permanent revolution', to paraphrase Lenin. However, the idea that something goes from A to B is not consistent with the traditional Chinese way of thinking. Everything is ephemeral; all events are part of a continuum without a beginning or an end. Everything forms part of the flow of the eternal stream of all things. Nothing is fixed, not even the truth – which is contingent by definition.

According to a former prime minister of the People's Republic of China, Wen Jiabao (2002–12): 'the complete wording of our economic policy is to let the market play its role within the allocation process of resources under macroeconomic policy and government regulations'. Any other country may comply with such a vague definition; there is no such thing as an economy that is market-driven on the one hand and command-driven on the other. There are, however, countries which are either market-driven or government-driven to varying degrees. If we were to draw a line where countries' economies are ranked according to whether they are market-driven or government-driven and include the United States of America (USA) and the United Kingdom (UK) on the one hand, and Cuba and North Korea on the other, where does China stand and in which direction is she moving?

Theoretically, a market economy should lead to capitalism and democracy (as proposed by Schumpeter). A market economy needs to be backed not only by private property, free prices, an absence of government interference and an absence of monopolies, but also by free enterprise, freedom of speech and freedom of innovation. Citizens vote with their ballot; consumers vote with their money. In a market economy, the leading forces work in a bottom-up scenario through the choices of decentralized consumers and entrepreneurs.

Given that words do not have the same meaning within the Great Wall as outside it, what is the status of a company both legally and actually? Every form of legal status is authorized: privately-owned companies, public companies, state-owned companies, individual companies; cooperatives; mixed companies, where private investors are owners together with the government itself; government agencies or local communities. But neither a monopoly situation nor public services are useful criteria in this matter since, ultimately, the government maintains a firm grip on any company, be it directly or indirectly. When the 1984 Company Law was passed, it was understood that the goal was to 'keep the large companies within government control and let the small ones go to the private sector'. But some 'small' companies have grown into 'large' ones, especially in the field of hi-tech or internet business: Alibaba, Baidu, Sina, Taobao. These developments take place while industrial sectors remain under direct government control, even though they have with public service or state monopoly. The legal statute does not provide any information as to the make-up of shareholders. A number of 'private' companies are actually owned by government entities. The government can interfere in many different ways and through many different intermediaries. In every case, the managers are appointed by the Party. In any company, there is a Party cell and a Trade Union cell, both reporting to the Party. There is a single Chinese Trade Union (the All-China Federation of Trade Unions – ACFTU) affiliated to the Party. Trade unions do not exist to support workers' interests but, rather, to prevent labour conflicts. A public company is not a company whose ownership has shifted from government to private investors, but a company which is run in accordance with the capitalist management model: autonomous management, competition, market-driven pricing, management targets expressed in terms of profits, market share, accountability, and so on. All major decisions, from the appointment of top managers to strategic planning, from investment programming to mergers and acquisitions, must be approved by the Party's Human Resources department or the Party National Development and Reform Commission (NRDC) – the powerful government agency which took the place of the former Planning Administration.

In the second half of the nineteenth century, China felt the urgent need to reform by importing Western technologies. Following the Taiping Rebellion which lasted 10 years (1854–1863), starting in Nanking, the Rebellion almost reached Beijing and almost toppled the Qing dynasty. The Imperial regime was seriously shaken and weakened, both internally and externally. The central government being too weak, the onus was on the local governors to break down the Taiping rebels by collecting taxes, raising money and armies, building up arsenals and shipyards, buying modern weaponry and recruiting foreign instructors. It was also the burden of the same generation of local Mandarins – such as Zeng Guofan (1811–71), Zuo Zongtang (1812–85) and Li Hongzhang (1823–1901) (who would go on to become Prime Minister) – to initiate the reform movement. After the disastrous Treaty of Shimonoseki (1894) which ended the Japanese war (1994), the local governors undertook the Industrial Revolution in their respective provinces, disregarded the central government's neglect along with Chinese merchants and foreign experts or mercenaries. 'Oversight by Mandarins, management by merchants'; 'Western technology, Chinese wisdom'. In 1918, thanks to World War I, Shanghai's shipyards were the largest in the world.

Under the rule of Chiang Kai-shek (Jiang Je-shi) (1927–49), the largest Western banks were, de facto, nationalized. They were under the control of the wealthy Generalissimo's brothers-in-law, T.S. Koong (the brother of Chiang's wife) and H.H. Kung (the husband of Chiang's wife's sister), alternatively and successively Minister of Finance and President of the Central Bank. Initially, Koong was Minister of Finance and Kung, a former banker was head of the central bank. Subsequently, Koong and Kung exchanged posts. War bonds were included in the bank reserve requirements. As the interest rates of the government bonds were higher than the interest rates charged to the customers, and because Chinese banks were required to subscribe to the government bonds, Chinese firms were starved of credit finance.

The 'policy of reform and opening' undertaken by Deng Xiaoping and his fellow reformists was mostly inspired by neighbouring countries such as Japan and the 'Asian Tigers' (South Korea, Taiwan and

Singapore). Reform was to support the concentration of big firms, one or two in each industrial sector behind the Great Wall of custom barriers such as the Japanese *zaibatsu* and the Korean *chaebols*. The plan was then to expose the most successful to the foreign markets and to international competition once they had achieved sufficient turnover and productivity levels.

Once state-owned companies are listed on the stock exchange, the aim is not to change ownership from that of government to private investors but, rather, to mop up the high level of saving by government target industries and to impose market discipline on management while keeping overall control of the companies. Whatever the company's legal status, it remains under government control. Only between 5 per cent and 10 per cent of the shares are floated. Of these, only one third of the shares are tradable. The volume of shares available to 'private' investors is quite limited and is sufficient to supply a fully-fledged, well-fed stock market. The stock shares owned by foreigners in Chinese companies cannot exceed 20 per cent, and such shareholders have no say regarding the company management. The newly issued bank shares are frozen by means of a three- to five-year lock-up provision. In joint ventures, foreign shareholders are always granted minority participations. Given the unofficial backing of the government and the quasi state guarantee, there is no major difference between stocks and bonds. In most cases, the new shareholders are government institutions. The public auction for new infrastructures (subsequent to the rescue package) is normally reserved to government-owned companies. In a 2013 directive, the government instructed state-owned companies to pay a minimum 5 per cent profit to the shareholders (including state and government entities).

The China Merchant Bank, a 100 per cent government-owned bank, was 'privatized' in 2003 through an initial public offering (IPO) on the Shanghai Stock Exchange and further, in 2009, on the Hong Kong Stock Exchange. No more than 15 per cent of the stock was sold and it was mostly subscribed to by *policy banks* such as the China Development Bank, state-owned banks such as the Bank of Communications (BOCOM), China Construction Bank (CCB) and Bank of China (BOC) or government entities such as the State Agency of Foreign Exchange (SAFE), the State-owned Assets Supervision and Administration Commission (SASAC), the China Investment Corporation (CIC), Huijin (which is part of CIC), and various large foreign banks subscribed to early IPOs through private placements priced below market value. These banks comprised, among others, Goldman Sachs in the Industrial and Commercial Bank of China (ICBC), the Bank of America and the Royal Bank of Scotland in CCB, the Hong Kong and Shanghai Banking Corporation (HSBC) in BOCOM, Crédit Agricole in the Agricultural Bank of China (ABC), J.P.Morgan in the China International Trust and Investment Corporation (CITIC). They soon realized that the price of shares was too expensive when compared with the expected benefits: their investment did not provide them any influence on bank strategy and did not open the Chinese market to foreign shareholders. More often than not, the companies with the most important shareholders did not hesitate to form affiliated companies with their competitors. Most of them tried to resell their shares once the lock-out period had come to an end.

Local communities were often shareholders of industrial or banking institutions. In some cases, the venture was initiated by local authorities to meet local needs. In the early 1980s, following agricultural reform (*household contract* or *household responsibility*), farmers were free to leave the collective *communes* and *production teams*. Most local communities had to form local companies known as 'Township and Village Enterprises' (TVEs) to meet the needs of the newly independent peasants. In the 1980s, the TVE sowed the first seeds of private capitalism 'with Chinese characteristics'. In a second stage, as a result of the 'period of political freeze' which followed the 1989 Tien An Men events, most of the TVEs were merged and 'privatized' (i.e. transferred to their managers). Some cities formed investment companies or private equity companies with a view to participating in local companies or external companies willing to invest in their territory – thus producing new jobs, new opportunities and new taxes. In 2011, the city of Beijing formed a private-equity company together with the American investment company Carlyle (the world's second largest investment company) to extend *ad hoc* financing to industrial investment in Beijing's Special Economic Area (SEA). Most of the local banks are partially or wholly owned by local communities; for example, the Bank of Nanjing is partially owned by the City of Nanjing and 20 per cent owned by the French Bank of Nanjing.

In any case, it is almost impossible to open a new venture in a local community without the active support and involvement of the local authorities. In case of trouble, there is no recourse before the Party or the courts unless the private investor is relying on a strong network of 'friends' (*guanxi*). In the countryside, the business community is also a mix of private initiative and local official involvement. The land is state-owned, as has been the case for centuries. The farmers are granted a piece of land by the local authorities in accordance with the needs of the household, the fertility of the soil and the distance of the plot from the village. Long-term renting allows farmers to invest in farming equipment and improving the fertility of their plot, with the expectation that they can harvest the profits of their efforts in due course. They can buy and sell, lease and rent the usufruct of their lots in order to widen the scale of the cultivated land for the buyer, and to collect savings to facilitate their migration to the next town or the seller.

Market mechanisms

The market has a dual function: it is both a price mechanism and a supplier of information – the latter being no more important than the former, as Hayek used to say. On one hand, it is the place where demand and supply meet to build up a common price; on the other, it is a source of information and data – a crucial ingredient to all market participants: consumer choice, producer investment, marketing strategy and government macroeconomic decisions are market-driven through the price process. Under one condition, the price mechanism should be free of any interference – that is, no market participant, especially the government, is strong enough to manipulate the price mechanism to take advantage on their own behalf. All market participants must have access to the same market data and information. In China, both the large state-owned enterprises (SOEs) and state-owned banks (SOBs) have a quasi monopolistic market share, with the government continuing to interfere with the price process.

Under certain conditions, government supervisors can prohibit, delay, or authorize new entrants to the market, such as foreign investors. Companies are kept under tight control through any of a wide range of legal constraints, existing regulations and informal guidance. The government supervizing agencies can use intrusive, detailed frameworks of regulation – often overlapping, or even contradictory – on behalf of some market participants at the expense of the others. Regulation – whether it relates to financial, banking, labour, legal, ecological, or safety matters – is arbitrarily used to support or eliminate a competitor. Whenever necessary, companies in a targeted sector, especially the banking sector, are summoned to join *ad hoc* meetings convened to convey government instructions. As a follow-up to the massive 2008 stimulus plan (Rmb 4000 billion, or US$650 billion), the banking sector (i.e. the four big state-owned banks) was instructed to undertake a dramatic increase in bank lending in support of the government's plan. Within one year, the volume of bank loans had more than doubled. Later, it appeared that most of the new loans that were granted to finance pointless local authority infrastructures were not going to be repaid. One year later, the banking sector was again recalled – this time it was instructed to refrain from granting fresh loans and being financially wasteful with regard to local authorities. Backed up by a gigantic domestic market (though not necessarily marketable), China's government imposed its own standards and criteria at the expense of international partners. Once authorization was granted, the investor – whether Chinese or foreign – had to apply to the local authority for a fresh round of groundless, duplicated enquiries. It is well-known that Chinese mining pits are poorly equipped, even dangerous. A number of manufacturing companies, including foreign companies, recruited youth and/or migrant workers without the required work permits. Migrant workers were unprotected: they had no binding contract, no social security, no access to schools, no health system, no pension scheme. As a matter of policy, the central government actively supported a consolidation process among the major manufacturing companies. Through merger, acquisition, regrouping and restructuring, under government or Party inducement 'national champions' emerged which had a monopolistic or quasi monopolistic market share. This was in order to compete 'evenly', or to benefit from 'fair' competition on the domestic and international markets. From then on, the new 'champions' will be in a position to dictate their wishes to business partners: suppliers, sub-contractors, bank institutions, distribution networks and/or local authorities.

The state-owned government trading companies no longer exist but the companies have kept some business practices inherited from the planning period. In order to guarantee access to the supply of raw materials, equipment and unfinished products at any given price, companies remained in touch with each other to bypass government constraints. During the credit crunch, corporations borrowed from and lent to each other, even though this is prohibited by law. For both lenders and borrowers, the spread was tightened (i.e. the interest rate paid by the borrower to the lender is higher than the bank savings rate and lower than the bank lending rate). It is estimated that business-to-business (B2B) transactions account in the region of 30 per cent of the overall amount of credit extended.

Thanks to monopolistic (a single seller) or monopsistic (a single buyer) market share, companies can increase or decrease prices over or under the otherwise free market price. In the Western world, such practice is prohibited by law as it bypasses the bank monopoly; in the Chinese market, it is a deliberate process undertaken by government on behalf of certain companies or industries at the expense of others. The rise of consumer prices is a way to transfer profits from the consumers to the producers, and vice versa.

Mao Yushi, an economist, tried to calculate the social cost of price distortion in China. According to him, estimated extra profits collected by government-owned telecommunication companies thanks to their monopolistic situation amounted to Rmb 31 billion (US$5 billion) per year from 2003 to 2010. This does not include the calls discouraged by the price level and estimated at a further Rmb 422 billion (US$ 60 billion). Depositor losses due to government regulation amounted to something in the range of Rmb 1,160 billion (US$184 billion) in 2011 (i.e. 2.5 per cent of the gross domestic product (GDP). Without free prices, companies cannot compare the respective costs of production factors, and prices do not reflect real costs; so are the economic actors: buyers and sellers, investors and savers, or lenders and borrowers. Companies are not provided with the data that they need to operate effectively.

In this respect, the price liberalization in banking in September 2012 was an historical event. Hitherto, the rate paid by banks to a customer's deposit account, the rate paid to the central bank for necessary daily refinancing and the rate charged to the individual or corporate borrowers were fixed by the central bank on the instruction of the State Council. From this point on, banks competed with each other to attract savings and deposits through so-called 'Wealth Management Products' (WMPs). These are a sort of subprime deal based on a certain range of loans which produce a rate higher than the usual bank savings account. Thus far, the rate scale was flat as all commitments were rated at the same level of risk (whether Treasury bonds or loans to government-owned companies or banks, whether short- or long-term) and, thus, at the same price. As a result, the banks allocated their liabilities to buy Treasury bonds rather than lend to companies as well as small and medium-sized companies or individuals.

The great return of the state

In 2012, more than 90 per cent of the 2,400 companies listed on the stock exchange were granted government or local authority subsidies amounting to Rmb 85 billion (US$13.8 billion) (i.e. a 24 per cent annual increase). This is while the profits of listed companies registered only a 13 per cent annual increase. In 2011, government subsidies amounted to 4 per cent of total companies' profits (3 per cent in 2010). Government aid is made up of all forms of subsidies: low land prices, below market prices, power prices, tax rebates, renewal of borrowings at a lower cost and so on. The major beneficiaries were the large state-owned companies such as China Yangtze Power (Rmb 2.1 billion grants), Chongqing Iron & Steel (Rmb 2 billion), China Eastern Airlines (Rmb 1.7 billion – i.e. more than the total annual profits), SAIC (Rmb 1.4 billion), TLC (Rmb 1.4 billion – i.e. more than the total annual profits), Air China (Rmb 1.8 billion). This time of crisis is an opportunity for the government to expand its sphere of influence. If the Chinese economy has recovered so quickly, this is mostly due to the government's prompt, far-reaching response, working in close cooperation with the State and the Party. As early as November 2008 – only weeks after the collapse of Lehman Brothers (18 September) – a stimulus plan amounting to Rmb 4,000 billion (US$640 billion) was set in motion. The rescue plan used the full range of government instruments: government subsidies, bank credits, local authority investment programmes, the building of infrastructure, public works and soft loans at interest rates lower than the market rate. If the banking sector has been more resilient, this is because of the low product diversification of bank products and tight government supervision. Foreign exchange controls have insulated the Chinese market from the spillover of the bank insolvency crisis. The Chinese banks have perhaps subscribed to a few billion dollars' worth of subprime vehicles, but the amount was not sufficient to diminish the overall solvency of the banks.

In the trading business, profits are generated from arbitraging one market price against another. Therefore, the constant interchange between markets accelerates the spillover process and makes liquidity problems worse. Market communication systems made the infection of a wide range of institutions by 'toxic' products easier. Several financial markets have been contaminated through the securitization process – connecting bank deposits, bank lending and financial markets. The relatively low integration of Chinese banking and security markets has spared the Chinese domestic market from the financial crisis.

The Chinese theory of government was designed during the periods 'Springs and Autumns' (722–453 BC) and 'Fighting Kingdoms' (453–221 BC). This was before China was reunited within a single empire (221 BC) ruled by a single Emperor, Shi Huangdi. Long before, China had been ruled by legendary dynasties (Shang, Zhu and Xia) which presented the ideal of a united China within a single empire, under a centralized government at the heart of the civilized world to future generations. In this interim period, Chinese thinkers had to redefine the very concept of State and government. While Greek philosophers pondered the role of the individual in the City, the Chinese were designing new methods of governance, the ways and means to strengthen the state apparatus and the kind of relationship between the king, the ministers and the subjects. The Chinese way of thinking is less speculative and more pragmatic. Socrates sought 'Truth' while Confucius sought 'Happiness' and, to this end, the best way to govern the people in the interests of the government. Chinese philosophers were less concerned by human nature (unless it intermingled with worldly issues), interesting themselves in the techniques of governance. In Greece, human relationships were perceived to be theoretically horizontal and equal, in China vertical and hierarchical. Every year, the Roman knights (a social category under the senators) were required to take part in a census. According to Chinese scholars, China before 1949 was 'feudal'. Technically speaking this is untrue. Feudality never existed in China. The concept of 'feudality' (decentralized and delegated power, hereditary fiefdoms) is contradictory with the very idea of a united country under a single all-powerful Emperor. This is the reason why, as opposed to the barbarian kingdoms which succeeded the Roman Empire, the imperial ideal of a united China has always re-emerged after all the invasions, rebellions and natural disasters which permeate Chinese history. Imperial ideology was Confucian by ideal but government practices were legalist by nature, in accordance with the Legalist thinkers – Yang Shang, Lu Buwei, Lizi and, above all, Han Feizi, an unsuccessful politician but great thinker.

A proper Confucian government is based on the 'virtue' of the Emperor, of the Mandarins and lower-level officials, the literati-bureaucrats (*shi*). Man was born with uncontrollable passions, but they can be tamed and turned into virtues thanks to education if he has the chance to be educated by a good Master. Through the 'rites' (*li*), Man can be taught how to behave properly in any circumstance. The *li* are a sort of code of good conduct which allows everyone to know exactly where they stand in the hierarchical structure; what he is expected to do or to say to anyone whom he may encounter. The detailed *li* prescriptions are a means of taking someone else into consideration while keeping him at a distance. But *li* is the opposite of two other characteristics. On the one hand, *li* is opposed to *ren* (the virtue of humanity) and, on the other hand, to *fa* (the formal law). The unwritten code of *li* is a way of life, a personal code of conduct to improve oneself, as well as a social code of good behaviour in society. The man from the street is governed by the law (*fa*), the literate and the cultivated man is governed by the rites (*li*), and the wise man by virtue (*ren*), a mix of honesty, generosity and a sense of duty.

In Western countries, every edict taken in accordance with the legal forms is enforced and no one is exempt, not even the government. Every form, whether a formal law, a king's edict or an official decree, belongs to a hierarchical order depending on who has initiated the prescription and in which form. By contrast, Chinese law is not rated according to the level of the issue; rather, all orders are enforced as an all-encompassing law since it is issued from the same common and single locus. Any official dispatched in a remote province is entrusted the same power as the Emperor himself.

As with Confucians, Legalists are searching for the most effective methods of governance but under a different premise working towards a different conclusion. Legalists have a nominal or formalist concept of law: the law is the law because ... it is the law. The law is not grounded on ethical substructure and moral principle. The law is nothing more than a form of government instrument among many others, such as the army and the bureaucracy. Hen Feizi had a low regard for human nature. An effective government of men must be based on the manipulation of basic instincts: hunger, fear and vanity. Law and order are based on the 'two jaws': punishments and rewards. Punishment must be totally disproportionate to the crime in order to make people so fearful that, ultimately, everyone complies willingly with the law. Eventually, formal law became second nature and the written law was useless. Local magistrates were both a judge and a manager enjoying the same power as the Emperor himself. Western companies tarred by official corruption should never bring the case before the judge. Instead, it is more effective to approach a Party member, since both of them are reporting to the same Centre.

The opposition of these two schools of thought (Confucianism versus Legalism) is a *topos* of Chinese rhetoric. But the two schools are not so different from each other. For both of them, education is the most important factor but something which should be reserved for the elite and dedicated to the service of the Emperor (or the State). Education teaches filial piety, respect of rites by learning the Great Classics. Legalists rely on reward and punishment, while Confucians rely on social sanction and consideration. As with all former dynasties, the Communist regime is trying to rediscover the spirit of Confucianism while practising the tough methods of Legalist methodology. Thanks to the hierarchical and decentralized ruling system, the Chinese government is likely to be more suited to combining China's short- and long-term aims. Thus, the policy of reform and opening-up has been implemented steadily but continuously since 1978. Every decision is processed by a consensus between clans and tribes which share the Party decision-making machinery. The 80 million Party members established all over the country make sure that the decision will be effectively implemented by local collectives.

The new planning system

Under the Empire, the 'official' calendar which regulated all the social and economic events of the year was fixed at the Emperor's discretion. Today, the country and government agenda is fixed by the Party. The Soviet version of the Five-Year Plan was meant to be a market substitute: a management tool based on recorded fact, designed to better coordinate all the industrial sectors and to save the 'transaction costs' of pointless intermediaries. Theoretically, the planning framework was more efficient than market forces thanks to the best possible resource allocation of production factors. During the Great Leap Forward of 1958, China aimed to overtake the British economy as Khrushchev announced that the Soviet economy would shortly surpass that of the USA. Mao decided that, from that point on, there would be two Plans rather than one: one based as usual on recorded statistics and reports from different levels of local administration, and another based on government targets and expectations irrespective of recorded data and resources. Local officials were obviously rated according to the latter. Eventually, following an inevitable escalation of the different hierarchical levels, officials reported a totally unrealistic volume of crops. There followed the Great Famine which caused something in the range of a minimum of 35 million deaths in two years (1959–60). Following the 1992 shift to the 'socialist market economy', the government was supposed to dispose of the former Planning Administration. But, as often happens in China's government business, it survived under another name: the National Development and Reform Commission (NDRC) is a very powerful institution involved in virtually every major decision whether political, social or economic (i.e. one child policy, *hukou* system).

Sometimes, the NDRC gets into the details of a critical decision (e.g. the privatization of a state-owned firm), or a much more macroeconomic issue (i.e. interest rates or foreign exchange rates). Far from being dissolved, the planning system is still very much alive; the NDRC is as effective as before, if not more so, since it is applied in a much more flexible way.

In China, the planning system is a political tool at the disposal of the government not subject to market constraints or political events. The Five-Year Plan is a combination of short-term and long-term objectives. It is a political issue as well as an economic survey. It is officially approved the year before the new government is 'elected', so that the new cabinet is tightened by the set of objectives set up during the previous administration. It is a written commitment and a compromise between the different factions challenging the top management. The Plan is split into different sub-Plans according to themes, regions and time schedules. The planning system is a way of ensuring that, whoever is appointed to the top positions, the long-term objectives will remain as before. In addition, the Plan is more flexible according to the industrial sector, the type and size of firms, and the province involved. The planning system is thus compatible with the market system: the more important the issue from a political point of view, the heavier the NDRC involvement and vice versa.

Accordingly, the planning system is a three-layer system: compulsory, contractual and indicative.

- At the upper level, the planning system is compulsory: documents outlining detailed sets of targets, including the human resources needed and the supply of raw materials and the financing needs, such as infrastructure programmes; development plans of the western provinces; education plans; health expenditures; research objectives, and so on. Generally speaking, included within compulsory planning are state-owned companies and banks and the monopolistic sectors under tight government control such as the Ministry of Railways.
- At the second level, the planning system is contractual: planning sets the objectives; the ways and means of a given industrial sector; and then negotiates with the corporations and the offices concerned to establish detailed objectives, as well as the allocation of resources to the targeted sectors.
- At the third and lowest level, the planning system is only an indicative: government schedule; industrial sector targets; the companies involved and inducement measures (government subsidies, tax exemption, bank lending and financial markets).

The Chinese Plan is an instrument of political and social control as well as a document including economic objectives, and the necessary ways and means and coordination processes. As opposed to the detailed and compulsory Mao-type Plan, the new system is based on involvement at any step of the participating entities through a top-down/bottom-up process before and after the Plan is finally disclosed. As a result, the Chinese economy is neither a market economy nor fully-fledged state capitalism; rather, it is something in between, something specific and far more complex.

Whether the companies are state-owned or not does not make a great difference from the point of view of overall economic control. The largest companies are maintained by tight government control, directly or indirectly, through local collectives, government agencies and SOE share-holding. At the other end of the government spectrum, small private companies are not under direct government control but still remain under control through the Party's tightly knit network. Party-State control allows the government to adjust the level of control according to the Party's range of priorities. This is more adaptable, more focused and more efficient.

The market economy is not a goal *per se*; market mechanisms are used on the fringes with a view to providing useful information and regulating the economy in accordance with the overall government directives. Market 'liberalization' is extended, as long as it does not infringe on the Party's monopoly of power. Banking and financial market reform is incomplete, mostly because the Party-State is not prepared to relax its control over a key industry on which all others depend. It is a key instrument of power. When the derivative contracts were first marketed, the government soon realized the speculative and risky nature of these new products and swiftly reversed their course. The market economy does not reflect a specific idea of man and society; it is nothing more than an extra tool in the governmental tool box.

The Party-State has committed a noticeable degree of interference and/or marketization in accordance with government policy and the critical nature of the industry. Following the collapse of the Soviet bloc countries in the late 1980s, China's leadership was not convinced that the Soviet model was wrong and that capitalism was the only alternative. Rather, at the time of a revolution in the information and telecommunication industry, economic management required more fine-tuning and a more flexible range of management tools. In China more than anywhere else, the state is not at the disposal of the people but, rather, at the Party's service. As for the Party itself, it is self-serving and committed only to its own survival.

2
The Transition Period

The only thing that never changes is that everything changes all the time.
(Yi Jing, hexagram 32, character Heng)

When Deng Xiaoping took over power, it is probable he did not know precisely where he was going. However, he knew that he was moving in the right direction. Like the *zen* archer, he had the chance to hit the target but only by adopting the correct stance. The 'policy of reform and opening' has been implemented through a set of experiments of trial and error which, over time, have generated a true mutation. It is a gradual yet pragmatic process, using a process of limited and tightly controlled opening. 'It was a step by step process thanks to which we continuously deepen our understanding – it was the experiment which allowed us to learn' (Zhao Ziyang, former general secretary and prime minister).

The Chinese way of thinking does not correlate with the Western thought of 'leap forward' found in Western experimental science, from paradigm to paradigm; rather, it functions through an incremental process, adding one more comment to the existing set of concepts. The Chinese thinker adds a new comment to the original statements of canonist texts through a chain of ever renewed questioning and proposals on common ground. For Confucians, the world is in a constant state of flux. Only a perverse and overambitious spirit aims to fix the process of evolution forever. Mao failed because he repeatedly tried to break down the system, to use force instead of letting the natural scheme of things achieve his ends. There is no such thing in the Chinese language as a question mark that demands a 'yes' or 'no' answer. Innovation does not process through a design followed by its implementation (doing by learning) as is the case with Westerners but, rather, through successive experiments out of which the cumulative effect produces something brand new (learning by doing).

The very wording of the 'policy of reform and opening' (*gaige kaifang*) refers to a method, rather than an objective. The final target is within the method itself. If you have the correct attitude, you know that you are moving in the correct direction. Both 'reform' and 'opening' go hand-in-glove. While they were shifting to a policy of reform, Chinese leaders rediscovered Ricardo's Law of Comparative Advantage (*On the Principles of Political Economy and Taxation*, 1817). Instead of covering the entire chain of production, it is more advantageous to concentrate on the industrial sectors where the emerging country has the strongest advantages.

Such questioning brought about fierce struggles amongst Party leaders. If words no longer have the power to kill, they can at least eliminate. In the days following his attainment of supreme power, Xi Jinping extensively used the pretext of a corruption campaign to eliminate his opponents. An ideological state which gives up its ideological background becomes a police state.

When Deng Xiaoping reached supreme power, he was already elderly (74). For the next twenty years, he would be the leading figure in Chinese politics. However, he never held a leading governmental position (general secretary, chairman of the Republic or prime minister). Deng was known to support the policy of reform; however, he was cautious in discussing reform. He had been a victim of the Cultural Revolution, but had no desire for revenge. He was opposed to a 'demaotization' policy, as he was opposed to any change of the one-party system. He was backed by the Party and the Army. He had lengthy experience of public service, as well as in military affairs, and he had in-depth knowledge of the Party apparatus.

Deng never held the same level of power as his followers Jiang Zemin, Hu Jintao and Xi Jinping. Though he was unquestioned as China's leader, he was not unchallenged. He was forced into endless negotiations to rally his supporters, to convince his colleagues, to mobilize the officials and to bolster his networks. Even inside the Politburo, he had to compromise with Chen Yun, a highly respected veteran advocating a cautious yet progressive reform policy; Li Peng, a Maoist prime minister; and Li Xianan, deputy prime minister in charge of economic affairs and a staunch supporter of the planning system. However, the two leaders never tried to eliminate each other. Rather, they were indispensable to each other. When the then prime minister Hu Yaobang, one of Deng's closest followers, was eliminated in 1987, his resignation was a by-product of a maoist-type 'anti-liberalization campaign' initiated by Deng himself with the aim of neutralizing the members of the conservative wing who had regrouped under Chen's umbrella. During the student demonstrations in the very centre of Beijing (May 1989), Deng and Chen worked out a trade-off: they both supported a dramatic shift in the course of reform policy. This involved the demotion of Zhao Ziyang, the newly appointed General Secretary and Deng's close disciple, but Deng remained leader. Three years later, stripped of any political mandate, the newly retired Deng embarked on his famous 'Southern trip' (*nan xan*) to resume the policy of reforms.

Deng was not a democrat but, instead, a true Communist who had devoted his whole life to the Party. He was not a liberal, whether in the European or the American sense. He was not a supporter of a market economy versus command economy. He had never supported the idea of a Western-style pluralistic democracy and had repeatedly stated that China was not suited for a multiparty system. Quite the contrary; he considered that the policy of reform and opening needed a strong centralized system to implement the new policy. The more open the market system, the more stringent the Party control should be.

Deng Xiao-ping (1978–97): policy reform and opening up

Chinese economists are accustomed to splitting the policy of reform into two successive phases: the first 'without losers' and the second 'with losers' meaning that, at the beginning, the status of workers remained unchanged while, in the second stage, workers were subject to the profit requirements of SOEs and, if necessary, dismissed. In the first phase, reform policy aims to revert from Mao's legacy and to improve the farmers' situation. Deng did not remove the 'iron bowl' (*tie fan wan*) – that is, all the benefits enjoyed by the urban workers provided by the SOEs (education, health and housing). In the second phase, the restructuring of the SOE from 1995 onwards led to a massive wave of lay-offs. As a result of growing urbanization, family ties were loosened. The first phase ('without losers') took place before the Tien An Men rising (1989) and the second phase ('with losers') took place after Deng's 'Southern trip' (1992).

Reform 'without losers' (1978–1989)

To exit the command economy and avoid the transition period, two avenues were opened: the 'shock-therapy' route (Russia, Eastern European countries) and the 'gradualist' route (China). Inspired by the works of Friedrich Hayek and Milton Friedman (of the 'Chicago school'), theorized by Jeffrey Sachs and the 'Chicago boys', supported by the American 'neo-conservatives' advocating the 'Washington consensus', shock therapy involved a one-shot transition to a market economy. It was intended that the whole process should be achieved as rapidly as possible and simultaneously in every sector since they formed a closely interwoven system. Within a few months, if not weeks, the following was implemented: currency convertibility, freedom of pricing, government subsidy cuts and the privatization of the loss-making state-owned companies. This process is supposed to be the most efficient, most comprehensive and shortest route from a command system to a market-driven system. But 'shock-therapy' entails a high degree of social and political cost: massive unemployment, closure of inefficient factories, a drop in purchasing power and the dismantling of natural solidarity links whether business, social or family. In contrast, China is putting in place gradual improvements in order to ensure that the new system works properly before it is imposed. This implementation is being undertaken gradually and over an extended period of time. In assessing the merits of the two approaches, it must be taken in consideration that the Eastern countries were relatively small-sized countries supported by massive European Union subsidies which were part of a much more comprehensive programme including market economy and political democracy. In Russia, where the social cost proved to be devastating, the government could only rely on the gas and oil resources, which accounted up to 95 per cent of government income.

In a country where 80 per cent of the population were still located in the countryside, it was natural to start with the area on which the fate of the farmers and the feeding of the towns would have the most critical impact. It was just the reverse of Mao's basic assumption: to transfer the burden of 'primitive capital allocation' from the agriculture sector to heavy industry. Over 30 years, Mao put pressure on farmers to transfer resources from the agricultural sector to the financing of industry and the feeding of the proletariat at the lowest possible prices. The agricultural work was organized by establishing working teams. The needs of the farmers were entirely fulfilled by the 'people communes'. Cooking implements were taken away to force the peasants to take their meals in the collective canteen. The peasants were granted no income at all since all their needs were supposedly met by the communes. Should they have some personal income left, since there was nothing to buy in empty shops, there was very little point in confiscating this from them.

Savings, if any, were deposited in the state-owned bank and earned only a very low interest rate.

In 1978, the land statute and production methods were very close to those in place during the Empire of 221 BC. The land was owned by the state. A piece of land was allocated to each family according to its needs, the quality of the soil and its distance from a family's residence. This was to ensure that a certain level of equality was maintained between the farmers' families. The slots were reallocated on a regular basis but were scattered all over the area of a farm, which did not encourage mechanization or improved productivity.

Deng approached this from the opposite direction, a necessary move since increasing the purchasing powers of farmers – who are, of course, consumers – and reviving agricultural production which had collapsed, were two very pressing issues. He did not suppress the commune system. Rather, farmers were permitted to leave their communes in order to cultivate their own piece of land. According to the 'household contract' system, every family was expected to offer the government a certain amount of agricultural produce at a given price, the rest being left at their disposal for sale on the free market. As a result, agricultural production leapt up and the communes disappeared by themselves. Step-by-step, the government increased the proportion delivered in cash instead of goods and the tax system steadily took over the commodity system. However, in the meantime, a rather complex dual-price system was operating – one government price and one market price. By shifting from one market to the other, the dual-price system was an obvious cause of smuggling and corruption. However, the market price was a useful index with which to establish the government price. When the level of the government price was raised to meet the market level, the whole market was unified. In addition, the 'housing contract system' paved the way for TVEs and rural credit cooperatives (RCCs) to service the manufacturing and financing needs of the local people, there being no nationwide market in existence into which they could integrate.

Deng used the same approach with the corporate sector. According to a contractual commitment, factories were requested to sell a certain amount of products to the government at the government price, the rest being free to be sold on the market at market price.

While passing through Guangzhou (Canton), Deng's attention was drawn by local officials to an appalling problem, both human and economic: every year a number of young people were killed trying to cross the border and reach the shores of the British colony Hong Kong by attempting to cross the Pearl River Straights. The only way to deter these young people risking their lives was to create job opportunities on the mainland. Deng suggested creating a free industrial area where foreign (as well as Chinese) companies were permitted to assemble foreign products, tax-free, in an offshore area. A little village of fishermen was selected, Shenzhen, which soon became a 17 million strong metropolis thanks to the Hong Kong/Chinese community which invested heavily in the new special economic area (SEA). Later on, the new system was extended to a ring of outposts along the eastern coast from Tanjin down to Hainan and up, having spilled over throughout the east coast from Mongolia down to Canton.

There was only one bank, the People's Bank of China (PBOC), which was then a mere department of the Ministry of Finance, and which fulfilled the functions of both a central bank and a commercial bank. All the company's receipts and expenditures were recorded in bank accounts on the instruction of the Planning Administration. All the deposits collected by the 'banks' (which were acting as mere central bank branches) were transferred to the PBOC and all the expenditures debited from the same account. 'Monetary policy' was limited to regulating interest rates (paid to the depositors and charged to the borrowing companies) since there was no market position to consider. Salaries were disbursed in such a way that primary needs were covered; any monies remaining were deposited in the bank and returned to the central bank. Were the central bank instructed to rein in inflationary trends, the rate was increased in order to attract excess liquidity. If the liquidity of the market was insufficient, the bank was instructed to decrease the interest rate so that cash was withdrawn from the bank accounts. In both cases, the aim was to maintain the money supply and the volume of currency injected into the cycle at the lowest possible level in order to prevent 'consumers' using their savings in a way which did not meet with the government wishes.

Reform 'with losers' (1989–2002)

In 1992, Deng Xiaoping turned 89 years of age. In 1987, he had relinquished all his public mandates. He enjoyed his retirement with his children (the elder had been beaten and crippled during the Cultural Revolution) and grandchildren. Together with members of his family, he boarded a train to go on holiday, the now well-known 'Southern trip' (*nan xan*). He was heading south, and then east, to the most reform-oriented provinces. Everywhere, even on the station platform if necessary, officials welcomed him. He knew them well; they had all worked under him; he spoke of the past, the good old days. Everywhere, to everybody, he repeated the same message; they should resume the growth policy against the wishes of the Centre, which had come to a standstill since the 1989 Tien An Men rising. 'Be innovative, go ahead and take initiative'. He ended his tour in Shenzhen; this was symbolic, as it was the city where the policy of reform and opening had started 10 years previously. Deng behaved just as Mao had when he had set in motion the 'Cultural Revolution'. He was circumventing the Beijing headquarters, the top management of the Party and the government. Initially, his speeches were erased by censorship. But Deng's initiative was very timely: the top management was about to be renewed; the roles of the governing body were split between General Secretary Jang Zemin, the 'politician', and Zu Rhongji, the 'technocrat' and 'economic tsar', then Chairman of the central bank and future prime minister. Zu was widely praised, since he had managed to save the highly indebted SOEs and the near-bankrupted state-owned banks. Since then, he has been widely recognized as the leader of the 'bureaucratic' faction, as opposed to the 'political' elite. However, in China everything is political. Above a certain level, a bureaucrat must be a politician. Each is in great need of the support of the other. Eventually, Zu turned to Jiang Zemin for backing. Soon, Jiang understood that there was a unique opportunity to strengthen his shaky position by jumping on Deng's bandwagon. Did Deng and Jang act in conjunction? Nobody knows, but it is possible. Deng died in 1997, a few weeks before the sovereignty of Hong Kong was handed back by the UK to the People's Republic of China. The policy of reform and opening has now recommenced, and cannot be stopped.

From 1978 onwards, the benefits of the policy of reform and opening had been enjoyed by all: farmers, workers and entrepreneurs. Deprived of their jobs, millions of migrant workers returned home to the countryside, where there were no job opportunities for them. Then, policy changed gear. From 1992 onwards, the number of dismissed workers was estimated to be something in the range of 50 million. Companies became subject to 'budget constraints': cost controls, risk analysis, subsidy cuts, increased competition and migrants (i.e. 100 to 200 million unskilled workers without working permits, social security or job contracts). Following the agricultural sector, the wave of reform turned to the manufacturing industry, exporting companies and capital expenditures. Between 1978 and 1998, foreign trade increased from 7 per cent of GDP to 27 per cent. Between 2002 and 2011, investments rose from 37 per cent to 50 per cent of GDP. Third and fourth generations of leaders (1: Mao, 2: Deng, 3: Jiang, 4: Hu Jintao) flooded the ultimate levels of power; a new generation of young and ambitious people who had not experienced the times of Mao knew only what their elders had told them – which was nothing, or very little. Former Red Guards tried to return to university after a 10-year hiatus but they were forced to compete with much younger students – more gifted, more sophisticated and more of the moment. Some turned to religion, most turned to the religion of money.

Jiang Zemin (1989–2002) and Zu Rhongji (1994–2002): exit from the Plan

Jiang and Zu were cut from the same cloth: Shanghai. Zu used to work under Jiang and they knew each other's ways. While Jiang was a politician, Zu was, instead, a technocrat. Both were reformist in economics and conservative in politics. Though his appointment was backed up by the most conservative members of the Politburo at a critical time (the Tien An Men rising), Jiang was a moderate who was trying to discover the proper balance between the factions which shared power. Zu was a strong character and an experienced manager who did not care much about ideology. In essence, he was a pragmatist and could rely on a wide network of bureaucrats at every level and, most importantly, in the central bank. In order to cope with the inflationary tensions caused by the decentralization process and the subsequent fast growth, his main achievement was to recentralize the powers released to the local officials to stimulate the economy. From this point on, the Centre had a budget surplus while the local authorities experienced a chronic deficit, which made them highly dependent on government subsidies.

Reforming the SOEs

Initially, the 'privatization' of the SOEs was not so much aimed at changing the ownership status as changing the management model to make it more efficient. Government-owned companies were converted into public companies. The shareholders were still government offices (the State-owned Assets Supervision and Administration Commission of the State Council – SASAC, for the manufacturing companies; Huyjin, for the bank and financial institutions) but the government was still deeply involved. The stocks were non-negotiable; the managers were appointed by the Party. Henceforth, managers had to manage as best they could with scarce human resources, fixed assets and financial means. Also, they were accountable to the Party Centre. The 'privatization process' did not really change the ownership hierarchy but it led to management rationalization. Local authorities 'privatized' companies or departments supplying a public service. Often, the former TVEs – initially formed by the local authorities to fulfil the functions of shops, stores and manufacturing units – were sold out or transferred free of charge to their managers. Some merged with other TVEs. The share of SOEs in GDP decreased sharply from 77.6 per cent in 1978 to 39 per cent in 1998. But the 'privatization' process had a high social cost. Millions of workers were laid off. From 1992 to 2005, the number of SOE employees fell from 35 million to 6 million. Those who were left behind no longer enjoyed the usual benefits attached to their status: lifelong employment, social benefits, a pension scheme, housing, a canteen, health care and schools.

Reforming the banks

There are two laws dedicated to the reform of the banks: the Central Bank (1985) and the state banks (1995). The central bank (the PBOC) was removed from the control of the Ministry of Finance and required to report directly to the State Council, the top-most level of government. Thus, fiscal policy and monetary policy were separated. Both report directly to the State Council, which takes basic decisions (interest rates, foreign exchange rates, lending quotas and reserve requirements). Although it is supposed to be independent, the central bank is tightly controlled by the State Council, which appoints the president and takes final decisions. Nonetheless, the central bank has become increasingly powerful. Each budget crisis, or liquidity crisis, or credit crunch which requires anti-inflation measures serves to reinforce the central bank's position in the balance of power, as its members have access to critical data, as well as the necessary ways and means. The members can trigger a policy shift and they have the necessary knowledge and means with which to proceed: the more sophisticated and more fined-tuned the macroeconomics, the more powerful the central bank. The PBOC relies on a very capable group of experts. Typically, the members of the PBOC are more market-oriented than the members of the Ministry of Finance, who are more state-oriented.

The 1995 legislation on commercial banking was the starting point of the 'privatization' process of the state banks. The four state banks were converted into public companies, but the hierarchy remained unchanged. Bank managers were appointed by the Party; they were all prominent Party members. But, from this point on, they were accountable. They were required to report to the Party, manage the resources allocated to them and generate profits. The loans were no longer authorized on a case-by-case basis by the Planning Office, but by the banks themselves, as they were in charge of risk management, credit analysis and marketing strategy. In the prospectus of the stock exchange listing, non-performing loans were withdrawn from the banks' balance sheets and transferred to an assets management company (AMC). AMCs are jointly owned by the banks and the central bank, and are funded through the issue of bonds subscribed to by ... the banks themselves. The whole situation is a mere accounting trick. In the next step, the state banks were recapitalized by Huyjin, a government holding company affiliated to the central bank. The bank was then ready to be brought to the market for sale. First, a capital increase was allocated to a certain number of institutional investors, including some foreign banks (a maximum of 20 per cent). The stocks were then listed on the stock exchange. To ensure that the issue was a great success, the initial selling price was much lower than that expected when the shares were finally listed. In addition, some 'political banks' fully owned by the government were established to manage the non-performing loans granted to the SOEs; these loans have never been paid back. Some 'privately owned' banks were authorized – although most of them were, in reality, wholly or partially owned by government institutions or officials (private banks with a 'red hat').

Mating the inflationary crisis (1986–8 and 1992–4)

The privatization of the corporations took place at a similar pace to that of the 'decentralization' of the local authorities, with the expectation that it would be more effective were the level of decision-making closer to the field of enforcement. The same cause produced the same effect, privatization led to the same result: waste, duplication and inflation. Central government had not yet set in place the tools of macro-economic control to take from one hand what it had put in the other. As a result, loans were allocated by the local branches of state banks, which are more sensitive to the lobbying of the local authorities than central government. A branch manager cannot resist the pressure of a local Party secretary who wishes to reward friends or relatives. Their promotion being linked to their achievements in terms of growth and employment, local Party secretaries competed with each other to draw fresh investments to their constituencies in order to provide jobs and taxes. However, the Centre eventually lost control over the volume of new credits and the money supply. In 1988, one year before the Tien An Men events, the price increase reached a rate of 18.5 per cent, and even higher for imported raw materials and food – for example, pork, which is a basic Chinese food ingredient. Zu Rongji used all the tools at his disposal, whether macro-economic or micro-economic, administrative or global – credit quotas, reserve requirements and interest rates – but he lacked the necessary macro instruments such as open market transactions, there being no market in existence at that time.

Overcoming the Asian financial crisis (1997–8)

Following the sudden withdrawals of dollar denominated credit, the crisis which had hit the neighbouring countries (South Korea, Thailand) spread throughout the whole region, triggering a deadly set of competitive devaluations. In view of the components of Chinese trade, the country was expected to follow suit. Not only did the Chinese government not devalue the competitive prices of Chinese exports in order to sustain them, but it granted sizable unconditional swap agreements (dollar versus local currency) to lighten the burden for foreign payments of their neighbouring export rivals. In future, the countries will not look to the IMF or World Bank for conditional loans (which is perceived as a breach of sovereignty) but, rather, to China. On the domestic market, Zu Rongji did not miss the opportunity of the Asian crisis to further re-centralize the local powers granted to local authorities as part of the growth policy.

Joining the WTO (2001)

Following lengthy bargaining with the USA, China joined the World Trade Organization (WTO) in December 2001. This step marked a breakthrough in the policy of reform and opening-up. The aim was to open the foreign market to Chinese products and to force Chinese companies to improve their competitiveness by meeting the standards of international competition while foreign direct investment (FDI) continue to flow into China. A five-year period of grace was granted to China, enabling her to open the domestic service market (including her financial services) to foreign traders and investors. But the Chinese government wasted no time in reaping the benefits of this agreement. In fewer than 10 years, China became the world's largest trading country and the largest target of FDI.

Hu Jintao (2002–12) and Wen Jiabao (2002–12): towards the socialist market economy and the 'harmonious' society

In 2002–3, a new team reached the highest echelons of power: Hu Jintao (General Secretary, President of the Republic and Chairman of the Party Military Committee) and Wen Jiabao (Prime Minister). Hu Jintao is neither a member of the Shanghai lobby as was his predecessor, nor a 'princeling'. He used to be the General Secretary of the Communist Youth League through which all future leaders had passed. Later, he was an energetic governor of Gansu and Tibet, among two of the poorest provinces in China. His iron clad fist in the midst of sensitive situations drew the attention of the Chinese leaders. Hu supported the idea of a 'harmonious society' (a very 'Confucian' ideal) while maintaining the pivotal role of the Party. As such, Hu had to keep the balance between the different factions, which gave him a very narrow window of opportunity. Wen led the government and the bureaucracy. While Hu appeared stern, Wen appeared more human – 'humanity' (*ren*) also being a Confucian virtue. Wen did not miss an opportunity to demonstrate his 'humanity'. When, in 2009, an earthquake killed 80,000 people in Sichuan – many of whom were children that were crushed to death under the ruins of their school – he went straight to the affected area to comfort the stricken population. Thanks to his caring nature, he is called 'Uncle Wen' (*bo, bofu*) or 'Grandpa Wen' (*zufu*). After 10 years of working closely together, the gap began to widen between the two leaders. As Wen called openly for political as well as economic reform, his speech was censored by the media.

Reforming the SOEs

With the legal and operational structures of the big SOEs set in place, the government aimed at reinforcing the SOEs by increasing their competitiveness, with a view to forming national 'champions' strong enough to compete with the large Western multinationals on the domestic market initially, and then on the international market when they were sufficiently strong. A handful of large SOEs with, *de jure* or *de facto*, monopolistic or oligolopolistic market shares had a dominant position in the Chinese market: computers (Lenovo), telecommunications (Huawei), petroleum (Petrochina, Sinopec), chemicals (Sinochem), public works (Sandy), aerospace (AVIC), shipyards (Ronsheng), steel (Baosteel), appliances (Haier).

The situation for foreign companies established on the Chinese market became increasingly difficult. Following the wave of salary increases, increasing transportation costs, shrinking profit margins and government discrimination – including access to government construction auction and public works as part of the recovery plan following the Sichuan earthquake and the international financial crisis – foreign companies became increasingly reluctant to settle down in such a difficult state-controlled market. Conversely, the Chinese companies were not only increasing their market share on the foreign markets, but had also begun to purchase foreign companies hit by the world financial crisis and the collapse of the stock exchange.

The government pursued and widened the 'privatization' of Chinese companies that became public while they remained under government control. Following the 'privatization' policy, the Chinese stock market broadened. In 2008–9, despite the global financial crisis, as the Western stock market experienced a sharp fall, the Chinese markets of Shanghai and Hong Kong were top-most in terms of fund raising through investors private offerings (IPOs). New products were marketed and traded on the Chinese stock market: private and public placements, convertible bonds, corporate bonds, start-up markets (Shenzhen) and commodity markets (Shanghai, Tianjin, Zhengzhou), as well as a widening range of derivative contracts. The Chinese market was steadily opened to foreign investors – not only in the Hong Kong Stock Exchange, but also in the Shanghai Stock Exchange (SSE). A very limited number of foreign companies were allowed to place bonds on the domestic market. The Hong Kong market was developing a Yuan denominated bond market ('dim sum' bond market). Also, an interbank payment hub was developed in Hong Kong and was subsequently extended to foreign markets: Taiwan and Singapore in the Chinese-speaking markets and, above all, London in the Western hemisphere.

However, it is difficult to sow the seeds of capitalism without capitalist rules. Government interference distorts market prices. Foreign companies were sued for illegal practices – Google, Danone, Siemens, Glaxo Smith and many others. A food industry group such as Danone, with lengthy experience in the Chinese market, was compromised when its patents were stolen by its Chinese partner: they discovered that their Chinese partner, Wahaha, was marketing a similar product through a separate wholly-owned distribution network. After a decade-long trial, Danone, which pursued a US$3.7 billion plagiarism lawsuit, was ordered by the Chinese courts to pay US$200 million in compensation to Zhong Qinhou, the wealthy Wahaha owner. Zhong Qinhou was said to be the richest man in China and an active member of the Central Committee, very close to the top political leaders.

A growing network of small and medium-sized privately owned companies

The 'private' sector grew far more rapidly than government-owned companies, whether in terms of GDP, capital expenditures or employment.

From 1978 to 1992, the number of privately owned companies rocketed up to 6.2 million in spite of the phase of repression which followed the Tien An Men rising, focused on privately owned companies or individual rural cooperatives. The move forward resumed in the early 2000s. All the fields given up by government industries were taken over by private firms, individual (services) or collective firms (start-ups) initiated by collective authorities and then transferred to private owners. Private companies which had no access to the supply of bank credit were forced to turn to informal credit institutions and pawnbrokers who charge usury interest rates on short-term loans. This is an old and traditional practice dating back to the early times of the Empire. In 2002, an informal credit entity became bankrupt, leaving behind it a chain of Wanzhou shoe manufacturers. Unwillingly, the government was forced to intervene in order to save workers' livelihoods. The estimated share of informal credit was somewhere in the range of 20 per cent to 30 per cent of the total volume of loans, not including inter-company loans (such as delays of payment) extensively used in periods of credit crunch, even though this was prohibited by law.

Reforming the legal status of land

Once pieces of land had been allocated to farmers, they were allowed to resell or sub-lease the lease agreement, but not the state ownership. Thus, the remaining farmers had the opportunity to enlarge the area of their farms, thus increasing land productivity. The seller or lender received a lump sum of money to facilitate either the formation of an industrial or commercial venture, or his settling in the next city as a waged worker. Those who became waged workers sent home part of their meagre salary to make up the family income. Some used the sum of money to open a little shop or a restaurant.

The legal status of land played a critical role in local authority financing, as they bought back the farmers' plots so as to resell them at a much higher price to an industrial or commercial firm, or to an individual entrepreneur. Once the available lands had been seized, local authorities could find themselves in a difficult situation, potentially drawing others into bankruptcy: the banks who granted huge amounts of lending to local authorities; property development firms; and the construction and public works companies; the whole property chain. The government endeavoured to deflate the property bubble with credit limits, increased down-payments and cancelled infrastructure projects. So far, this effort has been in vain.

Reorienting government investments

A massive development plan was put in place to reinvigorate the western provinces far from the wealthy and rapidly developing eastern and coastal provinces. As the work force grew and the coastal industries recovered, the lack of job opportunities forced those who were newly graduated back into the countryside or the western provinces.

Reforming the banking and financial sector

The new government continued to reform the banking sector through an ever widening 'privatization' process and the creation of stock exchange markets. Thanks to the development of an effective interbank cash market of a well-supplied government bond market, the central bank was in a position to use more diversified and more sophisticated management tools. They used global macro-economics (open-market) to regulate the money supply and to inject (or withdraw) liquidity funds into or from the market, while keeping control of the inflation rate.

The large and 'privatized' government banks were listed on the stock market through highly successful IPOs which provided unusually high profits. The listing of the SOEs and SOBs deepened and broadened the market and provided alternative investments to individuals and collective Chinese saving institutions. These institutions had so far been restricted to bank savings accounts or Treasury bonds rewarded at a rate below inflation. A set of supervizing institutions was settled with the subsequent regulation: the PBOC, CBRC, CSRC, CIRC, SAFE[1] and the National Development and Reform Commission (NDRC) – not including the local authorities. The rotten assets piled up on the banks' balance sheets were transferred to 'defeasance' companies and 'policy' banks. Privately owned banks were formed on the initiative of the largest banks (affiliated specialized banks) or the local authorities (local commercial banks). Following China joining the WTO, foreign banks were permitted to settle in China, although in a minority position (20 per cent in the largest banks, 49 per cent in the smallest: specialized credit institutions or regional banks). The foreign bank brings expertise and the Chinese bank a sales network, as well as critical connections with central and local government. In accordance with the 'Legalist' teaching, the government is powerful whether it is a shareholder or not. A mere suggestion from the right person in the right place at the right time is sufficient.

Converted into public companies, released from the burden of non-recoverable loans, recapitalized by the government through Huyjin (a central bank-affiliated holding company), opened to the foreign shareholders through the private placement of a capital increase, the large banks were ready to be listed on the stock exchange.

As the placement price was intentionally lower when compared with the market price, the early investors had the opportunity to collect a fair amount of profits. But the foreign banks which took shares in the early stages were locked into three to five years of lock-out provision. When the world financial crisis blew up, some of them tried to disinvest. Some made huge profits (HSBC, Temasek) whereas most experienced heavy losses (Goldman Sachs, Bank of America). From a 'financial' investment, the foreign banks turned to a more 'industrial' approach by forming specialized credit institutions with a Chinese partner, or by buying back regional banks with an extensive branch network and deposit base.

Opening the financial services

The policy of opening was an intrinsic part of the policy of reform. Jiang Zemin negotiated China's entry into the WTO to open foreign markets to Chinese export companies. From 1978 to 2003, Chinese exports increased by 28 times. In the meantime, the export share of GDP increased from 5.2 per cent to 23.6 per cent becoming, together with government investment, one of the main engines of Chinese growth. The expected goal was to expose Chinese companies to foreign competition in order to allow market forces to operate and constrain Chinese companies with the view to improving their management, productivity and competitiveness. After a five-year period of grace, China was bound to open financial services to foreign competition. But the government complied with great care and only very slowly. Some critical industries were kept outside the field of competition and WTO regulation, such as government public works. Some companies were even discriminated against under the pretext of health regulation, environmental standards, or safety regulation.

The global financial crisis

In China, as in many other countries, the global financial crisis operated as an accelerator, a revealing event. At the end of the crisis, China emerged as the world's second largest economy and on the way to overtaking the USA as the world's largest economy in the near future (2030). As the Western economies sank into the crisis, China became the second largest global economy behind the USA but leading Japan; the world's leading exporter before Germany and Japan; the world's leading manufacturer before the USA. Hardly touched by the financial crisis, the Chinese economy was hit by the declining Western markets. Very reactive in the short term, China's economy was forced by the crisis to redesign its long-term growth model. So far, the Chinese economy has been drawn along by capital expenditures and exports. The volume of foreign trade halved while the balance of trade remained positive, though sharply reduced. From this point on the economic engine moved from investment and foreign trade to internal demand and household consumption. As the Chinese growth model was more suited to facing a crisis by stimulating government (or quasi government) investments, it seemed less fitting to turn to the new consumption-driven growth. A strong and authoritarian government ruling a population of 1.3 billion people through a tightly knit net of 85 million Party members is more suited to stimulating government induced investments than a household's way of life and individual behaviour. It takes a considerable time to change direction and 'time' is likely to be what China most lacks.

The coupling and uncoupling theory

According to a World Bank report, the Chinese economy accounted in recent years for up to 50 per cent of global GDP growth.

On the one hand, the Chinese economy is highly dependent on other markets' demand. When Western markets slowed down, this affected the entire Chinese economy – or, at least, the exporting industries and the sub-contracting companies. When the global market slowed down, Chinese exports declined more than proportionally. The global growth rate slowed by 1 per cent in 2012 as compared with 2013, but Chinese exports fell by 50 per cent. However, the trade surplus, though halved, remained positive. The Chinese economy had so far been very sensitive to the growth and exports of the Western markets. In so far as China put emphasis on low-cost products, China's exports represented a substantial contribution to the fight against inflation. It is worth mentioning that, in spite of unusually high market liquidity and heavy cash injection by Western countries to cope with the economic recession, there have not as yet been any significant price increases.

On the other hand, as well as being the countries which produce raw materials, developed countries were thereafter increasingly dependent on the Chinese growth rate. In the event that China's growth rate slowed, or was merely expected to slow, raw material market prices fell too. Most multinationals and, generally speaking, most large companies are heavily dependent on the Chinese market. For many of them, the sales share of Chinese exports within the overall turnover accounts for more than the domestic share (GM, Volkswagen, Casino). The profits margins are higher, the Chinese market is growing faster and the profits generated by sales in China have overtaken all other sources of profits.

To cope with the new situation pending the recovery of the Western developed markets, China had to reorganize her export industries, to seek out new markets and to market new products. As China's economy still produces a significant trade surplus with the Western developed countries such as the USA and the European Union, it produces a trade deficit from the surrounding countries (including Japan and Australia) and the countries which produce raw materials. As a result, China had to redirect the flow of exports to new countries and to start trading with the neighbouring countries and the developing countries, which more than often lack the necessary purchasing power. Consequently, China had to back up and stimulate its exports to developing countries by granting export financing or infrastructure subsidies ('infrastructures versus long-term supply contract of raw materials' agreements). In addition, China had to increase the value-added content of the products manufactured in China. While China is the 'workshop' of the Western countries, a low-cost assembling factory manufacturing foreign designed and low-value, mass-marketed products, the terms of the trade are steadily deteriorating. Between 2013 and 2014, China's government had to grant substantial salary increases to cope with the growing dissatisfaction of its urban workers, the core of its supporting class base. The domestic share of the cost of goods 'Made in China' remains very low, as does average productivity. Facing the increasing competition of countries offering labour at a lower cost, China must move towards a more sophisticated range of products, including a higher proportion of goods manufactured in China.

However, China remains a powerful catalyst to neighbouring countries and a major exporter to those that are most developed, such as Japan and Australia (the latter mainly exporting minerals, and the former manufacturing products such as cars and machine tools). As experienced by the USA shortly after World War II, China must behave appropriately with regard to its neighbouring countries. This should be done either by producing a slight overall deficit of the trade balance to bolster markets with the necessary purchasing power and/or by transferring additional sources of financing (similar to the Marshall Plan). China's market is increasingly important to the large multinationals for extending the production chain and keeping manufacturing costs as low as possible.

Immediately the Western countries were hit by the recession, it was of the utmost importance for Western companies to expand their sales to the Chinese market as an alternative source of business.

Last, but not least, China is increasingly acting as a 'lender of last resort'. During the global financial crisis, China often subscribed to Treasury bonds issued by European countries (such as Ireland, Portugal, Spain and Greece) suffering from the debt crisis – not to mention the dollar denominated US$1.3 billion Treasury bonds stored in the coffers of China's central bank. On a bilateral basis, China demanded a foothold in the local distribution network (Pireus, the port facilities of Athens) to obtain access to the European market; on a Europe-wide basis, China's government demanded that the statute of 'market economy' be recognized; this entails some trade benefits and different legal practices. As the European Union (EU) was reluctant to grant such a statute, China withdrew its support to widely indebted EU member states. With regard to the surrounding south-east countries, China granted a set of swap agreements to cope with the shortage of international means of payment. It is worth noting that, despite sharp domestic recession, foreign direct investment (FDI) into China from the Western developed countries did not diminish but, rather, kept growing.

The recovery plans

Following the failure of Lehman Brothers (15 September 2008), the Chinese government managed to launch a comprehensive recovery plan as early as November 2008. The recovery plan was very 'Keynesian' by nature, including a massive cash injection into the Chinese economy, combining many types of instruments at the disposal of a centralized and authoritarian government such as China's combining fiscal, monetary and exchange policies. (See Table 2.1.)

Fiscal policy: To meet with the scale and the urgency of the crisis, the Chinese government used the quickest, easiest and most effective instruments; a programme of public works amounting to Rmb 4,000 billion (US$650 billion); that is, 40 per cent of the GDP spread over a two-year period, a budget deficit of up to 3 per cent of GDP and a doubling of the volume of bank lending (from US$800 to US$1,600 billion in 2009).

The Chinese recovery plan emphasized infrastructure, public works and low-cost housing. Infrastructure development programmes focused on communications: highways; railways (Pekin–Lhassa), high-speed trains (HST) – for example, the Guangzhu (Canton)–Wuhan route, which reduced the travelling time from eleven to three hours;

Table 2.1 Recovery plan (US$ billion)

United States	627
China	590
Japan	465
European Union	200 *

* This figure does not include the contracyclical social security payments.

telecommunications networks and the Internet. The Chinese HST network increased from 450 km in 2008 to 8,400 km in 2011 (the second largest network in the world) and is expected to reach 19,000 km in 2014. A US$23 billion development plan was disbursed to create a 100 per cent 'Made in China' version of the HST. With 500 million users, the number of people connected to the web overran the US market. In 2009, in light of the many wasted investments that had been made, the recovery plan was reoriented towards more social expenditures: education, health, countryside infrastructures, innovation, research and development (R&D) and regional subsidies in the western, less-developed provinces. Some items were specifically directed to improve consumption in line with the long-term strategy: distribution of coupons to those with low incomes, a 13 per cent premium on household appliances, US$50 billion tax cuts, cancellation of the centuries-old land tax and the lowering of the down payments for first-time buyers – none of which caused the existing system to fail. A sovereign fund, the China Investment Corporation (CIC) formed in 2007, was instructed to stop overseas investments (such as in the defaulting banks Bear Stern and Fortis) in order to re-orientate their investment policy towards the domestic market and the western provinces.

Monetary policy: As fiscal policy was designed to stimulate demand, monetary policy was expected to lower borrowing costs during the initial phase and maintain control of inflation pressures when growth bounces back.

Throughout 2009, the central bank (the People's Bank of China) worked out a plan including rate cuts to lower the cost of refinancing banks, as well as the interest rates paid on the bank deposits. The central bank held the view that they should make these funds available for corporate and individual borrowers, and then decrease the bank reserve requirements to decrease interest rates. On the government's initiative, commercial banks were instructed to implement a massive increase in loans, which doubled from 2008 to 2009. In order to support exporting companies hit by the crisis of the developed countries, the government tax on exports was lifted.

Foreign exchange policy: Furthermore, the government stopped the steady upward climb of the exchange rate which, again, was tied to the dollar rate. The US$/Rmb rate was frozen so that the Yuan followed the downward trend of the US dollar. Subsequently, all the other currencies, including the euro, were appreciated against the Yuan, disturbing the trade flows of goods.

In as early as the second half of 2009, the growth of the Chinese economy shot back up again. The growth rate of the 2010 GDP was back to 9.6 per cent but soon fell to 7.5 per cent in 2012 after a slight bounce in 2011. In light of price increases (food, housing and raw materials), the central bank was forced to increase interest rates and the reserve requirements to maintain control of inflation pressures. In 2010, the price increase reached 5.2 per cent. Fearing the coming of a housing bubble, especially in large cities such as Shanghai, the central bank had to implement credit restraints. As a tool against inflation, the Rmb was disconnected from the anchor of the US dollar and the government restarted the policy of slow-paced currency appreciation.

However effective the recovery plan was – with growth returning as early as autumn of 2009, public investment programmes nonetheless had their shortcomings: small and medium-sized companies, privately owned-companies and newly formed hi-tech companies that did not have access to bank credit were set aside by the rescue plan.

- Government subsidies, and also bank credits, were granted to large SOEs and the local authorities, leading to numerous areas of waste; useless infrastructures and production over-capacity. In a number of industries, over-capacity was a further burden on company balance sheets (cement, steel, aluminium, chemicals) and unsalable inventories grew. From 2008 to 2009, the volume of steel production increased from 600 to 800 million tons as the world market demand fell away. In 2009, the government and the Party sent several missions to audit investment and infrastructure projects financed by fresh loans or subsidies. A number of projects were suspended in more than 70 industrial sectors. Factories causing pollution and dangerous mines were closed.
- Millions of migrants were laid off and travelled back to their home villages, where they struggled to find work, becoming a burden to their families.

- The recovery plan, and the subsequent credit and fund allocation, was an inducement to further corruption and misappropriation of funds. The energetic and powerful Minister of Railways, Liu Xijun, once highly praised for his achievements, was arrested and sued for embezzlement to the tune of several billion dollars.
- The crisis was an opportunity for the government to reclaim centre stage and to recapture former powers of control. Maoist factions raised their voices (the 'New Left') and demanded that reform-minded policy be rejected in favour of the former state-driven governance, disturbing the sensitive balance between government regulations and market forces.

The double dip crisis and the second recovery plan

The sizeable injection of funds in the first recovery plan was effective as early as the second part of 2009 but, in early 2010, the growth rate fell once again from 11.9 per cent in the first quarter of 2010 to 7.4 per cent in the third quarter of 2012. China was hit by the overall trade slowdown. China's trade balance was halved but remained positive: exports were decreasing less than imports. Exporting companies were badly hit. In the eastern coastal provinces, a number of companies were forced to lay off millions of workers, starting with migrant workers; some were forced to close. According to the IMF, a 1.75 per cent decrease in the world GNP would lead to a 4 per cent decrease in China's GDP. The US economy had fallen below a 2 per cent growth rate and the European growth rate was close to zero. The member countries were involved in a deadly race for competitive decrease in fiscal policy. Although the European countries had been hit by a harsh recession, all of them simultaneously cut off social transfers and budget expenditures. Consumer demand was suspended while savings increased and capital expenditures were postponed. Subsequently, all Chinese industries issued (lower) profit warnings: airlines (Air China, Southern Airlines, Eastern Airlines), telecommunication companies (ZTE, Huawei), household appliances (Suning), television manufacturers (TCL), sports clothing companies (Li Ning) and cement (Anhui Conch Cements). The neighbouring countries (Japan, South Korea, Taiwan) were also hit. FDI decreased by 8.7 per cent in 2012.

Having learned a great deal from the first (2008) recovery plan, central government took more or less the same steps but with much greater focus than previously. With inflation under control, the central bank lowered the reserve requirements and interest rates again, in order to lower the banks' refinancing costs. Due to a limited budget deficit (which did not exceed 1.25 per cent of the GDP) and to central government debt (which remained low at 22 per cent of the GDP), the government enjoyed a certain freedom of action. Local authorities undertook a number of sizable infrastructure projects. But the government became increasingly concerned about the rapidly growing indebtedness of the local communities. As most local communities borrowed through special borrowing vehicles, the total amount was unknown but, according to some Western estimates, bank lending to the local authorities may have been as high as Rmb 10,000 (US$1,500 billion).

As the renewal of the leading team approaches, corruption trials are the best way to erase political rivals. Bo Xilai, a strong, powerful and brilliant 'neo-Maoist', secretary of the largest Chinese city, Chongqing, a candidate to the next State Council was arrested and sued for corruption and mistreatment. He was involved in an obscure affair – a mixture of sex, murder and corruption, a blessing for the Chinese and foreign press. As planned, the new team which emerged from the November 2012 'election' was headed by Xi Jinping (General Secretary, President of the Military Committee and President of the Republic) and Li Keqiang (Prime Minister). The number of members of the State Council was reduced from nine to seven, which gave some room for the new Supreme Leader to appoint new members closer to him or for a rival faction to demand compensation at some point in the future. The rise of the new team was followed by a wave of anti-corruption campaigns to eliminate the potential rivals.

Xi Jinping and Li Keqiang: the Chinese 'dream'

In November 2013, on the occasion of the semi-annual Central Committee meeting devoted to economic issues, the new government confirmed its commitment to the policy of reform. Attached to the final press release was a 30-page document including no fewer than 60 proposals of significant economic steps, few social measures and no political measures at all. A National Security Committee was appointed to involve the various factions. A Commission was formed to study ways by which to extend the scope of marketization. The Commission was chaired by Wang Ming, governor of Guangdong province who is said to be a staunch reformist and a close follower of Xi. The single-child policy was marginally amended. The cancellation of the internal passport was fettered (*hukou*) but no firm commitment was taken, given the sensitive nature of this issue.

China is changing course, starting a new venture with a certain level of assets: a relatively low central budget deficit and public debt, a trade surplus as well as a continuous flow of FDI (though a declining one), a large level of foreign exchange reserves (US$4,000 billion), a stable political regime, a new team in charge for the next ten years and a strong one-party system. There are, however, some shortcomings: a slowing growth rate (though still high by Western standards), a decreased export surplus (though still positive), a team of ageing leaders reluctant to advance any substantial innovation, an omnipresent and omniscient bureaucracy, widespread corruption from top to bottom of the hierarchical structure, a lack of democratic procedures, the lack of the Rule of Law, an unbalanced economy, and Party/government interference in all areas.

3
A Fast but Unbalanced Growth

Knowledge and action are two in the same.
(Wang Yanming 1472–1529)

Over the past 35 years, since the inception of the policy of reform and opening in 1978, China has experienced an exceptionally high growth rate. Over the first decade of the twenty-first century, China recorded a growth rate in excess of 10 per cent. The world financial crisis accelerated the process which, in effect, had already been in operation for some considerable time. Over the last few years, China has stepped up a breakthrough, leading to its emergence on the global scene. According to the '72' law,[1] China should overtake the USA within the next 10 or 20 years (see Table 3.4). In 2011, the IMF expected that China would overtake the USA in 2016. But the computing method was said to have been biased by two factors: a miscalculation of GDP and the foreign exchange rate. In 2009, China altered the calculation method but, as the foreign exchange rate used for the calculation is the prevailing rate, the actual growth rate was grossly underestimated.

Until the mid-nineteenth century, China was by far the world's largest economy. For a number of debatable reasons, China missed the Industrial Revolution. In addition to critical institutional reasons, suffice it to say that China experienced her most crucial and troubled century before the inception of the period of reform and opening-up. Following Japan and Korea, it is now China's turn to take off. After a full century of chaos and humiliation of national pride, China is now back in the game (see Tables 3.1, 3.2 and 3.3).

If an 'emerging' country is a country which has managed to transform the take-off period into a period of sustained economic and social development, China has all the attributes of an emerging economy: high

Table 3.1 China's share of world GNP (%)

	1700	1820	1952	1979	2000
China	22.3	32.9	5.2	4.9	15.1
Japan	4.1	3.0	3.4	7.6	6.6
Europe	24.9	26.6	29.3	27.8	21.1
USA	0.1	1.8	27.5	21.6	20.6
India	24.4	16.0	4.0	3.3	5.5

Source: Maddison (2007b).

Table 3.2 Average GNP growth rate

	1700–1820	1820–1952	1952–1978	1978–2003
China	0.85	0.22	4.39	7.85
Japan	0.25	1.70	4.78	2.53
Europe	0.58	1.71	4.37	2.00
USA	2.72	3.76	3.61	2.94
India	0.17	0.56	3.85	5.28
World	0.07	0.93	2.62	1.55

Source: Maddison (2007b).

Table 3.3 Average growth rate per capita

	1700–1820	1830–1952	1952–1978	1978–2003
China	0.00	- 0.10	2.3	36.57
Japan	0.13	0.95	6.6	92.11
Europe	0.14	1.05	3.6	31.79
USA	0.72	1.6	12.2	41.85
India	- 0.03	0.1	31.6	63.27
World	0.07	0.9	32.6	21.55

Source: Maddison (2007b).

growth rate, low income level per capita, an economy drawn by foreign trade and government investments, and a dual society which mirrors a dual economy. As such, China is a member of the BRICS club (Brazil, Russia, India, China and South Africa). Apart from the combination of a high level of growth and low income per capita, the BRICS countries have very little else in common. Their respective growth models are quite different. India and Brazil are federal democracies, whereas India

Table 3.4 Year when China overran or will overrun USA

	China–USA ratio
1999 Steel consumption	6.6
2001 Mobile telephones	3.3
2009 Exports	1.3
2009 Capital goods investments	1.4
2010 Manufacturing industry	1.1
2010 Energy consumption	1.1
2010 Sales of cars	1.2
2010 Number of patents	1.1
2014 Retail sales	0.7
2014 Imports	0.8
2016 GDP (PPP*)	0.8
2018 GDP (MR**)	0.5
2020 Stock exchange capitalization	0.3
2023 Consumption expenditures	0.2
2025 Military expenditures	0.2

Sources: *The Economist*, BP, CETC, IMF, Thomas Reuter, WIPO, World Bank, WFE. * PPP: purchasing power parity; ** MR: foreign exchange market rate.

has a parliamentary government and Brazil a presidential one. Russia and China are authoritarian regimes, Russia with a supposedly pluralistic democracy and China with a one-party system. Russia and Brazil are large producers of raw materials (oil and gas for Russia; coal, iron ore and oil for Brazil), while India and China are large consumers of raw materials. Every member country has developed its own model, a given mix of market forces and state interference, authoritarian and democratic regimes, statism and liberalism.

The Chinese growth rate is made up of a set of economic, social and polytypical specifics: unbalanced growth where savings exceed investments, investments that grow faster than consumption; growth which leads to inequalities, pollution and corruption; the constant threat of inflation; an economy threatened by the increase in labour costs; corporate relocations; highly dependent on the Western developed countries; a trade balance which is overwhelmingly positive towards the USA and the European Union, but negative with regard to China's neighbours (including Japan and Australia). The growth period is regularly interrupted by inflation which requires growth brakes: as further noted, inflation is a political as well as an economic event.

Growth components

China's unusually high growth rate is a kind of enigma. But one must always keep in mind that those figures are nothing but 'average' figures which hide wide discrepancies: between coastal and internal provinces, and between urban and rural areas (see Table 3.5). China is rich but the Chinese are not. China is becoming closer to the technological threshold where an economy should shift its emphasis from an exogenous growth model to a more endogenous one – from exports and government investment to household consumption and private investment. Last, but by no means least, we should take into account production factors in terms of energy consumption, labour costs, transportation costs, fiscal or social contributions and land prices, etc. Generally speaking, China is suffering from a rural to urban resident bias, from agriculture to industrial activities, from consumers to producers.

Until the emergence of the communication and information technology growth cycle, the industrial level of a given country was measured in terms of steel production. This was the basic ingredient of many key industries: construction and public works, housing, shipyards, automobile, armaments, and so on. In this regard, China is the world's largest steel producer, growing from one quarter (26 per cent) of the world's output in 2004 to nearly half (47 per cent) in 2012. Symbolizing the shift of manufacturing capacities from West to East, China is also the world's largest car market and the world's largest car manufacturer (27 million per annum) ahead of the USA (see Table 3.6).

Table 3.5 GDP growth rate (%)

2005	2006	2007	2008	2009	2010	2011	2012	2013
11.3	12.7	14.2	9.6	9.1	10.3	9.6	7.5	7.7

Source: OECD.

Table 3.6 Production of light vehicles (m)

	1995	2009
China	1.3	13
USA	14.7	10.4
Japan	6.7	4.6
Germany	3.5	4.0

Source: *The Financial Times*.

But China is moving into the upper bracket, into the most hi-tech of manufacturing industries: aerospace, aircraft, personal computers, research browsers, and so on. Following Japan's lead, China's range of products is also increasing. In December 2013, China landed on the moon and is expected to land a Chinese astronaut in the coming years. The world's most powerful computer is 'Made in China'. With 750 million internet users, China has overtaken the American IT market.

Based on the official exchange rate, Chinese GDP does not exceed 15 per cent of that of the USA, but in terms of purchasing power parity (PPP), the Chinese GDP per capita might be somewhere between one quarter and one third of American GDP. The average level of GDP per head teaches us next to nothing about the actual income per capita split between investment, consumption and exports and the distribution of the national income split between consumption, savings and imports (see Table 3.7).

As China is a dual society where the gap between the rich and poor is steadily increasing, the Chinese economy is also dual in the sense that the most developed industries coexist with the least developed. In the countryside, one may come across a Chinese family using a plough because the plot of land is simply too small to justify the use of a tractor. The grandmother is looking for the little (single) child at the end of the furrow ... close to a city in which is located the most advanced research centre staffed with white-coated engineers. In terms of value added – that is, the extra wealth produced by the Chinese factories – the Chinese

Table 3.7 GDP per capita (PPA) (US$ billion)

USA	45,935	Russia	14,913
Germany	34,388	Brazil	10,499
France	33,434	China	6,778
Japan	32,554	India	3,015

Sources: IMF, World Bank, OECD.

Table 3.8 Value added of the manufacturing industry (US$ billion), 2010

China	1,998
USA	1,952
Japan	618
Germany	408
Total	10,078

Source: Boston Consulting Group.

manufacturing sector accounts for 20 per cent of the world total which is equivalent to the USA (see Table 3.8).

Of the ten manufacturing companies which experienced the highest value added increase over the five-year period 2006–10, the top three were Chinese: Shandong Weigao (+92.2 per cent), Tencent HK (+83.4 per cent), Baidu (+72.7 per cent), all of which are involved in the IT industry. In addition, to measure Chinese GDP, we must take into account the respective productivity of the means of production.

A savings rate much higher than the investment rate

China is experiencing an unusually high savings rate unknown in other countries. Over the last thirty-year period of reform and opening (since 1978), the consumption rate has continued to decrease to something in the order of an average of 30 per cent while the investment rate has continued to increase, getting close to 45 per cent of the GDP with the savings rate now ranging over the 50 per cent level (see Table 3.9).

The Chinese have always being reluctant to entrust their savings to banks or state institutions – and not without reason. Deprived of alternative saving instruments for a long period, Chinese savers had no choice but low interest savings bank accounts and Treasury bonds. Deprived of the protection of social security net, Chinese households have to put aside enough money to cope with unexpected hitches in life (health, pensions) (see Table 3.10). Furthermore, the policy of reform and opening, together with increasing purchasing power, gave the

Table 3.9 Investment and savings rates (% GDP), 2010

	1993–7	1998–2002	2003–7	2008
Investment	36.1	36.0	42.3	43.6
Saving	37.0	37.3	46.1	50.9

Source: OECD, *China Economic Survey*.

Table 3.10 Savings rate distribution among industrial sectors (% GDP), 2010

	1999–2002	2003–8
State	3.6	2.8
Household	18.9	6.7
Corporations	13.7	13.7

Source: OECD, *China Economic Survey*.

Chinese more autonomy in spending their income. Most of the newly reformed companies have to generate profits and their management is accountable. Subsequently, social benefits such as schools, health care, retirement care and housing formerly supplied by large state-owned companies are now being marketed at market price. Each household must ensure its children's future (even though, in most cases, it is a child, rather than children): school, university and housing. A bride would hesitate to marry a young man who does not earn a good wage, preferring to choose a partner working in a government office or a state-owned company and being able to live in a private apartment to prevent friction related to sharing a home with the mother-in-law.

It is worth noting that half of China's savings are due to self-financing out of corporate profits, and urban and rural residents having very different consumption behaviours. An urban resident consumes three times as much as a rural resident. Urbanization is therefore highly important to consumption behaviour and the industrialization process. This situation is widely due to Mao's legacy where farmers and rural households were pressurized into financing the country's growth. Farmers were essentially paid in kind (housing, canteen, school provisions and health care) – savings having been useless since there was nothing for sale in the shops. Banks were required to mop up the excess unused income in the form of savings. When the institutional context changed, so too did the behaviour of the Chinese – although this took much longer.

High investment rate at the expense of consumption

Over a ten-year period starting in the early 2000s, the consumption rate continued to decrease as a percentage of GDP while investments, as well as exports, continued to grow. However, with the onset of the global financial crisis, the trade component began to decline. Though both exports and imports were halved, exports decreased less than imports so that the trade balance continued to provide a monthly surplus in the range of US$20–30 billion (instead of US$40–50 billion). As a result, exchange reserves keep increasing, albeit at a slower pace. Subsequently, the share of consumption in GDP continued to grow at a slower pace than the overall GDP and the investment rate (see Table 3.11). Government efforts to rebalance the Chinese economy towards a greater share of domestic consumption have not yet borne fruit (see Table 3.12). Household consumption is increasing in absolute terms but continues to decrease in relative terms as a percentage of overall GDP. Sooner or later, the government will have to take a much stronger direction

Table 3.11 GDP distribution (%)

	Household consumption	Capital expenditures	Trade balance
2000	62.3	35.3	2.4
2001	61.3	36.5	3.2
2002	59.6	37.8	2.6
2003	56.8	41.0	2.2
2004	54.3	43.0	2.7
2005	52.8	41.5	6.3
2006	50.7	41.7	7.6
2007	49.5	41.6	9.9
2008	48.5	43.8	7.7
2009	48.5	47.2	4.3
2010	48.1	48.1	3.8
2011	49.0	48.3	2.7

Source: National Bureau of Statistics, *China Statistical Yearbook* (2013).

Table 3.12 Distribution of GDP components (%, 2004–9)

	Consumption	Investment	Export/Import	Saving
China	50.3	41.2	8.6	49.7
Brazil	80.5	16.9	2.6	19.6
Germany	76.7	18.1	5.2	23.3
India	68.6	31.5	– 0.1	31.4
Japan	75.9	22.7	1.4	24.1
Korea	68.6	29.0	2.4	31.4
Russia	67.6	19.9	12.5	32.4
UK	86.2	16.6	– 2.8	13.8
USA	86.6	18.3	– 4.8	13.4

Source: World Bank, *World Development Indicators*.

than it has so far in order to reach its ultimate goal of rebalancing the economy.

In the long term, China's growth policy is a 'supply' policy as opposed to a 'demand' policy. But, in the short term, China's government has used all the tools at its disposal to stimulate demand in the economy, household expenditures and, above all, government and corporate capital expenditures – whether micro-economic or macro-economic, administrative, or global. They have followed a very pragmatic, demand-type approach. Though China's economy has changed considerably over time, the institutional framework remains highly Maoist in nature: a totalitarian one-party system. The government draws and reorients resources from the rural and agricultural sector so as to build up a strong manufacturing base.

Compared with other emerging and developing countries, Chinese GDP distribution shows a unique consumption/investment and savings/investment ratio. The consumption rate is lower and savings rates are higher than investment (see Table 3.13). In addition, the less protected rural savers have a higher savings rate than consumption-oriented urban residents. Subsequently, Chinese savings are invested in foreign countries as a financial investment, mostly in dollar denomination (Treasury bonds) and, to a lesser extent, in real asset investments (the acquisition of foreign companies and foreign properties). It is fair to say that the savings of the poor Chinese peasants are used to fund the pensions of wealthy retired Americans.

As a consequence, consumption prices do not show the information function they are supposed to indicate in resources allocation. In a market economy, the compared market prices should inform consumer choice, corporate decision in capital expenditure and government policy.

In addition, the growth rate is unevenly distributed. There is a widening gap between the rate of growth and the rate of income per capita in the different provinces (see Table 3.14). This is stronger in the coastal provinces than in the interior provinces, and stronger in the urban areas than in the countryside. Agriculture-oriented interior provinces have a stronger savings rate and a lower growth rate. In the 1980s, during the early stages of the policy of reform and opening-up, a farmer's income grew more rapidly than the overall GDP and a strong rural

Table 3.13 Household consumption rate and investment rate (GDP %)

	Consumption rates	Investment rates
2003	42.0	41.0
2004	40.0	43.0
2005	38.0	41.5
2006	35.0	41.7
2007	36.0	41.6
2008	35.0	43.8
2009	34.0	47.2
2010	35.0	48.1
2011	34.0	48.3

Source: National Bureau of Statistics (2014).

Table 3.14 GDP per capita by province (%)

	1978–2007	1978–87	1988–97	1998–2007
All provinces (30)	77.0	7.8	5.4	10.3
Coastal provinces (11)	8.1	7.8	6.1	11.9
Interior provinces (19)	7.5	7.3	5.5	10.9
Highest growth rate provinces	10.3	11.2	10.8	13.1
Lowest growth rate	6.1	1.9	1.1	8.2

Source: National Bureau of Statistics, *China Statistical Yearbook* (2014).

industrialization rate was provided through the TVEs. Following the Tien An Men rising and the frozen policy of reform, the emphasis was once more switched to the urban working class. From 2002–3 onwards, the newly appointed government team (Hu Jintao and Wen Jiabao) attempted to rebalance the economy, but so far to no significant avail. The gap between the growth rate of the interior and coastal provinces continues to widen with the exception of the interior industrial centres such as Chongqing, Wuhan, Kunming and Chengdu. In the coastal cities (former 'treaty ports'), a new strong middle class has emerged numbering between 100 and 200 million people. (The number of members of this new middle class depends on the type of goods used as the key indicator; e.g. the number of cars, or the number of freezers, or the number of private houses will each yield widely varying results.). This class is more exposed to Western consumption patterns which, in turn, nurture the local growth rate.

Once China has fully integrated the domestic market, Chinese multinationals will be in a position to compete on an even basis with the foreign multinationals. As with the USA, production lines are amortized on an ever larger domestic market so that Chinese companies are marketing their products on a marginal basis at a much lower price.

State investment overcoming private investment

Capital expenditures are mostly financed through government subsidies and development banks, as well as commercial banks in favour of local collectives and SOEs. This is a leading source of waste and misappropriation. A large portion of investment is dedicated to infrastructures and prestige investments, rather than productive investments. For example, empty highways where the only users are sweeping women dressed in a shapeless heavy lined coat with a wide straw hat tied under the chin by a ribbon. Most factories struggle with overcapacity (steel and cement industries, oil refining) and the corporate balance sheets are loaded by useless and ever-increasing inventory items.

Conversely, privately owned companies – and, generally speaking, the individual, small-sized, privately owned companies which are less investment consuming – are deprived of credits and are too small to tap into the stock exchange and the bond markets.

Restructuring of production lines

The production distribution between primary (agriculture and mining), secondary (manufacturing) and tertiary (services) industries is biased by state interference and investment flows. Theoretically, a developing economy puts emphasis first on the primary, then on the secondary and finally on the tertiary sectors. In the first phase, the agricultural sector provides an increasing contribution to the GDP at a low and decreasing rate of productivity, which then stabilizes in absolute terms or increases but at a much slower pace than the overall GDP, subsequently declining in relative terms. As a result, manufacturing grows at a higher productivity rate until it flat-lines and begins to decrease in relative terms. Finally, the tertiary sector increases both in absolute and relative terms but at a slower rate of productivity. Due to the high level of investment, China's secondary sector has remained at a high level (over 40 per cent of GDP) while the tertiary has continued to grow (see Table 3.15). The tertiary sector is very mixed, including both street-manufacturers of noodle soup and hi-tech start-ups staffed with highly skilled engineers in white coats.

Table 3.15 GDP distribution by sector (%)

	Primary	Secondary	Tertiary
2000	15.1	45.9	39.9
2001	14.4	45.2	40.5
2002	13.7	44.8	41.5
2003	12.8	46.0	41.2
2004	13.4	46.2	41.2
2005	12.1	47.4	40.5
2006	11.1	47.9	40.9
2007	10.8	47.3	41.9
2008	10.7	47.4	41.8
2009	10.3	46.2	43.4
2010	10.1	46.7	43.2
2011	10.0	46.6	43.4

Source: National Bureau of Statistics, *China Statistical Yearbook* (2014).

As the contributions of the tertiary sector showed an increasing contribution to the GDP growth rate (flow), the manufacturing sector kept an important share in GDP (stock) (see Table 3.16). This situation was due to political bias. From a political point of view, the Party–State is still very urban and working-class oriented. From an economic point of view, the Party leaders are all (or mostly) industrial engineers by birth and by education. Finally, it is a matter of policy that the tertiary sector should be backed by a strong manufacturing sector. Even though the

Table 3.16 Contribution to GDP growth by sector (%)

	GDP	Primary	Secondary	Tertiary	Industry
2000	8.4	0.4	5.1	2.9	4.9
2001	8.3	0.4	3.9	4.0	3.5
2002	9.1	0.4	4.5	4.1	4.0
2003	10.0	0.3	5.9	3.8	5.2
2004	10.1	0.8	5.3	4.0	4.8
2005	11.3	0.6	5.8	4.9	4.9
2006	12.7	0.6	6.3	5.7	5.4
2007	14.2	0.4	7.2	6.2	6.6
2008	9.6	0.6	4.7	4.3	4.2
2009	9.2	0.4	4.8	4.0	3.7
2010	10.4	0.4	5.9	5.1	4.1
2011	9.3	0.4	4.8	4.1	4.2

Source: National Bureau of Statistics, *China Statistical Yearbook* (2014).

Table 3.17 Foreign trade (US$ billion)

	Exports	Imports	Trade balance
2000	249.2	225.1	24.1
2001	266.1	243.5	22.5
2002	325.6	295.1	30.4
2003	438.2	412.7	25.4
2004	593.3	561.2	32.1
2005	761.9	659.9	102.0
2006	968.9	791.4	177.5
2007	1220.4	956.1	264.3
2008	1430.7	1132.5	298.1
2009	1201.6	1005.9	195.7
2010	1577.7	1396.2	181.5
2011	1898.3	1743.4	154.9

Source: National Bureau of Statistics, *China Statistical Yearbook* (2014).

tertiary sector (services) has doubled in the last 30 years, the secondary sector (manufacturing) is still overwhelmingly dominant and important for foreign trade (see Table 3.17).

It is of growing concern that China's overall productivity rate has been in decline over the last few years (official data are not published) as a result of the global financial crisis and the subsequent decrease in the global growth rate. This is also due to China's maturing economy and the decrease in productivity which had begun before the crisis set in.

A high but decreasing trade surplus

In the reform and opening policy initiated by Deng Xiaoping and pursued by his followers, the word 'opening' is tightly entwined with 'reform'. In the very early days under Deng Xiaoping's authority, a number of study missions were dispatched around the world to developed, emerging and developing countries, including China's neighbouring Asian 'Tigers' – Japan, Korea and Taiwan. Their purpose was to explore different policies and avenues for growth. In every country, export and government investment played a critical role not only in designing industrial policy, but also in reforming the methods of corporate management. When these tours were concluded, discussion groups gathered at the highest levels of government to study the reports.

Over the years, China has captured a growing share of world trade, ranging from 2 per cent in the early days of the reform and opening-up policy to 17 per cent in 2011, which makes China the world's largest trading partner (see Table 3.18).

From the beginning of the twenty-first century, Chinese foreign trade provided a surplus, though this has now been halved in the wake of the global financial crisis. But, if China accounts for a growing share of world trade, its share remains marginal by country (under 5 per cent) and is not sufficiently large to justify the shift of trade flows from West to East and to threaten the Western employment rate (see Table 3.19).

Table 3.18 Trade volume (US$ billion)

China	1,578 mds
United States	1,272
Germany	1,269
Japan	770

Source: OECD (2013).

Table 3.19 China's share of trade flows by country (US$ billion) (% export/import)

Japan	5.0	South Africa	1.8	Brazil	0.9
South Korea	4.0	Egypt	1.6	Saudi Arabia	0.9
Russia	3.8	Canada	1.5	Switzerland	0.8
Australia	3.7	Germany	1.3	Poland	0.7
Indonesia	3.5	Italy	1.2	UK	0.6
USA	3.5	Spain	1.2	Netherland	0.5
Malaysia	2.2	Argentina	1.1	Nigeria	0.5
Thailand	2.2	Sweden	1.1	Taiwan	0.5
France	1.1	India	0.4		

Vulnerable export industries

In the aftermath of the global financial crisis, Chinese exports decreased in 2009 but resumed growth in 2010, only to fall again in 2011 following the double-dip recession. This trend is not a hitch; rather, it is a long-lasting process. It is likely that China's foreign trade is in transition. To cope with the new situation, the government took a certain number of initiatives, both short-term and some long-term, with the intention of restructuring the entire export sector (see also Table 3.20).

- Initially, the government took steps in favour of export companies. The tax on exports was cancelled and replaced by a more neutral Value Added Tax. The US$/Rmb foreign exchange rate was frozen from June 2009 to July 2010. Therefore, the foreign exchange rate decreased against all the other currencies (including emerging and developing countries). Now that the Yuan's links to the US dollar have been relaxed, if the Yuan appreciates against the US dollar less than the other currencies, it is actually depreciating against the other currencies, such as the euro and the sterling. Some countries (Brazil) have complained and certain others have intervened in the foreign exchange market to lower their currency (Japan). But it is a very costly policy as the country is selling its own currency (yen) against the US dollar, bringing about inflation pressures, increasing interest rates, and so on.
- In order to compensate for the decreasing demand from developed countries (USA, the EU), China's exports have shifted to the neighbouring south-Asian markets (ASEAN) and emerging markets (Africa, South America). To support its exports, China is granting huge soft loans through the China Export-Import Bank, China Development Bank, and state-owned banks. When the world financing crisis erupted, the World Bank gave a warning to the developed countries not to cut off credit facilities to the stifled developing countries and raw material

producers hit by the credit crunch. In the USA's own backyard (Latin America), China granted a US$10 billion loan to the Brazilian oil company Petrobras to fund common exploration campaigns in new oil fields, thus becoming Brazil's largest trading partner. China is also the largest trading partner of Saudi Arabia, as well as a significant investor in the country. In Europe, China has purchased huge amounts of problem debt (Portugal, Spain and Greece) with the expectation of being granted a statute of market economy which enjoys a certain number of commercial advantages. China has built a new pier in the Pireus port facilities as a foothold in the European single market and is about to build another. A loan of several billion dollars (the aggregated figure has not been made public) has been granted to Greek shipping companies to purchase Chinese made tankers.

- To compete on an even footing with Western companies, China must raise the Chinese content in the added value of exports. It is a much broader issue which involves education, university qualifications, research and innovation. In 2011, for the first time, a Chinese construction and public works company (the Overseas Engineering Group) was granted a public works contract by auction in a European country (Poland) for the construction of a highway connecting Berlin and Warsaw.[2]
- As a result of the growing payment surplus due to the trade balance and foreign investment (whether direct investment or financial investment) causing strong inflation pressures, the government has

Table 3.20 Export distribution (%)

	Agricultural products	**Manufacturing products**
2000	10.1	89.7
2001	8.8	90.1
2002	9.7	91.2
2003	7.9	92.0
2004	6.8	93.1
2005	6.4	93.5
2006	5.4	94.5
2007	5.0	94.7
2008	5.4	94.5
2009	5.2	94.7
2010	5.1	94.8
2011	5.2	94.7

Source: National Bureau of Statistics, *China Statistical Yearbook* (2014).

maintained foreign exchange control. If and when the Chinese government is about to change its mind and begin loosening foreign exchange control, it is likely to be made for internal reasons (inflation), rather than external reasons (under foreign pressure). A heavy cushion of foreign exchange reserves (US$4,000 bn) is indispensable in order to overcome the transition from foreign demand to domestic consumption demand, and to shift emphasis from investment to domestic consumption as the new economic engine. For the time being, domestic policy is separate from foreign exchange, but once the Rmb is fully convertible, China will lose control over its monetary and fiscal policy. In the longer term, a substantial foreign exchange buffer is a strong asset when the time comes to rebuild the shaky International Monetary System.

- Fearing a nuclear attack – first, from the USA during the Korean war and, then, from the Soviet Union in the aftermath of the 31st Party Congress – Mao moved the factories critical industries to the internal western provinces. In contrast, following the new policy of reform and opening-up, Deng Xiaoping shifted emphasis to the coastal provinces. Once again, since 2002, the government has shifted emphasis to the internal provinces, where labour costs are lower (but the transportation costs are higher). In the meantime, China has improved her process of innovation and entered new markets which had long been beyond its reach: automobile (hybrid and electrical cars), aerospace, aircraft and bio-technologies.

High but decreasing foreign direct investment

Originally, China was looking for foreign investment, not only to draw on foreign capital, but also to catch new technical processes and new management techniques. At the time of writing, China is no longer interested in foreign exchange income but, rather, is looking primarily to technological transfers. The global financial crisis accelerated the existing process: disheartened by discriminative measures, some foreign investors refrained from investing, while some postponed or even cancelled planned direct investment in China – with some disinvesting by closing their operations.

Foreign direct investment in China

The flow of FDI in China has followed different trends and patterns over time. In the 1990s, following China's opening-up and joining the WTO, FDI enjoyed strong growth, reaching US$80 billion per annum. In a second step, from 2005 onwards, foreign investors participated in the 'privatization' wave of China's SOEs and SOBs, becoming public companies and listed on the stock exchange to take significant participation valued in billions of dollars. In the aftermath of the global financial crisis, some tried to withdraw – either because they were forced to, with the aim of focusing on their core business, or because they realized that the costly capital shares did not produce any significant dividend in terms of profit share or market share. The foreign banks which took significant shares in the state banks IPO and subsequent capital increase did not obtain any influence over the banks' management and strategy, or any penetration into the Chinese market.

Originally, China expected FDI to bring about capital funds, technological transfers and new management techniques. As China was piling up trillions of dollars of foreign exchange reserves, she lost interest in the transfer of funds, focusing instead on technological transfers, management techniques and international standards by selecting FDI. In addition, foreign investments are used by the Chinese government as an incentive to Chinese companies to put competitive pressure on the sectors targeted by the industrial government policy. The policy of a given industrial sector when opening up to foreign competition usually leads to a wave of government-sponsored concentration to build up large Chinese 'champions' to better compete with foreign multinationals – not only on the Chinese domestic market, but also in the international market and increasingly on their domestic market as well.

The foreign companies manufacturing tradable goods have quickly understood that they could not ignore a consumer market in excess of one billion. The trend was accelerated in the wake of the global crisis: as the Western markets were slowing down, the Chinese market became a crucial substitute market through which to compensate for the plummeting Western markets.

But Western investors face a certain number of obstacles: bureaucracy, networks, Western-made products unsuitable for the Chinese domestic market and Chinese consumers' taste, lack of the rule of the law, – in particular, a lack of protection of intellectual property, discriminatory measures – such as a lack of access to the auction of government-funded public works, salary increases, logistics problems, transportation costs and quality standards. Above all, most Western-style products were directed at a limited number of the Chinese population; that is, the 100 or 200 million people who have reached a Western level of income and consumer behaviour.

In the first phase, FDI increased faster than the already rapid Chinese growth rate. As a result of the global crisis, the flow of FDI slowed, the FDI growth rate being lower than the overall Chinese growth rate. FDI then resumed but at a slower pace than before. In the meantime, Chinese companies took advantage of the global crisis and the subsequent fall in the market price of foreign companies to increase their overseas acquisitions. This is despite Chinese FDI not exceeding one fifth or one third of the overall Western FDI in China.

Chinese overseas direct investment

In terms of the percentage of GDP, Chinese FDI has more than doubled since the early 2000s, from 2.6 per cent in 2000 to 5.3 per cent in 2011. Of a world total FDI, China is the second largest investment target (US$175 billion), far behind the USA (US$329 billion). Of this, US$106 billion is directed to mainland China (5th largest). Together with Hong Kong, China is also the second largest overseas investor, although far behind the USA. As both an investor and a target country, China already accounts for one third of the US figure (see Table 3.21).

In terms of geographical areas, Chinese FDI focused on Europe and China's neighbours, ahead of the USA and producers of raw material (see Table 3.22).

Table 3.21 Foreign direct investment (US$ billion), 2010

Investing countries		Target countries	
USA	329	USA	228
Germany	105	China	106
France	84	Hong Kong	69
Hong Kong	76	Belgium	62
China	68	Brazil	48
Switzerland	58	Germany	46
Japan	56	UK	46

Source: OECD.

Table 3.22 Chinese foreign direct investment by destination (US$ billion), 2010

Africa	215
Asia	8208
Europe	10429
Pacific	3225
South America	1950

Source: OECD.

Table 3.23 Some of the largest Chinese acquisitions of foreign companies

	Buyer	Seller	Amount (US$ billion)
2005	Lenovo	IBM	2.2
2010	Zheijiang Geely	Volvo	1.8
2010	Bright Food	United Biscuit	—
2012	Daliang Wanda	AMC	2.6
2012	Bright Food*	Weetabix	1.9
2013	Shuanhui Intal	Smithfield	4.7
2014	Lenovo	Motorola	—

In terms of industrial targets, Chinese companies, strongly backed by the Chinese government and government institutions, are targeting manufacturing industries: critical raw materials (iron ore, copper, bauxite) which are either missing or insufficient on the domestic market, suppliers of basic construction materials (cement, steel), oil companies, owners of promising production permits, or advanced technologies and hi-tech industries owning critical patents or processes, and so on (see Table 3.23).

Purchasing foreign industrial assets is a way of covering the foreign exchange risk of mostly dollar denominated foreign exchange reserves, either by investing in another currency, or investing in a company which is expected to offset the declining foreign exchange rate through the increase in asset price.

For Chinese companies, purchasing a foreign company is a means of: lengthening production lines, thus decreasing the average and marginal costs; accessing modern technology and penetrating developed markets; accessing the sources of raw materials; becoming involved in international competitive markets and meeting demanding international standards in term of quality or management. Purchasing a foreign company to establish oneself on a foreign market is a way to bypass the slowly developing Chinese domestic market and to gain time and experience. Due to the global financial crisis, Western companies listed on stock exchanges are very cheap – some priced below the capital base, or below the net asset valuation.

Some Chinese companies have been driven back on the grounds of data disclosure, national security or accounting standards. China is behaving in the same manner as Western countries, though to a larger extent. Nonetheless, in some cases, China's investment vehicles (CIC, Huyjin) have been approached by Western governments to bail out bankrupt banks or companies, but so far to no avail.

Pollution

China controls 21 per cent of the world population, 10 per cent of arable land and 7 per cent of water resources, but as far as pollution is concerned, China is a paradox. On the one hand, it is one of the most polluted countries in the world – if not *the* most; on the other hand, China is the world's largest investor in renewable energy and one of the most advanced countries in the manufacturing of wind power turbines. Though China is the world's greatest producer of CO_2 (overtaking the USA in 2011), China's wind power turbine manufacturers are among the leading firms in this field.

According to a report by the World Health Organization (WHO) in 2013, pollution in China has caused approximately 1.2 million premature deaths. In the most developing countries which are still at a very early stage of industrialization, growth targets have overcome the anti-pollution targets. They have to reach a certain level of growth rate and growth level before they can cope with the pollution issue and divert the necessary means. The failure of the 2010 Copenhagen summit was due to both the USA and China, the two most polluting countries – China positioning itself as the spokes of the developing nations. Both of the countries turned down firm commitments on volume and deadline targets. It is understandable that developing countries seek recognition of certain 'pollution rights' before their economies take off, that the costs of fighting against pollution be shared with the developed countries. In some developing countries, such as China and India, pollution is the bitter fruit of the rapid growth of industrialization (see Table 3.24). In this regard, China has inherited from the former Soviet countries the productivity bias, which put emphasis on quantity of goods instead of quality of life. In addition, China is the largest coal producer and most Chinese power stations are fuelled by coal (see Table 3.25). Quite often, the power stations are located in the very centre of the cities, as towns have been growing so swiftly.

It is worth mentioning that the pollution issue is not only a critical issue in China (as elsewhere), but is also one of the very few issues

Table 3.24 Greenhouse effect (m tons CO_2), 2009

China	6.921	Russia	1.779
USA	5.826	Japan	1.187
Europe	4.357	India	1.349

Source: International Energy Agency.

Table 3.25 Production of primary energies (%)

	1976	1986	1996	2006
Coal	68.8	72.4	74.9	75.7
Oil & gas	27.5	23.3	18.9	15.3
Other*	3.7	4.3	6.2	9.0

* Biomass (15%), gas(3%), hydroelectricity (2%), nuclear (0.79%).
Source: International Energy Agency.

capable of mobilizing the Chinese people which is occasionally tolerated by the Party leaders. Pollution is a critical, shared problem which may impair the expected growth rate above a certain level. Usually, courts and police forces are called to deal with demonstrations on a company's request. They are typically used to dishearten potential claims but, in some instances, the Party allowed leaks in the media so that, finally, an association of neighbours may obtain the closure of a polluting site, mine or factory. In 2011, a refinery based in Dalian (a north-east port city) was leaking a huge amount of raw oil. Surprisingly, the media were authorized to report the story. In 2013, Li Wen – the mayor of Kunming (the capital city of the province of Yunan in the south-west) – set up a website (through Weibo) to hold discussion with disgruntled citizens about the construction of a highly toxic paraxylen (PX) production unit.

China has the world's third largest coal reserves, behind the USA and Russia. However, the latter have plentiful oil and gas fields. In China, coal is still extensively used by thermal power stations. Coal still accounts for up to 75 per cent of energy sources (see Table 3.26). The use of coal has not actually decreased but, rather, is actually increasing. Water control is a critical issue and a strategic challenge for China. All the rivers in this region originate in the Himalayan Mountains, thus running through China from west to east. In 2004, the available water resources in China amounted to 2,200 litres per year per head (the world average is 8,800 litres). In 2012, the Three Gorges Dam, which led to the forced transfer of 2.5 million people, was inaugurated. China is one of the very few countries which did not sign the 1997 UN Convention on water sharing, which allows China to build a string of dams along the main rivers which pass through its territory (Yellow River-Huang He, Yangtze, Pearl River) and could be a source of conflict with neighbouring countries.

Due to its geographical location, China is exposed to climate change and natural and human disasters such as floods, drought, deforestation,

Table 3.26 CO_2 emission from coal (m tons)

	2000	2007
India	635	895
USA	2,120	2,115
China	2,460	5003

Sources: International Energy Agency and the OECD.

river diversion, soil exhaustion, urbanization, and exhaustion or pollution of ground water. Air pollution is causing 178,000 deaths each year and 300 million Chinese people have no access to tap water.

The Chinese perception of the threat of pollution has evolved over time according to the various accidents which have occurred. The first recorded wide-scale pollution accident in 1972 was caused by a leaking toxic waste pipe in Dalian Port. In 1978, legislation for protection of the environment was issued and, as a follow-up, a National Agency for Environmental Protection was formed. In spite of 1981 legislation which allows every citizen to sue the Administration before the Courts, legal cases have never led to any concrete steps being taken. In this kind of damaging situation, people turn directly to Party leaders and send a claim to Zhongnanhai (the Party Headquarters in Beijing), bypassing the bureaucrats and the local Party members. Some ecology-based non-governmental organizations (NGOs) have been formed to act on behalf of abandoned, remote people hit by environmental damage. In 1997, a petition issued by the city of Guiyang (Yunnan) near Chongqing was signed by over 10,000 people.

But China is not indifferent to the damage of pollution. Between 1978 and 1995, Chinese GNP increased fourfold, while energy consumption has only doubled. In other words, energy productivity has doubled in 17 years. The 2008 recovery plan would have decreased energy consumption by 20 per cent for each 1 per cent increase in GNP. The government formed the China Energy Conservation Investment Co., a type of investment company, to back up private initiatives and dedicated venture capital. Exchanges of carbon credits have been launched on the stock exchanges of Nanjing, Shanghai and Tianjin.

Solar power production capacity is expected to increase fivefold by 2020. By this time, China will be the world's largest manufacturer of photovoltaic cells. In 2011, Germany had a 54 per cent market share of renewable industries (wind power turbines, solar panels) but half of the wind power turbines installed in that country have been made in

Table 3.27 Major investors in renewable energy (US$ billion 2009)

China	34.0	Spain	10.4
USA	18.6	Brazil	7.4
UK	11.2	Germany	4.3

Source: *Les Echos*.

China. Chinese industry controls 89 per cent of the market share of the domestic market, 32 per cent of the US market and 32 per cent of the world market. Chinese prices are, on average, 30 per cent lower than Western competitors. Of the four largest turbine manufacturers, two are Chinese (Sinovel and Dongfang). As Chinese manufacturers are backed by a wide domestic market and substantial government subsidies, China is expected to capture a quasi-monopolist market share (see Table 3.27).

However, the global financial crisis has impacted the Chinese environmental industry as well as the Western companies. In 2011, over 85 per cent of the photovoltaic cells were produced in Asia. Consequently, most of the government subsidies granted by European countries to stimulate environmental industries were, in fact, allocated to Chinese or Chinese-owned companies. Following the global crisis, the government cut state aid (subsidies, soft loans and a higher purchasing power price). Subsequently, a number of ventures became bankrupt (Q-cells, Solon, Cionergy), including some Chinese companies (Suntech). In addition, China is now threatened by protectionist reprisals.

New independent workers trade unions

In 2012, a wave of strikes hit foreign companies located in China and, in particular, Japanese companies (Foxcon, Honda), which had been spreading all over China. The workers were demanding better working conditions and wages. It is not by mere chance that the workers' strikes burst out in foreign and, above all, Japanese factories. It is not by mere chance that the official trade unions linked to the Party (ACTUF) and the police forces have not been called to act (as would have typically been the case). Tolerated if not initiated by the Party-State, the strikes led to a salary increase of between 20 per cent and 30 per cent, which soon spilled out to all Chinese companies (e.g. mine workings, which are known to be very unsafe), in line with the government goal of increasing the purchasing power of low-paid Chinese consumers. Moreover, the government announced certain measures in favour of the 'migrant' population (*mingong*), the workers coming from the countryside and lacking the appropriate work permits. Their miserable wages are sent back to the family home as an indispensable extra income to make ends meet. They are poorly paid – usually in arrears, and sometimes not paid at all. Without the necessary *hukou* (the work permit), they are in an illegal situation at the mercy of dishonest employers, aggressive policemen or corrupt bureaucrats.

Unbalanced growth

According to the former Chinese Prime Minister, Wen Jiabao, the Chinese growth model is 'unbalanced, uncoordinated and unsustainable'. In Chinese, China is called *Zhong Guo* – which is usually translated as the 'Middle Empire' (literally the Land-Guo of the Middle-Zhong). But the character *Zhong* not only means 'centre' in the geographic sense of the word, but also the 'middle situation' in a moral or intellectual sense. In the former, China stands in the middle of the civilized world. In the latter, China's government keeps a middle position between factions. *Zhong* does not mean a shaky compromise between rival factions but, rather, a consensus between groups who share power. This is an unstable consensus that keeps moving to maintain its balance. 'Stability' is achieved by means of a continuous and flexible movement which is sensitive to the slightest breeze.

From this viewpoint, the Chinese growth model found the right balance between the state and the market. The Party managed to nurture a high economic growth rate, while maintaining political and social stability. The political regime and the economic model proved to be resilient to all sorts of crises: the inflation surge of the late 1980s; the 1989 Tien An Men rising; the 1997 Asian financial crisis; the burst of the Internet bubble in the 2000s; the world double-dip recession of 2008, which has not as yet unfolded its own impetus. In China, as in most developed countries, there is a risk of prolonged low-level growth similar to the situation in Japan.

4
An Uncompleted Banking and Financial Reform

All the leaves are printed with the seal of the Great Sire, if not they would be worthless ... nobody dares to turn them down since it would cost him his life.
(Marco Polo)

Money is a commodity unlike any other. It is the only one which can be traded against all others. Therefore, money not only has an economic function, but also social, political, institutional, even emotional ones too. The growing monetization of an economy is a form of rationalization of the economy and a strong integration factor. The monetary regime is a very accurate sign of the way a society is operating. From a historical point of view, money and credit have always been based on a highly centralized state, a strong bureaucracy and a legal framework. Under Mao's reign, money played a very limited role and was *stricto senso* restricted to the function of a *currency veil*; that is, a means of payment.

According to archaeological findings and numismatics, money came into being in China at more or less the same time as Greece (in the sixth century BC). Aristotle makes the distinction between *natural* currency based on the value of metal (*chrematia*) and the *artificial* currency based on law or convention (*nomos*). The law was made visible by stamping an image on the obverse of currency, either of the king or of the Athenian owl (representing the goddess of the city, Athena). Over centuries, historians and economists have debated whether the value of a currency is based on its intrinsic value (metal content), or on its nominal value, on a ruler's guarantee, or public acceptance. In Europe, most currencies were based on merchant acceptance, rather than the commitment of a ruler. China has never experienced such a situation. Money can never be anything other than an affair of the state. For centuries, China's monetary system was based on the silver standard; silver is rare in China and initially had to be imported from Japan and later from South America via the Philippines, together with copper, and traded against Chinese exports such as luxury goods (silk) or medicine (tea). Chinese currency was made of silver tael for large payments, and bronze sapeck (*tong qian*) for smaller payments. As a 'sapeck' has a very low value, the standard unit was the *splice* (*diao*) – a string of 1,000 sapecks tied together by a wire. In fact, the *diao* was never composed of the full number of sapecks. The actual number changed from one province to the other, from one city to another. As with Chinese painting or sculpture, the sapeck did not bear a portrait. Such was the strength of writing and the Emperor's power that the sapeck was simply stamped on one side with the year of the Emperor's reign, and on the other with the emblem of the minting workshop. The sapeck's function was as symbolic as it was economic: it was a widespread image of a unified China ruled by one man, the Emperor, and based on the Emperor's delegation of power even in the most remote parts of the Empire.

The banking sector and the financial markets were entirely dismantled under Mao's People's Republic of China (PRC), and have been rebuilt from scratch by the reform policy. This may explain why reform took place so late compared with the other economic sectors; i.e. agriculture and industry. This is because the banking sector and the financial markets would be the most difficult to reform and the focus of a potential power struggle. The way banking and financial reform has been implemented is a reliable mirror of the political, social and economic systems. It is understandable that, in such a context, the Party-State hesitated for a considerable time before releasing its control over such powerful instruments as the banking and financial systems.

Monobank system

In the 1980s, China inherited a Soviet-style banking system from Mao's government. The central bank (the PBOC)[1] fulfilled all the functions of a central bank, commercial bank, development bank and government bank. The PBOC was merely a department of the Ministry of Finance. The central bank operated the system of payment, as well as monetary policy, to the extent that there was such a thing as a 'monetary' policy. All bank accounts were opened in the central bank's books. The 'banks' were mere central bank subsidiaries collecting deposits to be transmitted to the central bank and granting loans to state companies in accordance with the instructions in the Plan. All payment transactions were centralized on the books of the central bank.

Monetary 'policy' was quite limited. Workers would be paid as little as possible, most of the primary needs being provided in kind by state-owned companies in the towns and by communes in the countryside. In so far as workers managed to put aside some savings, there was nothing to be sold in the shops. Proceeds of any savings were collected by the 'banks' and sent back to the central bank. The basic idea was to let as little cash as possible into the hands of individuals, 'available' cash being understood as the beginning of individual freedom. Treasury bonds were marketed by the banks but interest rates were lower than the actual cost of living. In addition, as there was no 'secondary market', savers were forced to hold their bonds until maturity. But the budget deficit, if any, was limited as the volume of government spending was fixed by government financing methods. The volume of tax collection was determined by the volume of planned government needs regardless of whether the actual tax capacity of the country was known. In any event, the tax level was very low compared with Western countries.

Once the Material Plan was approved, a Credit Plan was drafted to express companies' needs in monetary terms. There was no consumer credit. When a factory needed credit, the management had to follow a lengthy procedure involving a pyramid of decision-making levels and bureaucratic offices (the ministry of this particular industry, the Ministry of Finance, the Planning Administration, the local authority, the central bank, and so on) which were interwoven within each other. In most cases, when the money needed reached the company's central bank account, it was too late. This is the reason why companies used to barter transactions extensively, or initiated inter-company lending to make sure that raw materials, spare parts, equipment and components would be supplied in due time by suppliers and sub-contractors.[2]

Monetary 'policy' was limited to the use of interest rates: when, for whatever reason (e.g. inflation trends), the government wanted to mop up excess liquidity, the central bank lifted the interest rate paid so that people were encouraged to hold their savings in the 'banks'; when the government wanted to stimulate the economy, the interest rate was decreased to induce the people to withdraw their money from the 'banks' and use it to 'consume'.

Reform of banking sector

Generally speaking, reforming the banking sector requires a strong State and a strong Party to coordinate all the participating institutions and to ensure that policy will be duly and properly implemented by local authorities. The aim of banking reform was to give back more autonomy to banking institutions, including the central bank, to make competition more effective and banks more business-minded. Furthermore, this was undertaken to widen the range of market instruments at the disposal of the central bank to improve the efficiency of monetary policy.

Transition period

In 1978, the central bank was removed from the control of the Ministry of Finance. In accordance with 1984 banking legislation, the commercial functions of the central bank were transferred to the big four state banks. The central bank reported directly to the State Council, the highest level of government. This was the first step towards some form of central bank independence. From this point on, the central bank and the Ministry of Finance were on the same ministerial level. Any disagreement between the two leading institutions in the economic area – the more 'reformist' PBOC (i.e. more market-oriented) and the Ministry of Finance (i.e. more government oriented –and therefore more conservative) – could be cut short by the State Council. The central bank now had direct access to the supreme decision-making level and could afford to ensure that its point of view was well-documented by the best experts and correctly transmitted to the highest Party level.

Following Deng Xiaoping's trip to the South (*nanxia*) in 1992, the policy of reform and opening resumed after the static period in the aftermath of the 1989 Tien An Men events. The State Council approved a package of four laws concerning the status and functions of the PBOC (in March 1995) and the commercial banks (June 1995), and some other regulations regarding negotiable market instruments and non-banking financial institutions (NBFIs) (i.e. investment companies, brokering firms, funds management companies and insurance companies).

According to Article 3 of the 1995 law on the banking system (inspired by the European Central Bank statute then in the process of negotiation), China's central bank is in charge of price stability regardless of the other economic indices, such as growth rate or unemployment rate (in theory). The central bank is in charge of implementing monetary policy and bank supervision following the guidance of the State Council. According to Article 7 of the same law, the central bank is 'independent'; however, it is highly dependent on the State Council which appoints the chairman, the members of the Board and the Credit Committee. In any event, all management members of the PBOC are appointed by the Party. All the major strategic decisions are taken by the State Council: interest rates, banks' reserve requirements and the foreign exchange rate. Even though the central bank's duties are relatively limited, the PBOC has a growing influence due to the expertise it has gained over time and the numerous bank and liquidity crises – especially since the 2008 global financial crisis. The PBOC is now the main supplier of proposals and advice to the State Council in the monetary field. This is why the tenure of the chairman, Zhang Xiaochuan, has been renewed with the coming of the new team (led by Xi Jinping) even though he has been in charge for more than ten years.[3] He was appointed in 2002 by Jiang Zemin, a few months before the new team (led by Hu Jintao) was elected.

Also, the 1995 legislation on commercial banks has defined the nature and the functions of the different types of banks: deposit banks, investment banks, foreign banks, rural and urban cooperative banks, 'policy banks' and development banks.

The controlling power is shared between the PBOC and the China Banking Regulatory Committee (CBRC), both reporting straight to the State Council. The PBOC is in charge of oversight of banks (audit, refinancing); the CBRC is in charge of granting banking licences, authorizing a list of shareholders, capital increases, new capital subscriptions, public offerings on the market, mergers and acquisitions; the type of business (commercial banks, investment banks or development banks); and banking regulations (capital and liquidity ratios). The two institutions often overlap but they have to cooperate through meetings of the Special Party Committees (FPLG)[4] where all the parties involved are represented at the highest level, chaired by the Prime Minister or the member of the State Council in charge of economic policy. In the event of misunderstanding, they may take the issue to the higher level – the State Council.

A third wave of reforms took place between 2003 and 2005 following the appointment of the new team (led by Hu Jintao and Wen Jiabao). The large state banks (ICBC, BOC, CCB and ABC)[5] were 'privatized'. The privatization process was extended over several years. Initially, the banks were 'recapitalized'. The non-performing loans (NPLs) were transferred to four asset management companies bearing some very poetic names: Orient, Great Wall, Huarong and Cinda. Next, bank equity funds were reshuffled through capital increases subscribed by Central Huyjin Corp, a holding company affiliated to the central bank.[6] The capital was open to major foreign banks through reserved capital increases, the capital share owned by foreign banks being capped at 20 per cent: Goldman Sachs in ICBC, Royal Bank of Scotland (RBS) in BOC, Bank of America in CCB, Crédit Agricole in ABC and Hong Kong & Shanghai

Banking Corporation (HSBC) in Bank of Communications (BOCOM) and so on. The state banks were now ready to be sold out to the market. Well-funded and regulated exchange markets (Shanghai, Shenzhen and Hong Kong) were by now well-established and were available for public offerings. Everything had been arranged by the government and the CSRC to ensure that the IPOs were success. The opening trading prices were purposely fixed in the lowest possible bracket in order to ensure that the fortunate first subscribers make a substantial profit within a short period of time. As Chinese savings are plentiful, IPOs are subscribed to several times the original amount, an inducement to fraud and corruption. Some are allocated through a quota system; others are not. People lined up for hours before the bank offices to subscribe to the stocks on sale. Unrest erupted in the waiting queues. Foreign banks which had subscribed the previously 'reserved' capital increase are making huge profits. But a 'lock out' clause prohibits the resale of shares within three to five years (actually, by the end of the grace period of the IMF agreement). But why should they resell such a profitable participation? There was a huge (potential) added value and they were expecting to use shareholding to penetrate the Chinese market through the front door. But the global banking crisis blew up in late 2008 and the foreign banks were trapped by the 'lock out' clause. Some managed to sell in time (HSBC) and make huge profits; others were immobilized by the five-year lock out clause and made huge losses once they were finally allowed to sell (Goldman Sachs, RBS, Bank of America).

Originally, BOCOM and the China International Trust & Investment Co. (CITIC) were state-owned development banks, though they evolved in the opposite direction toward commercial banking. Although it has been 'privatized', HSBC[7] is the oldest Western bank established in China. Although 'privatized', BOCOM specializs in project finance, financing infrastructure and large development projects. CITIC is now a fully-fledged American-style investment bank. Along with CICC (affiliated to CCB and Morgan Stanley), CITIC catches all the mandates. Now that both banks cover a wide range of investment products and services, both Bank of America and Morgan Stanley have been advised to resell their stakes to non-banking investors such as Temasek and CIC, Singaporean and Chinese sovereign wealth funds less involved in the day-to-day business. Originally so-called 'policy banks' were loaded with non-performing loans transferred from the state-owned banks prior to being 'privatized'. They have subsequently evolved into fully-fledged commercial or investment banks, or both. The China Development Bank (CDB) is still wholly owned by the state. The CDB is prohibited from opening a customer's deposit account. The bank is funded through bond issues placed on the market.[8] The CDB is in charge of major project and infrastructure financing, such as the dam of the Three Gorges, the high speed train networks, highways and power stations. Also, CDB is required to follow up the BOC in export financing to the buyers of Chinese-made products, and providing large soft loans to build up infrastructures in exchange for long-term contracts of supply of raw materials (e.g. US$10 billion credit line to Petrobras).

Export/Import Banks back Chinese exporting companies by extending soft loans at low interest rates to buyers. The Agricultural Bank of China (ABC) extend credit to farmers and local enterprises, as well as supervizing the network of rural credit cooperatives. Its main foreign shareholder – Crédit Agricole – was also advised to resell its 20 per cent shareholding in ABC together with a 20 per cent participation of Morgan Stanley in CITIC. This was the counterpart of their selling to CITIC their affiliated and very successful investment bank in Hong Kong (Calyon).[9] Similarly, Morgan Stanley was requested to give up its 20 per cent participation in CITIC.

Regional banks – either 'public' or 'private' – are commercial banks often established by local authorities and/or local companies to service local firms, but they control a very low market share. Of the overall corporate financing, 80 per cent is provided by bank credit while the large four state banks account for a further 80 per cent; that is, two thirds of the total volume of lending. In any event, whether 'public' or 'private', it is barely possible to know who the true major shareholder is. No matter what the make-up of the equity fund holder, 'State Banks' (as they are still commonly called) are actually run by Party members appointed by the Party. Wholly-owned by the government, Minsheng Bank – which is now listed on the stock exchange (Hong Kong and Shanghai) – is said to be the best-managed and most profitable 'private' bank. Based in Shanghai, Minsheng is headed by a former member of HSBC, Eddie Wang, and specializes in foreign corporate and individual customers both in and out of China (80 million Overseas Chinese). Also listed on the stock exchange, the China Merchant Bank is another 'private' bank of which the equity distribution is unknown. In the 'private' banks, a variety of government agencies or institutions (SOBs and SOEs) have significant capital shares along with 'private' (individual or corporate) shareholders.

Some regional banks – such as China Everbright (wholly owned by the state-owned group Everbright)[10], Pudong Development Bank (Citibank), Guangdong Development Bank and the Bank of Nanjing (BNP) – have a wide branch network and customer base, a major asset for attracting foreign banks seeking business opportunities. Most of them have been formed by local authorities and are still wholly or partially owned by and highly dependent on local authorities. Foreign banks provide expertise and management techniques (such as risk management) with the expectation that sometimes they will be authorized to scale up and broaden the range of their banking licence. Most of these 'regional' banks are located in Jiangnan (south of the Yangtze River).

Rural and urban credit cooperatives are in the same situation. Originally they were formed by local authorities in the early 1980s, at the inception of the policy of reform and opening, to service the financial needs of the newly independent farmers free from the people's commune and the local firms (TVEs). Poorly managed and tightly linked to the local authorities and the local firms, they have been 'privatized', consolidated and sometimes 'sold' to their managers, if not merged with larger and more business minded banks. Non-performing loans have been transferred or cancelled through a massive government recapitalization programme (US$25 billion).

In order to comply with international standards (Basle I, II, III capital adequacy ratios), most of these banks – whether 'private' or 'public' – must proceed to capital increases. Most of the commercial banks, including the large state banks, had to increase capital as a result of the credit inflation of 2008, which caused a dramatic increase in the ratios of non-performing loans. After a two-year hiatus, the IPOs market has been reopened by the government. This may be an opportunity for foreign banks to get their foot in the door.

Opening of banking sector and business

The 'reform' policy is also a policy of 'opening-up'. Foreign banks are expected to play a key role in banking reform, but only under government conditions. Though there are 265 foreign banks in China (2012), they have only a 2 per cent market share (in deposit or credit terms). Originally, Chinese authorities expected an inflow of fresh capital and the transfer of technologies and management practices from these foreign banks. Today, China does not need any more fresh capital. Hence, the foreign banks are used to transfer new management techniques, new products and services, and new technology. Now that Chinese banks are run on an equal footing, foreign banks are primarily used to increase the competitive environment and to encourage Chinese banks to improve their management methods. This is especially true for the management of loan portfolios and credit risks, so as to extend the range of market products and services, provided that their market share remains marginal. Foreign banks (as with foreign companies) are allowed to penetrate the Chinese market on the proviso that they form a joint venture with a Chinese partner with a minority stake (20 per cent in the big banks, 49 per cent in small regional banks or specialized credit institutions). Foreign banks used to play the role of a banking university and training firm. Staff are better paid but turnover is high. As Chinese banks improve, competition is becoming fiercer. A number of foreign or Chinese-speaking students of Chinese descent become disillusioned when they move to the Chinese market with the expectation that they will be welcomed with open arms thanks to their experience in the West.

On joining the WTO in late 2001, China was obliged to open the domestic market of financial services to foreign institutions within a five-year interim period. From 2007 onwards, foreign banks were required to be treated on the same footing as the Chinese banks. Until that time, foreign banks could not collect Yuan denominated deposits or extend Yuan credits. They were restricted to foreign customers and foreign currency credits and deposits. When the interim period was over, China's government opened the market to a very limited number of foreign institutions and permitted the sale of a limited range of products within narrow credit limits. Following a lengthy procedure, foreign banks were allowed to open local subsidiaries or branches or take minority participations in Chinese banks. The largest and most diversified foreign bank in China, HSBC has built up a network of about 100 branches in 10 years, a very marginal market share compared with the 35,000 branches of the large state banks.

Foreign banks are subject to discriminative measures. For example, as foreign banks have not yet build up a clientele of customers or a broad deposit base, they have to turn to the domestic interbank market to acquire the necessary funding. But banking regulations stipulate that every branch or affiliated bank must provide a head office guarantee (which is legally meaningless, since a branch is by definition wholly owned by its head office which therefore has unlimited responsibility). As a result, foreign bank funding is more costly and cannot compete evenly with domestic banks. In addition, every foreign branch has to maintain useless 'capital' – useless, since the head office is by definition subject to an unlimited commitment. As a result of this extra cost, they are less competitive compared with the domestic banks.

Foreign bank strategy is moving from a 'financial' approach to a more 'industrial' approach. Initially, foreign banks were eager to participate in large Chinese banks, though it was narrowly limited to a minority share (20 per cent, 25 per cent in the case of a 'consortium' together with Chinese or foreign banks or companies). They soon understood that their participation was pointless, no matter the magnitude of the equity share (up to several billion dollars). This did not entail any benefit, whether in terms of sharing bank management and strategy, or in terms of penetrating the domestic market. Chinese banks with a foreign shareholder did not hesitate to form a joint venture with a competitor in some specific areas (investment banking, stock brokerage, fund management, credit cards, consumer credit, mortgage loans or life insurance, and so on). The Pudong Development Bank (Shanghai), whose largest shareholder is Citibank, formed an affiliated insurance company with a French consortium including BNP and AXA.

Later on, as the global financial crisis unfolded, most of the foreign banks sold back their participation – sometimes at a profit, sometimes at a loss. In 2013, Goldman Sachs sold out its participation in ICBC for US$9.7 billion which they had acquired eight years previously in 2005 for US$2.58 billion. Newcomers turned to a more 'industrial' approach by forming joint ventures in partnership with small regional banks or specialized credit institutions. In financial terms, the investment is much lower and the profits much higher. Foreign partners have a better say in a bank's management and greater potential for market penetration.

Initially, the Chinese authorities were strongly critical but, later on, they appeared to be much more supportive of the new approach. This was largely because the Chinese government was reorienting investments and credit institutions to the interior provinces and the countryside. In addition, the increased, tightened banking regulation required a majority of the banks to raise the level of their capital and other ratios and to improve their management know-how.

Banking reform led to a very peculiar banking system: the more banks are granted autonomy, the tighter becomes government control. For example, in 2013 the central bank (on instructions from the State Council) eased control over interest rates somewhat. Both interest paid to the depositors and interest charged to the customers used to be fixed by the government so that a certain interest margin was ensured, as well as bank profits. Chinese banks are now competing with each other fiercely to catch up deposits through Wealth Management Products, a sort of subprime-type of savings product based on the return of a given credit portfolio.

But the unofficial grasp of the central bank and the central government remain as strong as ever if not stronger: following the 2008 Recovery Plan, including an Rmb 4,000 billion increase in government spending, the banks were instructed to follow suit by dramatically increasing bank loans (mostly to local authorities and state-owned companies). In 2009, the volume of bank credit more than doubled (from Rmb 700 billion to Rmb 1,600 billion).

Informal credit sector

Non-banking credit (*shadow banking*) includes a variety of lending entities but fast growing ones. Banking credit fell from 96 per cent in 2011 to 65 per cent over the course of 2012, the balance being provided by informal types of credit. By tightening the volume of credit in the wake of the strong recovery, most companies had to turn to unofficial non-banking credit (*qian hui*). Most of the small and individual companies had no access to bank credit and were forced to turn to informal credit arrangements. Chinese banks claimed that accounting documents provided by small companies were not reliable, which may have been true. But, as usual in China, there are two different sorts of informal credit: one is illegal but tolerated; the other is legal but regulated.

The granting of funds by a group of relatives, friends or patrons is a very old practice in China which dates back centuries and is still used to finance new ventures today. A group of people put together a certain amount of money for financing a new venture (e.g. a café, restaurant, or laundromat in the many Chinatowns scattered all over the world). Every year, the group is invited to a banquet at which they draw lots. The winner enjoys either his money back, or the option of renewing his stake in the pool. Today, 95 per cent of small and medium-size companies are said to use informal credit of this kind. In addition, business-to-business (B2B) credit is increasingly used in the form of intercompany credit, though this is prohibited by legislation. Due to the increasing volume of informal credit and the increasing number of lenders looking for a better return than that offered by bank saving accounts, the government is considering regulating the informal credit sector. This step is being considered together with moves to prevent occasional failings, which draw high number of savers into bankruptcy – not to mention lending companies which are unexpectedly short of cash (Wangzhou 2013).

The other field of informal credit is legal and regulated. So-called 'trust companies' are lending to corporate customers and selling stakes to savers in search of more rewarding investments. Trust companies are offering a return of between 8 per cent and 10 per cent compared with 2 per cent to 3 per cent interest paid on bank savings accounts. For example, CITIC offered the steel maker Yichang Three Gorges affiliated to Quantong Coated & Galvanised Plate Co. credit of Rmb 1.13 billion when the company was on the verge of bankruptcy. The company's leading bank, CCB, was no longer willing to renew the existing credit line. One third of the total amount was finally provided through an *ad hoc* trust company formed by CCB and marketed among CCB's customers. Subscribers are unaware of the composition of the backing credits and are not concerned to do so. Over a certain size, all Chinese companies and banks are expected to be bailed out by the government in the event of failure, which leads to a steady worsening of credit rating ('flattening' interest rate curb). According to the Fitch rating agency, every Yuan lent and invested today produces one third of its performance in 2000 before the onset of the global financial crisis.

Creation of financial markets

In addition to bank lending, exchange markets are the major channels of savings to investments and entrepreneurs. Once it was decided to 'privatize' state-owned companies and banks, efficient (that is: deep and broad) exchange markets became indispensable. In the same way as banks, though in a different way, exchange markets have an 'intermediation' function collecting savings and allocating funds to the most profitable industries or, at least, to the companies that are sufficiently large to have access to the markets and meet investors' requirements. Stocks, bonds and derivatives prices are the key indexes which inform investors, companies and government circles. Given that 80 per cent of overall lending is provided by the banking sector (compared with an average 50 per cent in developed countries), the next step was to offer a direct investment channel (*bank disintermediation*) to the investors as an alternative source of funds for the companies and an alternative source of investment for those who wished to save. Not only are the sources of funds highly concentrated, but so are the users. Large SOEs have access to bank credit regardless of their solvency while small and medium-sized companies, individual companies, TVEs, private companies and foreign companies have no access to bank credit. They must switch to an alternative source of funds: the stock and bond exchanges for the larger organizations, informal credit for the smaller.

In China, more so than in any other country, exchange markets play a specific role in the mechanics of the financial system:

- Collecting savings by offering alternative investment instruments.
- Channelling savings to the most productive investment opportunities.
- Financing the pension scheme.

But Chinese exchange markets also have some more idiosyncratic functions:

- Subjecting Chinese companies to 'market discipline' (accountability, long-term strategy, cash management).
- Subjecting Chinese companies to international standards (information disclosure, management practice, internationally agreed ratios).

The policy of reform increased management autonomy to companies; however, on the other hand, companies are now subject to market requirements rather than those of governments.

In principle, the Chinese government did not need a strong exchange market: the budget deficit (if any) is low; government-owned companies readily borrow from the state banks, if necessary; they are able to rely on government subsidies or, in the event of an emergency (a liquidity or solvency crisis), on government or local collectives to bail them out. For the more conservative members of the Party, this is anathema; for the reformists, who have a more pragmatic approach, it is nothing but one among many other government instruments implemented in order to discover the best performance mix of state and market.

In every country, exchange markets were initially built on government debt, then on trading the shares of the first chartered public companies.[11] The number of stocks available was limited; fluctuations wide; and transactions informal.[12] The markets were illiquid and highly speculative. In late Imperial China, every war with Western Powers (or Japan) ended up with a treaty that usually included huge war indemnities. Western bankers established in Shanghai were more than happy to place vast loans on the Western markets on behalf of the Chinese Empire against juicy underwriting fees. Later on, borrowings were used to construct railways, shipyards and arsenals.[13]

In the wake of the policy of reform and opening, some Chinese local authorities formed local exchanges, in particular in the special economic zones (SEZs) such as Shenzhen, where Treasury bonds were traded. When the government regained control over tax and spending in the 1990s (under the authority of Prime Minister Zhu Rongji), local collectives were looking for new sources of funds. Some issued local Treasury bonds, similar to US municipal bonds, which were traded on the spot. Some companies that could no longer obtain credit as a result of the credit limits established in the framework of anti-inflation policy (put in place in the 1980s) turned to local sources of funds. Finally, once the Party was convinced of the merits of these exchanges, the whole matter was taken over by central government: marginal and peripheral wild (i.e. illegal or, more precisely, not unauthorized) exchanges were closed; stock and bond transactions were centralized on the Shanghai Exchange (1991) which developed a modern (quick, reliable, liquid) countrywide settlement system. Later, in 1997, the Shenzhen and Hong Kong exchanges were added to Shanghai, together with a handful of commodity markets: Dalian (coal, oil), Zhengzhou (agricultural products) and Baotou (mining).

A supervisory agency was formed, the China Securities Regulatory Committee (CSRC), which reports direct to the State Council – even though, according to WTO regulations, a request for a trading permit cannot be rejected as long as the recipient fulfils government law and regulation. The CSRC is powerful: it is in charge of implementing regulations, authorizing companies which have fulfilled a listing application and supervizing the markets. Usually, listing applications take several years to go through the whole procedure and be given the green light. The CSRC goes into the details: volume of traded stocks, percentage of the overall capital base on sale,[14] date of issue, location of issue (Shanghai, Shenzhen and/or Hong Kong), opening price, fee level, selection of advisory and underwriting banks (usually a team of Western and Chinese banks), distribution of the final issue between institutional investors (investment funds, insurance companies, pension funds) and individuals, *lock in* clause or *green shoes*[15] and allocation ratios in case of over-subscription.

Within a few years, the whole range of market instruments meeting the needs of both investors and fund raisers had been put in place: collective saving instruments, investment funds, brokering firms, asset management companies, private-equity investment funds, insurance companies and pension funds. Also, the markets have developed a range of financial products including derivatives: warrants, convertible bonds,[16] futures, options, futures of futures, options of futures and ETF (funds based on index(es) rather than securities) which are used on the part of companies in order to cover their exposure and on the part of investors to make a profit. The derivative contract provides extra liquidity to the underlying market but, due to the high leverage (1/10),[17] it is a very risky product. In addition, as all the securities are meant to be equal (whether state-owned or state-backed), price fluctuations are wholly artificial and do not mirror the actual growth and underlying risk.

However, the stock and bond markets are biased by government interference. The market is still unbalanced: the number, the volume and the range of securities available do not match Chinese savings (over 50 per cent of GNP) and investors' requirements. In Hong Kong, the volume of Yuan denominated deposits is about 10 times greater than the volume of stocks and bonds issued in the same currency in the same place. Even though the markets are still very narrow and illiquid, government regulations keep a close watch on the volume of transactions: the volume of float[18] is very limited (5 per cent against a minimum of 30 per cent in developed countries), the stocks of the large state-companies and banks are split up between negotiable (one third) and non-negotiable stocks (two thirds), the range of stocks are split between 'A' stock (denominated in Yuan and accessible to Chinese residents), 'B' stock (denominated in Yuan but paid in US dollars),[19] and 'H' stock (issued and traded in Hong Kong in HK or US dollars), 'red' chip stocks (large state-owned companies denominated in US dollars traded on the New York Stock Exchange). In the early stages, the government, through the CSRC, set a very low opening price, lower than the lower bracket determined by the underwriting banks on the basis of market perception, with a view to ensuring a large volume of subscription compared with the initial amount – hence the large profit of the first subscribers. Most of the initial subscriptions of state-owned companies amounted to several times the offered volume of securities. In the first days of trading, the price traded was significantly above the opening price, meaning that the first subscribers made a huge profit. The total valuation based on the stock price (capitalization)[20] was unrealistic (as had been Internet stocks during the 2000 bubble). Chinese stockholders are said to be very speculative and 'short-termist'. The average turnover does not exceed three months (as opposed to 18 months in the USA). The market lacks long-term savings to match the long-term investment, such as the financing of infrastructures and the funding of pension funds. The development banks (such as the CDB) are refinancing through the placement of short-term bonds (of up to five years) to match the financing of long-term infrastructures. Three quarters of the Chinese Stock Exchange capitalization comprises financial types of stock (banks, insurance companies and investment funds). In contrast, the share of institutional investors trading does not exceed 25 per cent, as opposed to 80 per cent or more in the developed markets. Institutional investor trading is indispensable for stabilizing the market and providing the necessary liquidity.

Chinese markets became very speculative. In 2008–12, the annual growth rate had been in excess of 7 per cent and the manufacturing growth rate over 10 per cent, while the Stock Market Index (SMCI) has been fluctuating, showing an 80 per cent drop in 2009–10.

Finally, foreign investors, and also foreign fund raisers, are kept separate. The Western investment banks are requested to provide expertise, know-how and placement capacity in the foreign markets, but they are not permitted to capture their business share. In the early stages of the reform policy, a number of brokerage firms mushroomed but soon experienced fraud and losses. Some went bankrupt with the owner disappearing along with the customers' cash. In most cases, Chinese brokerage firms have confused trading on clients' accounts and trading on their own account. The government intervened to close some of these brokerage firms, merged others, recapitalized most and opened the equity base to foreign investors such as well-known international investment banks, brokerage firms or investment vehicles (Merryl Lynch, Calyon). Some of them (Bank of America, Crédit Agricole and J.P. Morgan) have been strongly 'encouraged' to sell off once Chinese investment banks, such as CITIC or CICC, managed to cover the entire range of clients and products. Some investment permits (those for qualified foreign institutional investors – QFIIs) have been granted to a limited number of foreign institutions (mostly foreign banks) and a limited volume of transactions.[21]

Ultimately, foreign investors are increasingly concerned about China's overall indebtedness. The Debt to GNP ratio has been growing rapidly over the last few years (since the crisis erupted, compelling the government and the banks to inject huge sums of money into the economy). Though it is still moderate by international standards, government debt has increased by 50 per cent in the last 10 years alone (since the early 2000s) and 30 per cent since the global crisis began. Following the two Recovery Plans (2008, 2012), China's overall indebtedness (public and private) is said to have reached record figures but they are, alas, still unknown. The local authorities bypassed the compulsory authorization of the central government by forming empty shell companies, unofficial borrowing vehicles for the sole purpose of raising funds (LGFV).[22] Over the last few years (2011–14), the growth rate has dropped from 10 per cent to 7 per cent, while overall indebtedness (Treasury bonds, local authorities, state-owned banks and companies) may have risen to twice the level of GDP (25 per cent in 2012) (see Table 4.1).

If these assumptions are proven correct, China's indebtedness ratio would be nearing the most indebted developed countries and twice as much as other developing countries such as Brazil, India and Russia (see Table 4.2).

Table 4.1 China's overall indebtedness (% GDP)*

2002	139	2009	176
2003	151	2010	191
2004	149	2011	195
2005	147	2012	205
2006	146	2013	218**
2007	151	2014	230**
2008	148	2015	245**

* Not including informal credit;
** Forecast.

Table 4.2 Overall indebtedness (% GDP)

Japan	393 %	Germany	196 %
UK	298	Brazil	115
USA	250	India	111
France	250	Russia	56
China	203		

As a result – owing to the unknown but rapidly increasing local authorities' debt and real estate borrowings (due among others to the rocketing property prices in the cities) – rating agencies, such as Fitch and Moody's have lowered China's rating on the grounds that all the risks, whether private or public, are meant to be equally government owned or guaranteed.

In summary, the reform of the financial sector has demonstrated the mixed system of government controls. On one hand, the Chinese government has relaxed its control over a certain number of markets but, on the other, has retained tight control over a wide range of government or 'private' institutions. Following a set of trial-and-error processes, the Party-State found the most suitable – and, from this standpoint, the most effective – mix of state and markets shares. Such a 'hybrid' policy is in line with the policy of reform and opening. The government unleashed the market forces and mechanisms – within certain limitations – while keeping a close eye over credit institutions. On the side of the coin, it should be noted that, in spite of government involvement, the Chinese market is still threatened by massive but unknown indebtedness of local authorities, the real estate bubble and subsequent bank solvency issues.

5
Investment in Human Capital

Repressing one's passions is the best method to nourish one's heart.
(Mencius)

Over the centuries, Chinese capital was scarce while human resources were both plentiful and cheap. This may be one (amongst other) reasons why China did not experience the Industrial Revolution. At the present time, capital is plentiful and cheap; however, the human factor is becoming scarce in terms of both quantity and quality. In twenty-first century China, the government has to juggle with these two factors simultaneously: reining in the demographic growth while investing in the human factor.

A developing country cannot expect to take off unless it manages to take control of demographic growth. If not, the country cannot escape the underdevelopment trap. Economic and productivity growth are swallowed by demographic growth. Economic growth trails behind population growth. The economy is squeezed in a vicious circle brought about by underdevelopment. The middle-income trap freezes the whole country in a dual system in which the rich are getting richer and the poor are getting poorer, even though the overall growth rate is positive. Only the higher and middle classes, which managed to take control of reproduction rates, benefit from the economic growth rate; only they have access to better education while the poorer are trapped in a poverty cycle. At the poorest levels, children are required for the very survival of the household. Parents rely on children to take care of them in their old age, the older to take over the farm, the younger to catch whatever they can to supplement the meagre family income (rural exodus to the cities increases agricultural productivity). The girls marry and leave the family home to join their husband's household. A girl's

Table 5.1 Population (m) versus annual growth rate (2005–11)

	Population (m)	Annual growth rate (2005–11)
China	1,346	+0.51
India	1,241	+1.40
USA	312	+0.89
Indonesia	238	+1.07
Brazil	198	+0.94
Pakistan	177	+1.80
Nigeria	162	+2.50
Bangladesh	148	+1.12
Russia	141	−0.12
Japan	126	+0.02

education serves no useful purpose for the family. Otherwise, they take care of their ageing parents while the men leave the village in search of a better life.

But regulating population issues by law (or by force) – thus interfering in the natural demographic process – is highly dangerous as the resulting long-term consequences stretch out over generations and centuries. China's one-child policy was designed to accelerate and shorten the transition period. Thirty years later, the one-child policy is a time bomb. In a few years, China will not have enough adults to fund the pensions of ageing people. As opposed to Japan, China faces the threat of getting old before it gets rich (see Table 5.1).

In January 2013, for the first time since the one-child policy was put in place, the Chinese labour force (aged between 15 and 59) shrank (minus 3.45 million) according to the National Bureau of Statistics. The population reproduction rate was 1.47 per cent (i.e. well under the mere reproduction rate of 2.1 per cent). Without the one-child policy, the reproduction rate would have been only 1.62 per cent. To the 'natural' process, one must add the urbanization effect: urban jobs increased by 12,000,000 in 2011, while jobs in rural areas decreased by 9,000,000. Given that urban couples have a much lower rate of reproduction, it is understandable that the average rate of reproduction is decreasing steadily.

Demographic policy

Population growth is a recurring theme of totalitarian regimes. Women are created to 'produce' citizens, soldiers and consumers. Regulating the demographic rate is disturbing the most sensitive areas of social tradition, religious beliefs and private life. Birth control must be achieved by education rather than force. In China, birth control is enforced by a huge network of Party bureaucrats and government regulations.

Throughout, family values in China have been the social, political and even psychological background. According to the demographists, the Chinese family model belongs to the 'extended, patri-linear, hierarchical' family model;[1] as a result, some came to the conclusion that the Chinese are predisposed to an 'authoritarian' political model. The son is dependent on his father and the father is dependent on his own. The younger depends on the elder. The girl is always dependent on someone, whether it is her father, her elder brother, her husband. If a couple does not have a boy to ensure the 'ancient cult of family ancestors', or to take over the parents' farm or firm, they can adopt a boy – the child of relatives, neighbours or friends.[2] The boy is not uprooted: he maintains contact with his biological parents even though he has a deep emotional connection to the adoptive parents who have brought him up and educated him. Once she is married, a girl leaves the family home to follow her husband into his own family house. If she is repudiated for whatever reason (e.g. childless), she is not welcome back in her natal family home. She is condemned to a life of prostitution or, in better circumstances, a concubine. For a wealthy man, to have a concubine is a sign of his new status and living standards. The quarrels between a mother and daughter-in-law sharing the same home are classic features of Chinese literature.[3] A woman alone (whether a widow, or one who has been repudiated, today a late bachelor) is someone of whom to be wary. There are very few Empresses in Chinese history and all of them are perceived as evil or as usurpers who disturb the order of the cosmos and society. In the Emperor's family, concubines (especially if they have given birth to a boy) were more important than the Empresses themselves (but not the Dowager Empress, the Emperor's mother).

Birth control policy

After the Communist takeover (1949), when it was still possible to have an argument within the Party, 'pro-birth' supporters and 'Malthusians' argued between each other about the best demographic policy. Ma Yinchu, a 'Malthusian' who supported the family planning policy, claimed that economic take-off was not possible unless China took control of the population growth rate. From an historical point of view, he was right economically, but politically he was wrong. He was swept aside by Mao and rehabilitated once the dictator was dead. Since the 1980s, family planning policy has been part of the reform policy (see Table 5.2).

According to the 2010 census published by the National Bureau of Statistics in April 2011, China's population has reached 1.370 billion but the growth rate has begun to decline. Within a few decades, the whole population will begin to decline in absolute terms (see Table 5.3).

Over the last 10 years, the Chinese population has risen by 0.57 per cent (i.e. half the number of the preceding 10 years). The Chinese population is ageing: in the same period, the share of seniors (60+) rose from 3 per cent to 13.3 per cent, while the share of youths (–14) decreased from 22.9 per cent to 16.6 per cent. In 2012, for the first time, the share of population aged between 15 and 25 decreased (by 3.5 million). The reproduction rate (1.47) is now below the renewal rate (2.1) (see Table 5.4). The reproduction rate is even lower in big cities (0.7 in Beijing and Shanghai). There, the population growth is attributed to rural depopulation, rather than natural growth. Immigration is a two-step process: from the village to the next town to search for an increased income and from the regional town to the metropolis to start a new way of life.

Table 5.2 Birth rate (000s)

1949	6.1
1960	4.0
1970	5.8
1980	2.2
1990	2.2
2000	1.8
2010	1.7

Source: State Population and Planned Parenthod Commission.

Table 5.3 Population growth (%)

1970–80	+20.00
1980–90	+16.00
1990–00	+11.70
2000–10	+5.84

Source: National Bureau of Statistics Census (2010).

Table 5.4 Distribution per age (%)

	1964	2000	2010	2035
0 - 14	40.0	22.8	16.6	17.0
15 - 59	54.0	66.9	70.1	59.0
60 +	6.0	10.3	13.3	24.0

Source: National Bureau of Statistics Census (2010).

According to official data, the ongoing decline of the birth rate is due to economic and social factors rather than police interference, which has served only to accelerate the natural process. Actually, this steady decrease in the population growth rate is the combined effect of the one-child policy, the increase in living standards and the end of poverty. Thus, the one-child policy has impacted society far beyond a mere demographic effect.

The one-child policy

Just behind land expropriation, China's one-child policy is the main source of disorder and violence. The one-child policy had gradually been set in motion (1975–1980) starting in the late years of Mao's oversight. It reached full-speed under Deng Xiaoping's leadership. Infringers are exposed to harsh sanctions: loss of child benefits, housing, health care, jobs, and fines ranging from Yuan 500 to Yuan 70,000.[4] Extra children are not allowed to enrol in school and university. The Family Planning Commission is a state within a state comprising 500,000 staff supported by a two-million strong network of local auxiliaries. The Commission presides over a US$ 3 billion fine chest. According to the Health Ministry, in a thirty-year period (1980–2010), 281 million abortions would have been processed, as well as 516 million contraceptive and sterilization operations. Party members' annual appraisals include several points about their commitment to applying the one-child policy. Local authorities are allocated part of the funds raised by the fines. The one-child policy is an opportunity for corruption and many types of pressure, including violence. In 1996, the Deputy Chairman of a hospital located in Hunan was sentenced to death (and executed) for taking Yuan 200,000 of bribes (US$30,000) over a five-year period for granting 448 false sterilization certificates. In the rural areas, it is not unknown for a pregnant woman to disappear for a given amount of time: her 'forbidden' baby having been born in another constituency so that no one could be sued, the Party secretary of her housing therefore not responsible since the 'crime' had been committed in another constituency while the Party secretary of the place of birth is not responsible for the woman's misconduct because she is resident in another constituency.[5] The media report an increasing number of child abductions or criminal organizations 'importing' foreign women from neighbouring countries.

Population 'policies' are very slow to have the desired effect but they become very difficult to uproot once they have started to impact on society. China is getting closer to the 'Lewis turn', when the benefits of a lower population growth rate become a drawback. Young couples have internalized the one-child policy. It is perceived as the only way of social promotion. An extra child is expensive. Following the 'privatization' process, large companies have cancelled the usual benefits (health, schools, holidays) aimed at freeing parents and, in particular, require mothers to dedicate themselves to 'productive' work. The market of home-servicing is still non-existent. Last, but not least, the rapid urbanization process has cut off links with the family. In the rural areas, grandparents and relatives take care of the children while their parents move to a city to improve their way of life. In addition, the one-child policy is tightly linked to the land policy of financing local authorities: in China, the land is state property. Plots of land are leased to the household for a given period of time. On maturity, the plots will be reallocated in accordance with the needs of the family, but on the condition that a male is in a position to cultivate the land. To make matters worse, local authorities expropriate the farmers' plots for resale to an investor – a main source of resources for the local authorities. As land becomes scarce, local authorities are threatened by bankruptcy.

The psychological and social disturbances caused by the one-child policy have not yet been scientifically studied, but subsequent damage will be high in terms of health and education. Everyone remembers the 'little emperors' wrapped up in several layers of stuffy coats born to the whole family as an icon. Also, everyone remembers the uneducated, noisy children they saw on public transport. Once they have grown up, they threaten social links because of their exacerbated individualism, which is inconsistent with the dominant Chinese traditions.[6] The 16 per cent increase in the divorce rate is said to be due to young couples' inability to compromise. Children born after the one-child policy was implemented are more pessimistic, more anxious, less social and less self-confident. Overprotected in their childhood, they are less disposed to innovation and creativity, and lack a business and risk orientation.

Over time, the one-child policy has been relaxed (see Box 5.1). Minorities are exempt from the one-child policy. In the urban coastal cities, some families are wealthy enough to pay the fines. In the rural areas, families who have a girl are allowed to 'try again' to have the boy they need to keep the slot of land allocated to the family. The two parents of a couple who are themselves single children are allowed to have a second child. Following the meeting of the Central Committee in November 2012, parents of a single child are now permitted to have a second child. In Shanghai, where the population share over the age of 60 was already 21 per cent in 2008 and is expected to rise up to 34 per cent by 2020, a new system has been trialled. But, given the vested interests involved, it would seem to be very difficult to cancel – or even to modify – the one-child policy as a whole. In 2013, in an attempt to regain control over the Family Planning Commission (and the 'war chest'), the Commission was once more put under the auspices of the Health Ministry. But, as nothing is that simple in China, the Head of the Family Planning Commission has been appointed Minister of the Health Ministry. However, on the occasion of the 2012 meeting of the National People's Congress, the demographic policy was transferred to the powerful National Development and Reform Commission (NDRC), the new Planning Office, which reports direct to the State Council.

Box 5.1 The Yicheng experiment

A 300,000 strong rural district in Shanxi, Yicheng is the site of a 30 year long experiment ... in the rural areas and upon very stringent conditions, inhabitants are permitted to have two children, a boy or a girl ... In spite of the looser regulation, Yicheng has a population growth rate lower that the neighbouring districts. The boy–girl baby ratio is 105 as opposed to an average 117 in the whole of China.

Ageing population

In the meantime, the age pyramid is becoming increasingly stretched out of shape; wider at the top, narrower at the bottom, with a male contingent than the female. The ratio of the number of working people (15–65) compared with retired people (65+) is expected to decrease from 9 in 2010 to 4 in 2050. Since the Communist takeover in 1949, China has experienced a steady increase in life expectancy which lifted China up to 106th position in the world (out of 200).

Table 5.5 Life expectancy (%)

1950	46.0
2010	72.4
2035	76.3
Population over 60 (m)	
2010	155
2020	260
2040	400
2050	437

Source: National Bureau of Statistics.

Following an improvement in their quality of life, the aged population over 60, which now accounts for 7.7 per cent of the total population, should increase rapidly in the coming years. Subsequently, the ratio of aged people compared with young people should also increase (see Table 5.5 and Figure 5.1).

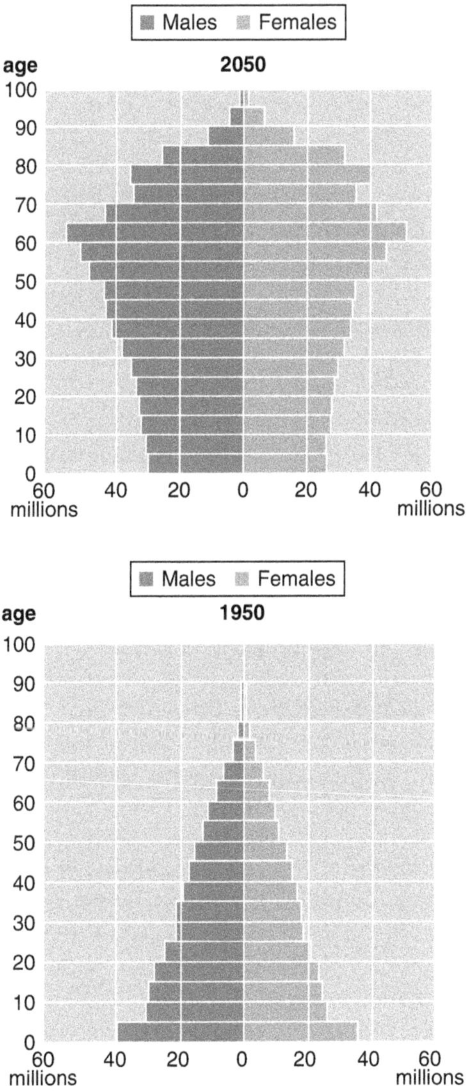

Figure 5.1 Male and female births
Source: Les Echos.

Table 5.6 Population aged over 60 (%)

2001	10.3
2005	11.0
2010	12.6
2015	15.2
2020	17.0
2025	20.4
2030	24.5
2035	27.5

Source: China Population Research Centre.

The one-child policy has led the country into a problematic situation known as '4–2–1' (four grandparents, two parents and one child). The one-child policy, which was initially designed to facilitate the transition period (to have an economic growth rate above the population growth rate), has turned on itself. As the share of the aged population is growing faster than the young population, the reproduction rate is below the renewal rate and the population is steadily ageing. The Chinese government is facing a thorny problem: how to fund the increasing volume of pensions. As opposed to Japan, who got rich before it got old, China is threatened to get old before it gets rich (see Table 5.6).

On a regular basis, it is unofficially said that China is about to abolish the one-child policy, as if the Party were testing public opinion. Shanghai postponed the retirement age of city staff from 60 to 65. Over the last few years, the government tried to put in place a universal pension scheme to unfreeze household savings and boost household domestic consumption. The aim is to be less dependent on foreign demand, which is decreasing due to the global crisis in the short term, and to take advantage of the the urbanization process and increased living standards in the long term. The urbanization process has broken down the former networks of solidarity. The retirement age is now 60 (employees), 55 (workers) and 50 (women, as they have to take care of young children due to the lack of household services). This system is based on working conditions in the past when social benefits were taken over by SOEs and life expectancy did not exceed 50 years.

Today, the pension scheme is duplicated: a 'national' system and a loan-back supplementary system. The 'national' Social Security system is broken down into region and into industry, which ignores the population of 800 million. Though the national pension fund, the National Social Security Fund (NSSF), is one of China's biggest sovereign wealth funds, it includes no more than a marginal share of the overall savings. Nowadays, large state-owned companies, large 'privately owned' companies, foreign companies and labour contracts include funding provision for a supplementary loan-back pension scheme. Put forward by foreign insurance companies (such as AXA) jointly with domestic insurance companies (Ping An, China Life), pension funds such as Tai Ping (*Peaceful*) Pension Assurance are managed by management companies and investment banks. The premiums are paid by both the company and the employees. This inhibits a worker's freedom of movement[7].

Development of human capital

It is widely agreed amongst economists that the return from investing in human capital is greater than investment in real assets. In a country deprived of natural resources, it was understandable that the government was naturally inclined to invest in health and education. Dismissed and exiled, Deng Xiaoping was about to rejoin the core circle of the Party in 1978 – two years after Mao's death – claiming that he was disinterested in supreme power. His only ambition was to devote himself to educative and scientific problems which he felt to be of utmost importance following ten years of Cultural Revolution. Placing emphasis on education in the widest possible sense – including not only education proper, but also physical and mental health – is part of a very ancient Chinese tradition. For a Confucian, 'virtue' is understood both as self-improvement and personal qualities to fulfil one's role in society. Based on filial piety and the cult of ancestry, 'virtue' proceeds from education. Regardless of innate qualities, a child requires the mediation of a master to reach knowledge and wisdom.

Health system

As was the case with the first Emperor, Qi Shi Huangdi, the 'Great Helmsman' – as Mao Zedong was known – was surrounded by a number of shamans providing recipes for long life or even eternity. Over centuries, in line with Taoist tradition,[8] many Chinese thinkers searched for the ways to live a good life. In effect, Chinese medicine is much more compliant with natural flows and streams than Western medicine, which is based on chemical drugs and violent surgery.

Since the inception of the policy of reform, health policy may be summarized as a continuous and steady withdrawal by the government from the health market. Following the 'privatization' of the large SOEs, the share of state spending in the total health expenditure has shrunk from 90 per cent to 17 per cent. This government share in the total health expenditures is less than India, two-times less than Thailand and three-times less than Brazil. The ratio of private/public health spending is 60/40 per cent in China (as opposed to 80/20 per cent in France). Average health expenditure accounts for US$350 per head and 4.5 per cent of GDP. With 60,000 hospitals, health centres and clinics and 4,000,000 employees, the health infrastructure is far below population requirements (2.3 beds per thousand as opposed to 7 in France). That situation continues to worsen and it will be increasingly difficult to catch up as rapidly as the population is ageing. In order to compensate for the fall in government subsidies and the privatization of large SOEs, hospitals have been forced to find alternative resources: overbilling of services, the sale of graduation diplomas and the sale of pharmaceutical products.[9] As used to be the case in the past, private charitable organizations are taking over government duties.

The rural population (half the total population) is not shielded by social security schemes. Urbanization has broken down solidarity networks. Urban apartments are too small to accommodate the whole family. A number of lonely women –divorced, separated, or widowed – are penniless. Since 2005, the rural population has enjoyed a cooperative insurance system on a voluntary basis (10 Yuan per annum or US$1.5). But the refund does not exceed 60 per cent of the fees charged by rural hospital and health centres. In towns where prices are much higher, refunds do not exceed 30 per cent of health care fees and 10 per cent of hospitals fees. In 2008, within the framework of the recovery plan, a US$124 billion budget was allocated to the health sector over a period of three years, but the whole system needs restructuring – hospital infrastructures, staff training and social security schemes.

Education system

Educative values make up intrinsic parts of the Confucian legacy. Education is not only a method of moulding pupils' minds with a view to fulfilling their social and professional functions, but also, out of the raw materials of natural passions, building up an accomplished man, able to acquire virtue and wisdom. Education is the heart of the bureaucratic system. Officially created in 605 (under the Sui dynasty) but actually dating back as early as the Han dynasty (206 BC–220 AD), imperial examinations were designed to select the best and the brightest, and to sweep aside the sons of the great and ancient aristocratic families. Writing – which requires a lengthy and painful teaching process[10] – holds a particular place in Chinese identity. Historians know that writing is a powerful instrument: writing allowed rulers to record essential data in order to exercise power, to complete population censuses so as to identify the number of conscripts and to calculate population wealth so as to extract tax resources. From the fourteenth century onwards, under the South Song dynasty (Hangzhou), teaching and culture, arts and literature were separated from state bureaucracy. In addition to the public (i.e. government) schools, there were blossoming private institutions funded by wealthy families. Private 'academies' coached pupils for government examinations. Having withdrawn to their luxurious villas in Suzhou, retired or exiled bureaucrats who displeased the Court or the ruling Emperor enjoyed a life devoted to the arts, music and letters with a select group of cultivated friends who shared the same values. The image of the wandering poet who failed to pass imperial examinations,[11] too cultivated to work and too poor to make a living out of his talent, is a *topos* of Chinese literature.

Following ten years of Cultural Revolution (1966–76), schools and universities were ruined. A whole generation had been sacrificed. Teachers were humiliated. Some died, most were traumatised for life. Everything had to be rebuilt. Huge subsidies were allocated to the education system. Between 2002 and 2010, the number of students registered at universities more than doubled, rising from 13 per cent to 26 per cent in each age group (see Box 5.2). In the meantime, the

Box 5.2 Education in a growth model

Economists tried to calculate the 'return' on education through correlating the level of education and the level of growth. The 'knowledge premium' measures the extra income produced by a more skilled worker. The Mincerian return on education (after the name of the economist Jacob Mincer) is more uncertain. Through a regression process, based upon a set of factors known to contribute to the growth rate, a 'remainder' is obtained which accounts for the percentage assigned to 'education'. According to a US report, a 10 per cent rise in the number of secondary school graduates in 1980 produced a 6 per cent increase in growth rate between 1980 and 2000. In the counties which showed a 10 per cent share of secondary school graduates, growth reached 72 per cent between 1970 and 2000 as opposed to 37 per cent in the counties where the population share of secondary school graduates was below 5 per cent.

Source: E. Glaser, *Triumph of the City*, Penguin, 2011.

number of university institutions doubled, rising from 1,022 to 2,305. With 2,000,000 students more per year, China needed to build two universities capable of accommodating 20,000 students every week. Over the last ten years, the number of graduates has increased sixfold. In the top 500 of the Shanghai rating, there are 150 American universities, 42 Chinese, 37 British, 21 Japanese and 10 from South Korea. In 2011, the number of Chinese students pursuing their studies in foreign universities accounted for 510,000 of 3,300,000 students (see Table 5.7).[12]

If a university degree is a requisite, it is not sufficient to find a job. In sharp contrast with Western developed countries, in China the number of those unemployed increases with the level of qualification obtained. Students graduating from the most reputable universities can expect a starting salary of no more than 10 per cent higher than those graduating from lower rated universities (see Table 5.8).

This does not induce students to start their own business, or to search for a job in privately owned companies or foreign companies where salary levels are usually 40 per cent higher. They would rather apply to government bureaucracy or large state-owned companies where the salary level is lower but where a career is guaranteed.

In the framework of a questionnaire, Tsinghua University graduates (Beijing) and Stanford University graduates (California) were asked how

Table 5.7 Number of university students (25–35 years old)

	2000	2010	2020
America	25.2	23.1	19.8
Europe	29.3	28.1	22.4
China	16.5	17.8	28.5
Japan	9.8	6.9	4.1
India	6.0	11.4	11.6
Total (m)	91.00	129.00	204.0
Total (%)	32.96	39.90	47.0

Source: OECD, *China Survey* (2013).

Table 5.8 Unemployment rate (21–25 year olds, %)

Elementary	4.2
Secondary	8.2
Professional	11.3
University	16.4

Source: Gan Li, 'China Household Finance Survey', *Wall Street Journal* (2012).

Table 5.9 Employment expectations and achievements

	Job sought %	**Job acquired** %
State enterprise	32	35
Administration	32	10
Start-up	11	4
Private sector	4	36

many of them wished to create or to join a start-up company. Compared with 3 per cent of Tsinghua graduates, 22 per cent of Stanford graduates said that they would. They were then asked how many wished to join the government administration: only 2 per cent of graduates from the University of Stanford answered positively, compared with 52 per cent of graduates from Tsinghua University. The one-child policy backfired: parents who have only one child wish for him to join a government office and benefit from safe and secure employment. On the marriage market, government bureaucrats enjoy a premium. In the same questionnaire, graduates were asked what they would wish to do, as opposed to what they actually do (see Table 5.9).

The Chinese education system is a mix of government and private institutions. The government sector has inherited some prestigious institutions (Tsinghua in Beijing, Fujian in Shanghai) but, although the number of educative institutions is rising, they are becoming more and more private, and less and less public. As a legacy of the Soviet Union, most Chinese political leaders are engineers, though the number of leaders with a non-scientific background has been increasing – such as the Prime Li Keqiang, who is a lawyer and an economist. Most needed at the present stage of development are managers, lawyers and economists, rather than engineers and technicians. In China, education is expensive. A number of private business schools have been founded at university level, most of them in conjunction with a Western university or business school. But the marketization of education did produce some illegal practices, such as the sale of university degrees (a very old practice which was already in use in imperial times).

Chinese overseas diaspora

Officially, the number of overseas Chinese would be something in the order of 20,000,000. Based on the most conservative estimates, Chinese diaspora account for some 80,000,000 people. Chinese-speaking communities (so-called 'Chinatowns') have settled all over the world, but especially in South East Asia and Western Africa, where they have captured the economic sector (Malaysia) or commercial networks (Indonesia, East Africa). Most of them stay in close touch with their family and province. In the Communist Party, a special department is devoted to maintaining links with the overseas Chinese community. In addition, some foreign countries are Chinese-speaking (Taiwan, Singapore). Taiwanese businessmen have invested heavily in China, in Fujian province in particular, opposite the island, across the straights, where they can rely on family connections who speak the same language. The success of the Hong Kong experiment ('one country, two systems') will be critical to the repatriation of the island to the motherland.

The one-child policy is not the only feature of the Chinese politics of investing in human capital. However, it is one of the most enlightening of the Party goals and methods. The demographic policy is highly sensitive, as it is impacting the way of life of many generations ahead. Whatever the policy – whether 'Natalist' or 'Malthusian' – it has a great impact on a wide range of side-effects: political, social and economic, not to mention psychological. Government interference in such a sensitive area is destructive in what is the most sensitive area – private life and feelings. Therefore, the 'demographic' policy, the investment in human capital, is much broader than the population policy: one-child policy, urbanization, living standards, millions of graduates entering the labour market every year, the funding of pensions, and the privatization and marketization of education. In such an area, it is understandable that the Party and the government are facing a strong reaction from the attitudes of local communities.

6
The Knowledge Economy

I pass on but I do not create.
(Confucius)

Devoid of raw materials, China developed processing industries before it turned to an economy of knowledge. Theory states that developing countries are supposed to go through three economic sectors of growth return: primary (agriculture, mining), secondary (manufacturing), tertiary (services), if not quaternary (digital economy) where the share of intellectual development is overwhelming. The service sector includes several types of activities: from the noodle soup vendor who has set up a shop around the corner, to the hi-tech company staffed with highly skilled manpower. Western countries that were increasingly moving towards a tertiary, if not quaternary, economy realized that a strong tertiary economy must be backed by a strong manufacturing sector. Most of them have undergone a 'reindustrialization' process by pulling back some of the manufacturing units formerly transferred to emerging or developing countries. China is working the other way around. Manufacturing industries account for an unusually high share of the economy. Therefore, salary increases must be compensated through increasing competitiveness. The policy of research and innovation is aimed at raising the added-value of Chinese output and the profile of the range of Chinese-made products.

As with the other areas, the government plays a key role in the development of an economy of knowledge. The distribution of government R&D expenditures, as opposed to expenditures in the private sector, is approximately 80/20 per cent in the USA, 20/80 per cent in Europe and in China is wholly funded by government subsidies. The R&D programme extends over the whole chain of knowledge: school and university, the training of scientists, the spreading of R&D throughout industries, the creation of national 'champions' and the consolidation of firms from the same sector to reach a critical size.

In a command economy, issues related to quality, management and marketing are unimportant: overall production is the priority. But, in a partially or fully market-driven economy, companies need managers rather than engineers, especially in the sensitive transition period, people who are able to manage a 20 per cent or 30 per cent growth in turnover per annum. When you are driving a racing car instead of an ordinary car, you need a much swifter reaction time. In China, there is an increasing number of business schools, mostly designed along the American university model. Chinese universities are often organized on quantitative obsolete models, while American and European universities put emphasis on cross-cultural specificities, network development, interactivity and creativity. This herd instinct may be a hindrance to collective decision making and the spirit of individual creativity.

In order to broaden the market share of a foreign economy, a company must be backed by a strong market share in the domestic market, and vice versa. A company can lower the range of prices on the domestic market by extending their overseas market share. Pending the development of domestic consumption, Chinese companies made a detour through the overseas markets. As a result, this policy lengthened production lines, reduced overheads per unit and lowered marginal prices. What Japanese *zaibatsu* did in the 1960s and Korean *shaebos* did in the 1980s, the great Chinese SOEs are doing in the 2000s. For developing countries, it is cheaper and quicker to buy or obtain advanced technologies from developed countries at any price and by any means, rather than to build them up internally from scratch. Lacking the implementation of the Rule of Law system and the protection of patents, it makes it easier to catch up with Western technologies.

Rightly or wrongly, the Chinese often complain about the reluctance of Western companies to share their know-how. The very idea of intellectual property is hard to understand in a country where knowledge has always been a common property. The knowledge process is completed by increment, rather than breakthrough. In Western countries, scientists who have made a discovery are honoured by both their peers and the public. In China, a discovery is not an epistemological breakdown but, rather, a new order in an existing set of knowledge, the final result of an endless set of comments compounding on each other around a consistently developing core. When Deng Xiaoping initiated the policy of reform and opening-up, he used Mao's quote ('progress based on facts') to respond to and sweep aside his competitor, Hua Guofeng, the then General Secretary. Hua had been appointed by a dying Mao and wrote an article using the wording 'neither right nor wrong', meaning that he was neither prepared nor willing to give up Mao's legacy.

The landing of a satellite on the moon drew the attention of the entire world. In just a few years, China has joined the most advanced group of countries in the scientific field and become a leader in some selected areas: chemicals (fertilizers), pharmaceutical laboratories (Hangzhou), high-speed trains (Beijing–Shanghai–Canton), high-speed computers and aerospace to name but a few. The next human to set foot on the moon will probably be Chinese. The strongest and fastest computer is Chinese (Tianhe-1A),[1] even though the components are foreign-made. The Chinese Internet community is the largest ahead of the USA (700 million). The third largest aircraft company in the world is Chinese – AVIC, whose affiliated company COMAC is about to launch a new mid-range airliner (the C919) which is expected to be marketed in 2016. For some considerable time, Internet industries were not intended to be among the so-called 'strategic areas'. But, as the small hi-tech became a worldwide colossus, government institutions subscribed heavily to the capital increase so that management remains under government control, while the management techniques remain the same. Alibaba, the world largest website, is expected to place a record US$2 billion IPO on the stock exchange (13 September 2014).

Research and innovation policy

In 2012, China devoted Rmb 1,000 billion (US$160 billion) to research and development – a 20 per cent annual growth rate. Between 2000 and 2005, the volume of R&D doubled and increased again by 50 per cent between 2006 and 2010. China is targeting a R&D budget amounting to 3 per cent of GDP in 2020. If so, China will become the world's largest country for R&D expenditures.

Though China has initiated a number of discoveries – the compass, gun powder, paper (in fact, writing paper), the banknote and so on – unlike the Western world, China does not honour those who make discoveries[2] The discovery process is a joint venture, like European cathedrals, and not a personal contribution. Greek thought is speculative; Roman and Chinese thought is basically practical. Greek philosophers are searching for 'truth' while Chinese or Roman philosophers are looking for 'happiness', or the solutions to practical problems: how to behave in society, how to rule a country, how to make the best use of existing tools. According to Sunze, the military goal of war is not to crush the enemy as happened in the

Napoleonic wars of attrition, but to bring him to surrender – the enemy of today is the ally of tomorrow, the foreign conquered land of today is tomorrow a Chinese province or a tributary country. In China, someone making a discovery does not create an invention out of fresh air, he has simply put forward a new set of interpretations or arrangements. 'I pass on but I do not create' (Confucius).[3] The Chinese are learning by doing; Westerners are doing by learning. The Chinese education system does not aim to nurture creative spirits. Most Chinese scientists have been trained in foreign countries. Moreover, Communist education does not induce students to critical behaviour. Some Chinese companies – such as the Beijing Genomics Institute (BGI), the world leader in genetic sequencing[4] – usually hire undergraduates leaving college rather than university graduates who have been 'distorted' by the prevailing methods of learning or management techniques.

Every year, the education system 'produces' 23 million graduates (five times more than ten years ago in 2004) from 1,700 universities. 'The Long Term Development Plan of Science and Technology' (2006–20) established a set of objectives and priorities for developing 'innovation with Chinese characteristics': priority was given to national innovations, focusing on a limited number of key areas; priority was given to the contribution R&D makes to economic and social development, as well as technologies of the future.

The government has put forward a broad range of measures to support the development of advanced technology (see also Table 6.1):

- Tax cuts or exemption for R&D expenditures, for all income produced through the sales of technology and for the import of research equipment. VAT has been brought down from 17 per cent to 3 per cent for Chinese-made software and integrated circuits.

Table 6.1 Number of registered patents (2010)

	Number of patents	**Growth rate 2006/10 (%)**
China	12, 698	54
Korea	12, 342	21
USA	60, 588	12
Japan	41, 917	10
Germany	33, 139	9
EU	82, 828	5

Source: OECD.

- Loans and subsidies to innovative, hi-tech companies, softening interest rates for financing R&D programmes and Import-Export Bank guarantees to imported products related to meeting the needs of research.
- Prioritization of hi-tech companies in the allocation of government public works.
- Hi-tech companies are allowed to take 5 per cent off the tax base, the net value of asset increases dedicated to the distribution of stock options and other types of profit sharing schemes.
- Accounting rules have been amended to include industrial properties among fixed assets[5] investment funds are formed to back up hi-tech companies (most of them are affiliated to government agencies, universities or Academies of Sciences); creation of a stock exchange specialized in hi-tech stocks (Shenzhen) similar to the American NASDAQ.

The lack of protection of patent rights

A lack of the Rule of Law means that the protection of intellectual property is not guaranteed. This is harmless to Chinese companies where knowledge sharing is widespread, but it could be extremely harmful to foreign companies which are often stripped of their patents.

Should a foreign company establish itself in China, it is obliged by government regulation to form a joint venture company with a Chinese partner in the minority position 51/49 per cent. At first sight, in view of the peculiarities of the Chinese market, this sounds natural. The foreign partner provides the product, the technology, the know-how, while the Chinese partner provides his market knowledge, the marketing network and connections with the right people in the right places in government and the Party. In some cases, the foreign partner is compelled to provide the source code (such as Eurocopter) which allows them access to the software. If the Western partner is reluctant to disclose the software, the Chinese government turn to a less demanding competitor (such as US Westinghouse in lieu of the French 4th generation Areva EPR). Following the construction of the Three Gorges Dam (again French), Alsthom (later sold out to GE) refused to share the technology of the large power turbines and thereby lost the high-speed train contract. Ultimately, China developed a less sophisticated, home-grown version (Maglev) of the German magnetic suspension high-speed train. Following several months or years of happy cooperation, the Western partner discovers that its Chinese partner is manufacturing or selling the same products through another company of which it is the sole owner (Danone *v.* Wahaha). After an attempt at conciliation, the Western company brings the case to the court. Following an endless legal procedure, the Western partner is found guilty of stealing its own patents which, in the meantime, have surprisingly become 'Chinese' and is forced to pay substantial 'compensation' (Schneider *v.* Clint). Dreading an endless and unfair trial, most Western companies would rather compromise.

But there is another way consistent with imposing 'Chinese' standards. 'Standard war' is not new in international competition (such as TV sets in the 1960s). A country which plays this game must rely on a large domestic market to impose its own standards. It is a double-edged sword: as with countries which use the English language in international trade, a country which is strong enough to impose its own standards benefits from an extra trading asset. However, if a country imposes a set of standards on domestic products which are not up to the established foreign standards, its products may be difficult, if not impossible, to sell on the international market. Another version of this behaviour is to impose a set of specific legal constraints such as safety and security regulations, ecological norms and labour regulation. SINOPEC, one of the largest Chinese oil companies, 'demanded' that the government enquire about the corruption practices 'imported' by foreign companies (Daimler, Rio Tinto). A 2009 government directive aimed at prioritizing Chinese hi-tech start-up companies. China used the 2008 anti-trust law to push aside foreign competitors (Anglo-Australian Rio Tinto, American BHP, Brazilian Vale with regard to iron ore mining).

R&D expenditures

In terms of R&D expenditure, China is far behind the USA but has already caught up with Japan as the second world leader on an even footing with the European Union (see Table 6.22). R&D spending decreased in the USA in the wake of the global financial crisis (because most R&D expenditure is privately funded), it stabilized in the EU and it increased in China (where R&D spending is wholly funded by government subsidies). Chinese R&D is said to be less productive. Chinese laboratories wholly funded by the government focus on a limited range of supposedly 'strategic' areas, especially defence. Therefore, the volume of R&D expenditure is relatively less sensitive to the overall economic trend. American R&D expenditure is focused on mass market products and thus is more sensitive to economic growth. In Europe, R&D programmes are

Table 6.2 R&D world total expenditures (%)

	USA	EU	China	Japan
R&D expenditure	32.8	23.4	11.8	13.2
Scientific publications	30.8	33.3	7.8	7.6
European patents	28.9	37.3	1.3	18.1
Numbers of scientists	22.6	21.3	18.1	11.4

Source: OECD.

designed on a national basis which leads to overinvestment (as in the case of ITER) and duplication (aerospace), while strategic fields are neglected.

Today, Chinese R&D expenditures are increasing at an annual growth rate of 10 per cent. The number of scientific articles issued by Chinese researchers is five times greater than ten years ago in 2004; however, some members of the scientific community are questioning the quality and innovation of Chinese contributions. Based on GDP, the number of Chinese scientific contributions accounts for 53 per cent of the rate of American scientific contributions (127 per cent in Germany, 123 per cent in France).

Lifting the market range of Chinese products

As the world's largest manufacturing industry before the USA and the EU, China must cope with the legacy of obsolete Soviet-like 'bricks and mortar' heavy industry. By investing in R&D, China tries to short-circuit natural development and reach the tertiary sector (services) and quaternary sector (digital). Though the share of the manufacturing industry in GDP is the world's highest, the industrial sector is capped at a given level, instead of decreasing as in developed markets.

In order to lower manufacturing costs and, above all, labour costs, China's industrial sector has two alternatives: either to move factories inland to the western provinces, or to relocate manufacturing units to neighbouring countries (Vietnam, Cambodia, Burma, Indonesia, the Philippines) where labour costs are lower. New graduates are induced to move to these inland provinces where the salary range, as well as the cost of living, is much lower. They move with the expectation that they may be able to return to a more attractive coastal city in the future.

Chinese groups are expanding overseas thanks to an aggressive price policy based on a large domestic market, credit conditions, dumping practices by transferring costs and profits from one product to another, from one industry to another in a diversified consortium which is concealed from the public. For example, Haier, a manufacturer of housing appliances, is now the world leader of 'white' products, having moved up from a 1.7 per cent market share in 2001 to 5.7 per cent in 2012, overriding the American company Whirlpool, and the Korean company LG. But in light of the size of the country, China has been investing hugely in transportation industries. In addition, less sophisticated but more solid Chinese products can be successfully marketed in emerging and developing markets.

In information and telecommunication (ITC) industries, China is the world leader in terms of exporting hi-tech products and electronic components. China adopted the idea of 'Silicon Valley' by creating a string of 'technological parks' which put together firms, universities and research centres not only in the view of creating skilled jobs, but also to trigger a spillover process among the other industries. The cost of learning and finding a job is decreasing in so far as the related activities themselves are concentrating and diversifying. Townships are competing with each other to attract a wide range of industries through tax exemptions and land allocation. Companies in the same industry are concentrated in the same area in the same way as in Soviet times – for example, the car industry is centred in Wuhan, oil and coal in Dalian, chemical industries in Hangzhou.

On the other hand, pending the development of a domestic market, some Chinese companies are tapping into the foreign market before they shift emphasis back to the home market as did the American company Dell and the Taiwanese company Acer. A former affiliate of Beijing University, Lenovo acquired IBM's PC department in 2005. Coping with declining prices, IBM wished to give up the low margin PC market to shift to the more rewarding consultant business. Lenovo used the same technique to buy Motorola (the iPad manufacturer) from Google in 2014, which gave them access to a promising but very competitive market. The labour cost premium turned out to be a management premium. Now that Lenovo is a dominant partner on the international market, the Chinese company is in a position to take advantage of the rapidly developing domestic market.

With an Internet community in excess of half a billion people, China is the dominant country in the mass production of ITC-related products. China Mobile is the largest manufacturer and distributor of mobiles. Formed in 1988, Huawei, a manufacturer of telecommunication equipment, became the world's second largest manufacturer in

2009, capturing a 20 per cent market share behind Ericsson (31 per cent) but before Nokia and Alcatel Lucent. Baidu is the world's largest search engine company and Alibaba is the world's largest company of online sales websites. In conjunction with the Chinese government, foreign competitors Google and YouTube have been driven out of the country.[6] Now that Chinese companies control the hardware market, they are moving onto the software market. Chinese-made broadcasts are steadily taking over the former Japanese- or Korean-made media programmes.

The railway industry is a critical area in such a large country with such a centralized government. For centuries, geography was the main obstacle to the extent of the Emperor's power. When, in 1912, Sun Yansen gave up his position as the first President of the Republic of China (in favour of a General Yuan Chekai, to prevent a civil war), he dedicated himself to the extension of the Chinese railway network until his death in 1925. He rightly found this a key condition of economic growth. Over the last few years, China has managed to build up 100 per cent Chinese technology. The first Chinese high-speed train (HST) connects Guangzhou (Canton) and Wuhan (inland). It now takes three hours to make this journey instead of eight. Another HST track has been completed which connects Beijing, Shanghai and Guangzhou in just eight hours (two to three hours by plane). Managers of the powerful Railways Ministry think HSTs will prevail in any connection of less than five hours. In view of the costly fares, HSTs still represent a prestige means of transport, too expensive for the average citizens. A 300,00 km track construction plan accounting for a US$500 billion investment programme has been approved in spite of the crash in Wenzhou and the arrest of the Minister of Railways. The Chinese aircraft company COMAC, an AVIC affiliated company, is about to market a mid-range liner (C919). In the aerospace industry, China is one of the few countries which can launch heavy satellites into space. Now that the USA has ceased its NASA programme due to lack of government funds, the next person to walk on the moon will probably be Chinese. In 2015, the Shenzhou programme (*'Heaven Ship'*) is expected to launch a heavy rocket which can drive a 25-ton satellite into space. This lags, of course, far behind Saturn V of the Apollo project (100 tons) but it should be sufficiently powerful to reach the moon by combining several rockets together. As with the USA in the 1970s, investment in the moon race does not provide a high return in term of scientific or economic profits, but in terms of image, the 'return' could be very high.

In the car industry, where China benefits from some comparative advantages, Chinese manufacturers have focused on lower- and mid-range vehicles. This has forced foreign companies to focus on lower-priced vehicles (where profit per unit is small) and on higher-priced vehicles (where profit per unit is greater but where a much more sophisticated technical input is required), giving up the mid-range. Chinese companies are therefore extending their range of products to the two extremes in order to compete on an even field with foreign brands, especially on the developing and emerging markets. It is very likely that shortly the government will focus on SAIC (Shanghai Automobile Industry Corpn) as a 'national champion' to reach its critical size and production level to decrease costs and increase margins. Some have already undertaken similar moves, such as GAC (Guangdong Automobile Corpn) and Chery/Geely – which has acquired Volvo, the troubled Swedish car manufacturer, while others such as Qoros have put emphasis on the higher-priced range of cars. And yet China is at the forefront of car technology: the first ever fully electric car was designed and manufactured by BYD, of which the main shareholder is Warren Buffet's Berkshire Hathaway.

In 2010, with total sales of 13.8 million vehicles, China overtook the USA to become the world's largest car market. It is expected to reach 40 million by 2020. At the moment, 30 per cent of the domestic market is covered by Chinese car manufacturers, small cars at low prices but of poor quality and unattractive an unappealing appearance – comments levelled at Japanese car manufacturers in the 1970s. But the foreign manufacturers continue to invest in new production units though the industry is threatened by overproduction and overcapacity (31 million vehicles – i.e. twice as many as the annual demand). Economic growth slowed and the car market shrank before growth resumed in 2013. Foreign companies, such as Toyota (no. 1) and GM (no. 2), are already selling more cars in China than in their own countries. The powerful Planning Office, the NDRC, has already dispatched a circular letter 'instructing' foreign car manufacturers to produce 'Chinese' cars instead of importing foreign vehicles under 'Chinese' brands capable of being sold overseas (see Table 6.3). But so far the export of Chinese-made cars has failed to take off.

To cope with the limitations (overcapacity, low average purchasing power) of the domestic market and in spite of a high growth rate, Chinese manufacturers are shifting to foreign markets. However, they must acquire Western technology and local marketing networks. Chinese car manufacturers are increasingly buying suppliers, manufacturers and designers of car components and equipment (such as the French Faurecia, a manufacturer of spare parts), rather than attacking

Table 6.3 Car production (m units)

	2009	2010
China	10.4	13.8
Europe	14.1	134.0
USA	10.4	11.6
Brazil	3.0	3.3
Japan	2.9	3.2

Source: Car manufacturers throughout the world.

large well-established and politically more sensitive targets. This is the exact opposite of the foreign banks' in coping with the Chinese market.[7] When GM sold out the troubled Swedish car maker Volvo to Geely (Zhejiang Geely Holding Group), synergies were not that obvious but it worked in spite of very different technical and managerial cultures. The two partners are now extremely complementary: Volvo having access to the Chinese market, Geely having a bridgehead on the European market and the high-end market, as well as taking advantage of Volvo's image and sales network. In contrast, the acquisition of Saab, another troubled Swedish car manufacturer, led to a rapid failure because the buyer, a Chinese investment company involved in a number of different areas, had no experience in this field.

Industrial strategy

Though Chinese industry is suffering from a relatively low rate of productivity, Chinese industries have managed to penetrate the Western developed markets. As the case in other fields, the global financial crisis accelerated the closing up of the gap between these two areas. In 2009, following the financial catastrophe, the productivity of Chinese manufacturing companies increased by 8.2 per cent at the same time that overall world productivity was decreasing by 1 per cent (+2.5 per cent in the USA and –1 per cent in Europe). However, although the right definition of 'productivity' is arguable (GDP per head, GDP per assets, power productivity, and so on), Chinese productivity, in general terms, remains extremely low (about 15 per cent that of the USA). China needs three times more power to manufacture the same product as the USA. Meanwhile, China is now the world's 27th most productive country (India being the 51st), due to the rise in productivity in certain specific areas – such as infrastructure, education, the institutional framework and health.

But such an astonishing productivity growth rate is owed to overwhelming government interference which, in the long term, may be harmful. Not only is R&D wholly funded by the government, but also the government is actively involved in every step of the innovation process in defining priorities, in concentrating the ways and means, in using the leverage and spillover effects and in priority fields – transport, communications, education, nuclear, aerospace, aircraft, techno-biology, and so on. But, in the long term, R&D requires not only good management and heavy subsidies; it also requires a certain freedom of thought, a spirit of creativity – which, at first sight, seems to be incompatible with a totalitarian economic and political regime.

Government interference has followed the Japanese path. The NDRC is playing the same critical role as the powerful Japanese Ministry of International Trade and Industry (MITI) in the post-war period. As with the MITI, the Chinese government proceeds step by step: concentration, integration, expansion. First, concentration: the government takes the initiative to build up big 'national champions' enjoying a monopoly or near monopoly at home. Next, integration: industrial groups acquire neighbouring industries up and down the production line: suppliers and marketing networks. Then, expansion: through direct investments abroad, Chinese 'champions' acquire market shares and technical know-how. For this purpose, Chinese companies can tap into an unlimited amount of foreign exchange reserves (US$4,000 billion). As the Japanese in former times, Chinese companies can afford to overpay for Western companies which are up for sale), because the buyer and the seller have not the same goal. Japanese companies did the same in the 1970s: they overpaid for foreign companies to acquire a foothold in foreign markets and purchase technical expertise. As they were practising a policy of lower prices, they kept all local competitors at arm's length. Once they had reached a dominant position, they could afford to increase the market prices steadily. When a US company did not reach a 15 per cent return in a given market to reward the equity, it was sold to move into a more rewarding market. It was given up to a more competitive company that could cope at that price level. When IBM sold out its computer section (which was initially the most profitable section) because the return was no longer in line with their financial targets, Lenovo bought it and became the world's largest PC manufacturer within a short period of time.

The Chinese model has adopted the Japanese experience of the 'wild goose flight unit', defined in 1937 by the Japanese economist Kaname

Akamatsu (1894–1974). First, the manufacturing strategy focuses on a low-cost item that has low added-value and requires low working power and which has been designed for export. The next step is to take control over the whole manufacturing process in an integrated industrial and financial model. The final step is to raise the profile of the range of products, as long as manpower, cost and productivity is increasing. A leading company practising an aggressive price strategy penetrates the foreign market bringing with them the other companies in that sector.

The government is the core element of such an industrial strategy, which requires a high degree of integration. The government selects the priority sectors, builds up national 'champions', provides financing and supports overseas direct investments through a number of government offices: state banks, development banks, 'political' banks, sovereign wealth funds, attractive lending conditions, import–export guarantees, and so on. However, the development of an innovative system and mentality requires certain other assets. The domestic market is not sufficiently mature; the penetration of foreign markets is increasingly felt as intrusive by local consumers (and governments), and under-priced currency has led to protectionist reactions. Finally, social inequalities at home may hurt the domestic market base.

7
Growing Inequalities

People full of humanity extend their love from those they love to those whom they don't.
(Mencius)

The average income of the upper 20 per cent of the population accounts for 133 times the average income of the lowest 20 per cent. Not only is the degree of inequality in China high, it is also worsening: the richest 10 per cent own 45 per cent of the national wealth while the poorest 10 per cent own only 1.4 per cent (see Table 7.1). In January 2013, for the first time since 2000, the National Bureau of Statistics (NBS) published China's Gini index,[1] a measure of the level of inequality. The Gini Index increased from 0.30 in 1978 to 0.474 in 2012[2] (0.22 in Japan), well above the 0.40 which is considered to be the threshold of social troubles. According to UNO,[3] China is placed 143rd out of the 177 recorded countries in terms of inequality. According to some economists, China's Gini Index may be as high as 0.61, which would make China one of the most unequal countries in the world. According to data published by the Ministry of Interior and Security, 'violent' (this is the Chinese definition

Table 7.1 Income scale (average income per head of every 20 per cent group (US$)

Upper group	21,776
Upper-middle group	6,029
Middle group	2,860
Lower-middle group	1,138
Lowest group	163

Source: National Bureau of Statistics (2014).

of social troubles) demonstrations (over 500 participants) numbered 8700 in 1993; in 2005, 87,000; and, in 2011, 180,000.

Inequalities are both caused by and contribute to economic growth. In a first step, growth brings about inequalities, some benefiting from the fruits of growth, some not, until increasing purchasing power spreads itself over the whole population. Higher income increasing faster than the average, increasing income acts as an incentive for the most enterprising members of the community to advance. In a second step, as the richest people dedicate an increasing portion of their income to saving in the 'best' case and to buying luxury goods in the 'worst' case, the momentum of growth is threatened by increasing inequalities which divert an increasing share of the income to non-productive fields. Such a situation requires government intervention to spread the increasing purchasing power to lower brackets in order to keep the consumption engine working through fiscal means (income and wealth taxes) and transfers (social security, pensions funds, unemployment benefits, family allowances). Otherwise, the country may be threatened by the 'middle income gap' – the overall economy is working in two separate circuits of a dual society: an upper level and a lower level, instead of spilling over the whole population as a fully integrated economy. Moreover, the income inequalities are reducing much more slowly than wealth inequalities. It takes a lifetime to ruin an individual but it takes several generations to ruin a wealthy family. In other words, over a certain level, inequalities are an obstacle to economic growth.

A 'Kuznets curve'[4] (1955) is an inverted 'U' which shows the ratio between the inequality rate and growth rate. In the pre-industrial stage, everybody was poor and the inequality ratio was relatively low. When the Industrial Revolution came, peasants moved to the cities and industrial centres, where salaries were higher. As far as the spread of urbanization, an increase in income spread over an increasing portion of the population and income gaps shrank. The number of farmers with a low productivity rate decreased, while the number of workers who had a higher productivity rate increased. Lower working classes benefited from tax rebates and social transfers. But, starting at the beginning of the century, there was a resumption of the increasing income gap, the Kuznets inverse capital 'U' became an inverted 'N'.

The American ratio is getting closer to the Chinese ratio. The tail of the 'Kuznets' curve is heading upwards again, a 'services' economy is turning into a 'digital' economy, where highly qualified workers take the place of the less-skilled workers of the old style ('bricks-and-mortar') industry. The gap between the highly qualified workers and those lower qualified is increasing. The unemployment rate is growing in the old industries and dropping in the new IT service industries. It is a generation gap as well as an income gap. Moreover, since the beginning of the nineteenth century, financial income has grown at a much more rapid rate than labour income. In previous times, free exchange used to increase the average income by spreading wealth over the populations integrated in the world market; in today's times, free exchange is working the other way round (i.e. pushing everybody's salary down to the lowest competitive level). The income gap is widening not only between countries, but also within countries – the industries directly or indirectly exposed to international competition being more vulnerable.[5]

The Chinese model fits more or less with this scheme. In a first stage, following the implementation of reforms, the poverty rate (under US$1.25 per head per day) fell. Over the last few years, poverty has begun to increase again. The 'elasticity' of the poverty ratio to the Gini rate is close to 3 (a 10 per cent increase in inequalities entails a 30 per cent increase in the poverty ratio).[6] China's case is remarkable in the sense that an increase in income gap is both wider and swifter. According to some economists (Levy and Temple, 2007), society is more tolerant to growing income gaps as long as the average income keeps growing. Actually, the specificities of China's model are amplified by both short- and long-term factors.

Regional inequalities

A sketch of China's inequalities can be mapped out according to three vertical arcs: the developed coastal provinces (from north to south: Shandong, Jiangsu, Shanghai, Zhejiang, Fujian, Guangdong), the less-developed central provinces (Liaoning, Beijing, Tianjin, Shanxi, Henan, Hubei, Hunan), and the least-developed western provinces (Sinkiang, Gansu, Qinghai, Tibet, Yunnan, Huizhou, Chongqing), Sichuan in the south-west being an island of prosperity. The GDP per head in provinces such as Shanghai (US$2,200) and Guangdong (US$844) are 2 to 7 times higher than Huizhou (US$428) or Gansu (US$333).[7] Even when we take into account the price differential between the two areas, the income gap is still wide.

China's historical heart is the Yellow River (*Huang He*) delta where the capital city Peking (Beijing) can be found. China's capital cities have been moving throughout history in response to invasions, dynasties, strategic priorities and provincial resources: from Shang'an (Xian) to Luoyang, Kaifeng, Hangzhou, Beijing, Nanjing and back to Beijing again. But China has always been defined as a centre (*zhong*) surrounded by concentric circles on which the Empire's power weakened as the further one moved from the centre to the periphery.

King Zheng's kingdom of Qin, located in the mountainous Ordos provinces on the eastern curve of the Yellow River, was a border kingdom at the junction of the Chinese (civilized) and Barbarous (uncivilized) worlds. King Zheng smashed one neighbouring kingdom after the other and rebuilt the Empire, a symbol of unity and stability. King Zheng became Emperor Qi Shi Huangdi. For the Chinese, the idea of an empire is connected with a united country, ruled by a centralized and strong government, managed by an army of cultivated bureaucrats-literati put together by a common language (Mandarin), writing, education, way of life and culture. From this point on, China's history became tales of endless conflict between unity and fragmentation, centrifugal and centripetal forces, centre and periphery. Since the founding of the Empire (221 BC), China has experienced a countless number of barbarous invasions, foreign occupations and foreign dynasties, civil and foreign wars. However, China has never experienced feudalism or federalism; China has never been colonized; China has ever been united as a cultural area and institutional framework; China has remained the same, always fragmented, always to be reunited.

However, regional solidarities are very strong in China. Everybody belongs to one (or several) networks, most of them united by a common language and dialect. Members of these networks do not necessarily come from the same province or city, or even village, but they share some common features and provide assistance to each other in any circumstances. Mao's birth place was betrayed by his strong Hunan accent.

North–south axis

All Chinese rivers run from west to east, from the Himalayan Mountains to the Sea of China, bordering several natural regions ranging from north to south. In the north, the Yellow River cuts across Beijing and Tianjin, where it flows into the Boha Gulf. In the centre, the Blue River (which Westerners call Yangtze and the Chinese call *Chang Jiang*) cuts across Chengdu, Chongqing and Wuhan, and reaches Shanghai where it flows into the Sea of China. In the south, the *Xun Xi* river flows into the Pearl River (*Zhu Jiang*) near Canton (Guangzhou) and Hong Kong.[8] The north–south axis is rooted in the very foundations of the Chinese mentality.

Straddled over the Yangtze River, northern China (Beijing) and southern China (Nanjing)[9] belong to the same country but each has a very different history, culture and even language. In the north, great windswept loess plains, battered by frozen, sandy gusts of wind from Mongolia; in the south, tropical hilly and green landscapes – the China of wheat, corn and millet against the China of tea, cotton and rice. From the north comes all the evil: cold winds, barbarous invasions; from the south comes heaven: 'streams' (sources of energy: *qi*). All the houses, temples, palaces, government offices and office buildings open to the south, including the Beijing Party headquarters (*Zhongnanhai*). The Emperor's throne faces south and is shielded from the evil north by a screen decorated with shamanic writings. In the Forbidden City, a succession of courtyards and pavilions is constructed, facing south to protect them from evil influences. From the South Gate, from which Mao proclaimed the People's Republic of China on 1 October 1949, visitors walk further north, from gardens to courtyards, from pavilion to pavilion lined up along the north–south axis, up to the Emperor's private quarters where only eunuchs were permitted entry. The Emperor's quarters are protected from northern influences by the green covered 'Coal Hill',[10] an artificial hill made from the spoils of earth excavated from the nearby West Lake.

The two major public works of China (i.e. the Great Wall and the Great Canal) are both made for protection, similar to the useless and expensive French 1940 *Ligne Maginot.* Northern and eastern borders protect from barbarous invasions, the Great Wall from the Mongolians, the Great Canal from Japanese (and Chinese) piracy. The Great Wall is not only a line of defence (designed to stop not only men, but also their horses – in principle, horses cannot climb walls), but is also a means for transportation: a paved road is built on top of the Wall for delivering reinforcements, supplies and weapons. The Great Canal is not only a means of transportation[11] of the southern products (rice, tea, cotton) to the northern armies garrisoned on the northern border, but also a line of defence to avoid the sea and its dangers.[12]

The Kingdom of Chu (south Yangtze) was the last to be conquered by King Zheng of Qin, the future Emperor Shi Huangdi. In 1127, the invasion of the Mongol tribes, Juins, forced the Court to run away from the capital city, Kaifeng, and to seek refuge south of the Yangtze (*Jiangnan*) in a new imperial city, Hangzhou, developed around an artificial lake (the Lake of West: *Xi hu* named after the same West Lake near Beijing's Forbidden City) which enjoys a southern climate and way of life. The court members, high ranking mandarins and bureaucrats, wealthy land owners and ancient families owning huge estates followed the Emperor's family along with the literati, and those practising arts and crafts, who developed a new, rejuvenated style of art and language which was more refined, more flexible and more subtle (e.g. 'neo-Confucianism'). When the new Manchu Qin (*tchinn*) dynasty invaded China, the Emperor fled to the south-west (Sichuan), where an independent Ming kingdom managed to survive for a while against the Manchu 'banners'.

Barbarous invasions to the south had a deep impact on the Chinese mentality. Literati and bureaucrats had to choose either to remain faithful to the 'Chinese' Ming dynasty, or to join the new 'foreign' dynasty with the expectation of keeping their northern estates and privileges. Some chose to retire from public life and withdraw to luxurious, comfortable homes in the countryside, or in a provincial city (Suzhou), and dedicate themselves to poetry, music, letters and friendship. The image of a poet or a thinker (often one and the same) who withdraw to the mountains of Yunnan (on the Yangtze's southern shores) to devote themselves to meditation and art far from the illusions of city and court, became a major literary theme and a way of thinking.

East–west axis

Traditionally, in China danger stems from the north and the west, a line of defence against the Northern Barbarous, an expansion area to the remote western mountains and deserts. Buddhism came in the sixth century by land and sea with Arabian and Indian merchants. When the Westerners landed in the port cities of the east and south-east, they opened a new penetration axis bringing with them the best and the worst of things: science and technology, the Bible and opium, commerce and industries, democracy and imperialism. Wrapped up in the northern and western threats, located in Beijing in the far north, the Court did not care for these newcomers, merchants and missionaries – a despicable kind of people only looking for trade and money. There was nothing to fear. When Emperor Qianlong responded to the British envoy, McCartney (1793), China was self-sufficient and did not need foreign goods (or ideas). Danger came from the north (Siberia, Mongolia) and the future lay in the far west (beyond the Gobi deserts). An appointment in the western provinces was a sort of exile far from the cultivated and civilized eastern port cities opened to the outside world. Today's young graduates who cannot find work in the eastern cities are migrating to the interior cities (Wuhan, Chongqing, Chengdu or Kunming, where the French-built narrow, one-line railway track from Hanoi and the port of Haiphong in Vietnam terminates). The Party nurtures this 'settler' spirit among the young pioneers, who are encouraged to settle in the remote western provinces, and further to Tibet and Xinxiang, with a view, ultimately, to increasing and inter-mixing the

Han settlers with the native dwellers. Every Five Year Plan includes a heading about the development of interior provinces.

From the frozen lands of Siberia to the scorching deserts of Xinxiang, China stretches over five time zones, but all the Chinese are subject to the same hour – the further west, the poorer the province; the further south, the richer the province. In the south-east, Guangdong has a per capita income 10 times greater than that of Gansu or Shaanxi in the north-west. Western mountains and deserts are the Chinese 'Far West', a territory of expeditions, explorers and settlements.

Centre and periphery

The Middle Kingdom (*Zhong Guo*) regarded itself as the centre (*zhong*) of the Chinese world and China as the centre of the world. The bordering countries and foreign countries in general were nothing but tributaries. Some adopted the Chinese language and writing. When Manchu banners invaded China, when the new Manchu dynasty settled in China in 1644, the Nurhaci[13] kingdom was already using ideographic writing, Confucianism ideology, and Chinese rites and government techniques, which made their settlement in China easier. The Middle Kingdom was also the heart of a number of foreign non-Han ethnic minorities, most of them settled on the borders. But, due to the increasing and more rapid means of transportation, the very idea of a centre and periphery is now more political than geographic. China's flag is red with five yellow stars, one large star surrounded by four smaller. The symbol's meaning is multi-faceted. Red is the symbol of the Revolution and yellow (like the sun around which revolves the stars) represents the stars of the Party surrounded by the smaller parties united in the 'National Front', or the Han people surrounded by the minority ethnic groups (Mongols, Tibetans, Manchus, Uyghurs). Red is also the colour of joy and prosperity,[14] and yellow (an Emperor's colour) is the shining sun – denoting China lighting and warming up the world.

The centre-periphery axis is a founding feature of Chinese identity and mentality. Even though it is China's historical centre, the Yellow River delta is located in the north-east. The central provinces mostly inhabited by the Han peoples are opposed peripheral provinces: Manchuria, Mongolia, Xinxiang, Tibet, Sichuan and Yunnan where ethnic, linguistic and religious groups are still active. China includes hundreds of dialects (Northern, Wu, Guangdong, Hunan, Jiangxi, Hakka,[15] Fujian) and non-Han ethnic groups (Thai Zhuangs, Turk Uyghurs, Burman Yis, Tibetan Zhangs, Muslim Miaos, Manchus, Mongols, Koreans), several minority religions (such as Muslim Huis and Miaos) out of the traditionally dominant religions (Confucianism, Buddhism, Taoism) are split between several 'schools' (Buddhist Mahayana, Varajyana, Lama Tibetans). Previously, local solidarities were strongly rooted among family or linguistic links. Today, thanks to the short- and long-term migrations (rural depopulation, urbanization, tourism), Chinese people are increasingly spread across the country (see Box 7.1).

Box 7.1 Holidays in China

Now that they are allowed to do so, the Chinese have been gripped by a travelling frenzy. On the occasion of New Year and 1 May, millions of Chinese return to their place of birth and visit their families. Every New Year, the central bank must allow for extra means of payment to the banks to meet with the seasonal cash withdrawals and upsurge in consumption. The Chinese government understood that official holidays (two weeks) could be the source of a prosperous tourism industry. For a few days, airlines are fully booked, trains are crowded and tourist sites are invaded.

In addition to the remoteness and the linguistic or religious features of the border provinces, capital transfers (towards the west) do not compensate for the population migration (towards the east). Provinces and province leaders are reluctant to transfer some of their resources to the neighbouring provinces. Local authorities fiercely compete between each other to draw or divert savings, jobs, investments, subsidies, taxes and loans. A province secretary is more powerful and influential than a minister. This 'autarchic' bias is a hindrance to capital transfers. As opposed to Europe (but as in the USA), population migration compensates for the lack of capital mobility. Chinese migrants do not hesitate to abandon their family (and children) to move eastward to the city in search of jobs or a better life, with (or, more often, without) the required working permit (*hukou*). Government is supporting the population transfer to the remote empty border provinces, the 'new frontier', 'new territories' (literally *Xinjiang*).

Ethnic minorities

In China, there are 57 officially recognized ethnic groups. Minority populations account for a marginal portion of the total Chinese population (below 5 per cent), but the minority policy is entangled with other considerations which make settlements difficult: ethnic groups and religions are often located in strategic areas, border provinces with abundant raw materials and natural resources invaded by Han settlers who took over local businesses and bureaucracy. Minority problems entwine with other political, economic, social and religious issues. The local secretary is expected to maintain a firm hand, a tight control and avoid troubles, especially from irredentist groups, if he wants to move up to a national career on the back of this assignment (such as Hu Jintao in Tibet).

To most Chinese people, minority groups are not grateful for economic and social investments granted and funded by central government. Minority groups are not subject to the one-child policy (as, formerly, minority women were not subject to bound feet or men to the long back plait). Minority groups benefit from quotas in schools, universities and local administration. To the ethnic minorities, the border provinces have been invaded by the Han population through a settlement policy. The best jobs, local businesses and the highest positions are taken by Han immigrants. Local culture is destroyed, since the Chinese language is imposed in schools and government offices. Han settlers respond by saying that they cannot hire local people unless they speak and write Mandarin. It is a never ending road of trouble.

Social inequalities

The former Prime Minister, Wen Jiabao, stated that, with a growth of 8 per cent, China was no longer in a situation to absorb the millions of young people entering the labour market every year and the millions of migrants coming from the country (rural depopulation). In 2013, the growth rate decreased to 7.7 per cent and is expected to reach 7.5 per cent in 2014. According to the World Bank, China's growth rate may stabilize in the range of 5 per cent in the near future, which is well below the sensitive 8 per cent growth rate. We have seen that China is already well above the 0.40 Gini Index, which mark the threshold of social disturbance. To the traditional inequalities (peasants, workers and women) must be added the emergence of a middle class which does not fulfil its historical 'reformist' or 'revolutionary' function as it used to in developed countries. In contrast, growing urbanization is a source of economic development and social revolution. Economic growth is accelerating social revolutions which reverberate with the economic situation and so forth.

Urbanization

For centuries, China was a mostly agricultural country inhabited by land owners, farmers and peasants. Traditional opposition of city dwellers and peasants is a classic theme of the Chinese culture. In painting, sketching or poetry, land is meant to be a heavenly and idyllic shelter against the urban troubled life. To the farmers, land is a site of hard labour, servitude and uncertain future. In China, more than anywhere else, the city is the site of power, social promotion and cultural life - in a word, of civilization. Since 1980, on the eve of the reform policy, built-up areas have quadrupled and continue to grow rapidly. From the beginning of the century, the urbanization process has grown at an annual rate of 3.5 per cent. Urban citizens comprise 53 per cent of the population and are expected to reach 75 per cent (i.e. over 1 billion) within the next ten years.

In 2010, the urban population overran that of rural areas. As a matter of comparison, the UK breached the same level in 1841, the USA in 1920 and France in 1931. Having only just been elected to the Politburo in November 2012, the new Prime Minister, Li Keqiang, published an article in the *People Daily*, the official Party newspaper, which put emphasis on the role of urbanization as 'an essential growth engine'. The current (12th) Five Year Plan (2011–15) brought forward urbanization as a national 'priority'. Indeed, urbanization is not only caused by rural depopulation. On the rural side, young people moving to the towns increases the rural productivity rate, but they join urban industries where the productivity rate is higher. In economic terms, urbanization means housing construction, public works and infrastructures to keep up with the increasing urban population. For example, there is a close connection between the construction of houses and the consumption of cement and steel. Local authorities are rapidly developing urban facilities at the expense of a balanced environment. Drawing on natural resources such as water has reached critical levels. All around the city of Peking, circular highways (as in Moscow) are crowded with millions of vehicles at a standstill in huge and smoking traffic jams. The times of millions of cyclists invading streets and avenues are over. In spring 2013, a high level of toxic gas forced the government to impose a system of dual traffic (cars are permitted on the road only every other day according to the registration plate number). On the eve of the Beijing Olympic Games and the Shanghai Universal Exhibition, car traffic was prohibited in the surrounding neighbourhoods several days, and even weeks, before. In addition to the economic impact of the urbanization process, urban middle classes nurture consumption and growth (housing, cars, appliances, health and schools) at the very moment when the Chinese government wants to move from one growth model to another by means of domestic consumption and demand instead of investments and exports.

Rural depopulation

In 2004, according to official data, the average annual income in the countryside amounted to 2,936 Yuan (US$400) against 9,422 Yuan (US$1,500) in urban areas (i.e. a gap three times greater than that needed to produce a continuous flow of people to the towns). From 1992 to 2002, 66.3 million farmers were expropriated (*China Leadership Monitor*) and the number continues to increase. In 2011, 50 million peasants were forced to move and the number continues to increase by 3 million each year. Rural depopulation is a common feature of all the developing countries. But, in China, it is faster and partially uncontrolled.

The Maoist policy of industrialization was based on confiscating the agricultural 'surplus' and redirecting it to the urban manufacturing sector. Compared with the rest of the population, urban workers were privileged: state companies used to provide jobs for life and 'iron, rice and bowl' (education, health, entertainment and holidays). The Great Leap Forward was not only a growth target ('to overtake the UK', as Khrushchev announced that the Soviet Union would soon overtake the USA), but also a management method: funding industrialization processes through transfers from the agricultural sector. This was supposed to be the final stage of development from 'socialism' to 'communism': the transfer of all production means to the State, to the 'people's commune' in the countryside and the state companies in towns; workers assigned to production teams; compulsory communal canteens; the separation of the families. These measures were aimed to ensure the transition from the 'collective means of production' to the final stage of 'people means of production'. The aim was to break down traditional social links such as the family, which was an obstacle to the implementation of a communist regime. Thus, the first step of Deng Xiaoping's reform policy was to free the farmers from the people's communes and to allocate a piece of land to each family to make sure that they could make their living from it and produce a surplus, delivered either to the government or the market. However, even among the most reformist leaders, it remains a leftover from the former productive, Maoist-type policy. Investments in urban industries, property and infrastructures increased from 36.5 per cent of GDP in 2001 to 48 per cent in 2011.

Rural depopulation affects mostly young adults but is often expected to be temporary. The land is state property and is allocated to each family according to its needs; but the presence of a son is required to take over the farm in due course, Therefore a young man may be tempted to move to the city with the view to making some money to help his family back home before he returns to the farm. The young women take advantage of the interlude between the end of compulsory schooling (at age 16) and their eventual wedding to make money to help their parents and to collect some savings of their own before getting married. But, in some cases, migration is a one-way street for those who cannot expect to find work in their birthplace, or who seek a better life in town. Factories are full of young people who have been uprooted from their family environment. Some of them have been picked up at school and sent to the factory, the salary (if there is one) is paid directly to the parents. Usually migration is a two-step move – first to the next town, then to a larger and more remote city, where migration may become permanent if there is no job available at home: landless peasants, farmers deprived of their land by local Party officials, business men or property developers. In this case, assuming that the farmer is paid the 'right' price, a migrant can collect some money to facilitate his settling in a town. On the other hand, the new land status allows the farmer to sell the lease or to entrust his plot to a relative, friend or neighbour to cultivate his land so that the average cultivated acreage of land per head is enlarged, thus increasing the productivity of the land.

Rural depopulation is also tied up with land ownership status, to the allocation of work permits and to the financial resources of local authorities. The land is owned by the state in a town or by a local authority in the countryside, either of which has the right to expropriate the land for any other purpose: infrastructure, public works, the construction of a manufacturing unit or tourism complex, and so on. A farmer needs to have a son to take over the cultivated land which has been allocated to him when he retires. Any further child – whether a son or a daughter – is forced to migrate. On the other hand, the local authorities are not officially permitted to borrow the land. Since the old land tax (which dates as far back as the foundation of the Empire) was nullified in 2006, the only way to collect unauthorized additional resources to finance unauthorized expenditures, in addition to the government subsidies, is to seize farmers' land and sell it to business people, making a juicy profit in between. It is estimated that the arable land purchased from farmers is priced at 2 per cent of the value of building land,[16] which leaves a hefty profit for the local communities or local authorities which have granted the building permits. Based on an enquiry in Yunnan provinces, out of the purchasing price to the farmers, 60–70 per cent is paid to the commune or the county, 25–30 per cent to the village, and only 5–10 per cent to the farmers from whom the land has been purchased.[17] According to data by the Ministry of Finance, the proceeds of land sales provide 26 per cent of the total resources of local authorities, 40 per cent according to the *Financial Times*[18] and 74 per cent according to Pr Guan Qingyou of Tsinghua University. The unavailability of lands may cause a major borrowing bubble for the local authorities. If and when they can no longer rely on land sales to repay the bank loans, the banks will be pulled into a chain of bankruptcy.

Last, but not least, the rural depopulation led to a growing class of 300 million *untermensch* without work permits, a *lumpenproletariat* of miserable ghost workers or migrants (*mingong*). Without a domestic passport or work permit (*hukou*), migrants are deprived of any protection, are subject to forced repatriation and lack social security or a labour contract. But the cancellation of the *hukou* system is a delicate issue as all the regulatory city holders of *hukou* (by birth) are hostile to the migrants, delinquents and competitors on the labour market. In addition, due to the lack of up-to-date land registration, allocating the land to regular owners is quite impossible as nobody knows who is, or used to be, the owner.

Working class

Before the global financial crisis exploded, the official unemployment rate was 4.1 per cent. Following the 2008 crisis, a number of exporting companies hit by the plummeting demand from developed markets supposedly sent 50 million migrant workers back home. Due to the recovery which brought the growth rate back up to the 7–8 per cent range (7.7 per cent, in 2013) the hiring of workers has resumed. In contrast, companies are now hit by unavailable labour supply and subsequent salary increases. Since the constitution reform of 1982, strikes are illegal. In effect, strikes are not formally prohibited but neither are they permitted. As a result, official data has registered an increasing number of labour conflicts, some of them violent. In 2009, an official of the Jianlong group (Jilin), an affiliated company of the steel maker Tonghua Iron & Steel, was beaten to death by workers in front of hundreds of colleagues –none of whom intervened. The root of social troubles can be traced back to the 'privatization' of state-owned enterprises in the 1990s (50 million dismissed workers according to the Ministry of Labour), then by a second wave of mass dismissals following the 2008 global crisis, especially in coastal exporting industries. Furthermore, most strikes have blown up as a result of late payment of salaries – or no payment at all, arbitrary salary withdrawals (housing, canteen) or compulsory overtime (textiles, toys).

It is widely known that numerous Chinese companies (as well as some foreign) do not apply labour regulations. In 2007, in an enquiry by the People's National Assembly (PNA) on a sample of 2,500 companies in seven different provinces, 80 per cent of the private companies were found to be delinquent. In 2004, the volume of late or unpaid salaries in the private sector was over US$10 billion (car, property, light industry and textile). Most of the workers did not have written labour contracts and thus were not eligible to claim social benefits, any jobless indemnities in case of dismissal, any health care in the event of a labour accident or any subscription to a pension scheme. Paid wages (when paid) were below the minimum legal wage. Most labour contracts included an illegal provision according to which workers committed themselves to give up the right to sue the company in the event of a labour accident or illness in the workplace (an example is Huawei, the world's second-largest manufacturer of electrical equipment, well-known for misconduct).

Following its enquiry, the PNA passed a law (put in force on the 1 January 2008) which set the base of a national labour regulation. From that point on, all workers must be given a written contract. All workers who have worked for over 10 years or had two limited labour contracts should be granted an unlimited labour contract. The trial period has been reduced. The labour contract must include some provisions regarding dismissal indemnities (one month per working year). At the same time, the single and compulsory trade union affiliated to the Chinese Communist Party (the All China Federation of Trade Union – ACFTU) announced the possibility of electing local officials. Nobody knows to what extent the labour regulation has been put in force but, in some cases, it has been used as a retaliatory measure, especially against foreign companies (out of the top 200 exporting companies, 153 are foreign).

This all started back in 2010, following a wave of suicides on the Shenzhen industrial site of Foxcon, a Taiwanese chip manufacturer, then a manufacturer (Foshan) of auto parts affiliated to Honda. Strikes burst out in a number of manufacturing sites, mostly foreign companies such as Oxcon (Taiwan), KOK (Taiwan) and Foshan Fengfu Autopart (Honda). For the first time, the labour movement did not address late salary payment or labour contracts but, rather, salary level and working conditions. It is somewhat puzzling that strikes burst out in foreign companies and, especially, Japanese companies where salary and working conditions are supposed to be better than Chinese companies – such as private mining pits. As the government did not react at this early stage, the strike movement spread rapidly to other industries. The media were allowed to report on the strike movement. Official trade unions intervened to offer arbitration services. But the movement was not only directed at the employer, but also to the official trade unions. Strikers demanded elected representatives and legal procedures for collective settlement of labour conflicts. After two weeks of strikes, the government put an end to the movement. Honda workers got a 33 per cent salary increase which brought the minimum salary up to 2,000 Yuan (US$350) per month. In 2011, wage increases reached an average 20 per cent. The legal wage was raised in most of the provinces: from 660 Yuan (US$106) to 1,030 Yuan (US$150) a month in Guangdong, to 960 Yuan in Beijing and 1,120 Yuan in Shanghai.[19]

Migrant population

The household registration system called *huji* or *hukou* dates back to the very beginning of Chinese history – probably from the times of the 'Fighting Kingdoms' (481–221 BC), but certainly from the foundation of the Empire (221 BC). From the beginning of the *hukou* system, the purpose was to keep the population under control in accordance with the collective responsibility principle. A census of the whole population was implemented to fix the basis of tax collection and the recruitment of conscripts. The *hukou* system already existed under the nationalist regime with a view to keeping the population managed and supervized. The *hukou* was re-established by the Mao regime in 1958 as a domestic passport. Today, the *mingong* are said to account for 270 million (OECD, 2013) or 350 million people (Beijing University). Between 1970 and 2010, 70 per cent of the growth of the cities was due to migration and only 30 per cent to birth rate. Every Chinese citizen was allocated a place in which to live (usually the place of birth) and a job (usually the father's job) for life. By retaining the rural population in the countryside, the government's intention was to keep the peasants away from the town and to keep the workers away from the peasant competition. However, it did not prevent migrants (*mingong* – literally 'working people') from crowding together in the towns. The *hukou* system was designed to keep the two communities away from each other, a sort of apartheid ('equal but separate'). In a country where 80 per cent of the population is comprised of rural people, rebellion was always 'rural' by nature: the Maoist Party was *ruralist* to take over the power but *urbanist* to keep it.

As social benefits are linked to the place where a person is registered (i.e. the place where they live), the *mingong* lose all their rights (housing, social security, health care, school and pension) in a society where the state is supposed to provide all the necessary means for living. The *mingong* no longer have an identity card. Legally speaking, they no longer exist. They could be dismissed without warning, arrested on the occasion of a routine police check or sent back to their place of birth even though their family may have been resident in a town for several generations. Work permits are allocated sparingly (only to highly skilled or well-connected people) according to a number of 'points' related to education, job, qualification and residence. Newcomers are not welcomed. For the local communities, migrants are a source of additional financial burden. By definition, migrants do not pay taxes and they are perceived as unfair competition on the labour market. In any event, whatever their personal feelings, Party members are restricted by Party instructions. In the best scenario, since 1985 migrants have been able to obtain a three-month work permit on an employing company's request, granted at a huge price by the local authorities. A *hukou* may cost up to hundreds of thousands Yuan. Quite often, farmers are forced to sell their land to pay for the *hukou*. This is a major source of corruption. In Shenzhen, the number of *hukou* holders is only 1.6 million out of a population of 10.5 million. As a result, the delinquency rate is growing to a record level. In most cases, migrants are not willing to give up their land rights together with their rural residence, which they consider to be a last resort in the event that their migration to the city fails.

As mentioned, the *hukou* system is not easy to displace as most of the parties involved are reluctant to make sacrifices: the *hukou* holders, who fear the growing competition of migrants on the labour market; the migrants themselves, who are not prepared to relinquish their land rights; and the government, which is not prepared to give up the monitoring of population growth and movements. Today, the *hukou* system is still a means of social and economic control. Given that the magnitude of arable land is 0.1 ha in China (23.9 in the USA), further peasant migration is inevitable to increase land productivity. Originally, due to the fast growth of export industries in the coastal provinces (Jiangsu, Shanghai, Zhejiang, Fujian and Guangdong), millions of workers were hired who came from the interior provinces (Sichuan, Chongqing, Huizhou, Henan, Hubei, Hunan, Guangxi, Anhui and Jiangxi) and mostly worked in textile industries (68 per cent of the total workforce), construction (58 per cent) and catering (50 per cent). It is the *mingong* who made China the workshop of the world.

Usually, migration is a three-step process. First, jobless peasants move to the next cities to find a complementary source of income for the family. Second, migrants move to a metropolis with the expectation of making money to return home when they have earned sufficient to take over the farm or for their retirement. Finally, some remain where they are, either because they have found a better way of life, or because they have married. But a curse hangs over them and their following generations: their children cannot register in schools and universities. They cannot obtain social security benefits because employers are not willing to register them and, thus, make the salary costs greater. They cannot expect to buy a house or an apartment because most of the urban apartments are either sold by the companies who own them, or allocated by the local authorities – both types of residence being reserved to the local *hukou* holders.

Tolerated because they are needed but remaining unrecognized, migrants live a very precarious life. Near railway stations, bus stations or highways terminals, you can find them with their meagre belongings, showing a piece of cardboard where their specialty is written (most of them unable to speak the local language). This labour black market is ruled by Mafiosi (*gongtou*). In the event of an accident at work, late payment of salary – or no payment whatsoever, or illegal additional working hours, they have no recourse and no access to health care. Most of them are lonely, leaving their children behind in the care of grandparents, relatives, neighbours or strangers. Of 160 million recorded migrants (out of an estimated total of 350 million), only 33 million live with their family. The number of migrants living alone is much greater due to the high level of non-recorded, illegal and paperless migrants. According to official data, 58 million abandoned children live far from their parents (i.e. 1 in 5).

In the event of economic downfall, they are used as an adjustment variable: they are hired on a last in/first out basis. Following the 2008 global financial crisis, 325 million migrants returned home. Two years later, when the recovery was well under way, recruiting teams were wandering the countryside in search of young peasants willing to move to the city. Some were hired straight from secondary schools. Housed and fed by the company, salaries were paid directly to the parents (minus the deductions). In such a context, it is understandable that the turnover of migrant workers is high. A *mingong* will not hesitate to move to another company or another city if he can expect a better life and working conditions. In Shenzhen, 4 million workers have worked for less than one year.

With some grounds, conservatives have suggested that the *hukou* system prevented the growth of overcrowded shantytowns, which spread around most of the major cities of the developing world. But, in effect, *hukou* have given birth to a *lumpenproletariat* deprived of any rights, who suffer degrading working conditions. They pile themselves into insalubrious shelters,[20] deprived of any public utilities, threatened by hostile residents. As a gesture, the government decided that the Chinese National Assembly should include three *mingong* representatives out of 3,000 members (i.e. one representative per 100 million). Some experiments have been undertaken in Shenzhen and Guangdong (Canton) for the allocation of *hukou* to the migrants who own their apartments, or those who have invested more than Rmb 5 million in the city (US$784,000). In Suzhou, the local government granted *hukou* to the *mingong* who have been living and working there for a given period of time. In 2011, the government created a three-month provisory *hukou*; this failed to solve the issue as most of the employers, as well as the *mingong* themselves, are unwilling to register them. On the other hand, the new system widened the range of opportunities for corruption.

Pending a reform which is regularly announced but never carried out, NGOs and charitable institutions have taken charge of some of the migrant services, such as schools or clinics. In many cases, such institutions have been closed by local authorities or due to harassment by neighbours. In September 2011, 23 migrant schools located in the suburbs of Beijing were hit by power and water cuts and strike pickets. But the second-generation *mingong* will never return to their registered village, where they feel and are perceived as strangers. This is despite them never being fully integrated in towns, where they continue to be looked on with suspicion.

Middle class

The policy of reform and opening gave birth to a middle class. A market of between 100 and 200 million people (Consultant GaveKal Dragonomics), the Chinese middle class accounts 20 per cent and 30 per cent of the urban population – i.e 110 million (2009) to 240 million (2011) – and should reach 75 per cent in 2023 (372 million) (see Table 7.2). This equates to a market as large as the European Union enjoying a purchasing power similar to Mexico or Turkey. Even though less than 8 per cent of the total population is earning more than 100,000 Yuan (US$15,000) and the average consumption expenditure (purchasing power parity – PPP) per capita does not exceed US$2,199 (35,577 Yuan), Chinese consumers are already purchasing more cars, mobile phones and computers than the Americans. They can be found primarily in coastal cities and their way of life is growing closer to that in the Western developed countries. But it is difficult to define the Chinese middle class other than through economic criteria, as it is a somewhat diversified and fragmented social group which lacks a sense of common interest.

Table 7.2 Middle classes as number of households (m)

	2010	2020
Wealthy	1	12
Upper-middle class	48	134
Lower-middle class	61	66
Poor	93	62

Sources: Boston Consulting Group, McKinsey, World Bank.

`The Chinese middle class is extending both upwards and downwards. In the upper direction, a minority of leading positions enriched through guaranteed government income, rather than risky innovation: company managers, high-level civil servants, leading figures sharing company management and/or political assignments. In the lower direction, a variety of management positions which do not derive from government circles: small and medium-sized entrepreneurs, middle-rank managers, university professors or foreign company managers. In any event, all of them are more or less dependent on government officials.

The acquisition of an apartment is a good index of the growing middle class. Usually, development companies sell the property to a company (sometimes the company have commissioned the apartment from the development company which is building it on its behalf) who, in turn, rent the apartment to their employees and, sometimes, in the event of a shortage of cash, sell it to the tenants at a very attractive price. More recently, development companies have acquired large tracts of land from local authorities to build huge complexes of shopping centres, housing and offices. The final purchase price depends on the availability of credit. The banks are very reluctant to loan to households and they impose stringent criteria. Mortgage loans and mortgage companies are still uncommon. Most of the consumption credit companies are foreign joint ventures together with local banks. Furthermore, the average Chinese person is very reluctant to apply for a bank loan and prefers to pay in cash. A bank loan is solicited only when the house is considered a more rewarding investment than a bank savings account or Treasury bonds, and less risky than stocks and bonds. Investors are betting on an average 10 per cent + annual return (in urban settings).

There is no data concerning empty offices and apartments, but there are 65 million unconnected power cables, which demonstrates overcapacity and may be the beginning of a property bubble. Regardless, the

12th Plan has devoted a substantial amount in government subsidies to housing. The construction of housing raises a complicated issue for central government and also local authorities. Either they give financial support to the construction of housing, especially for the poorest bracket of the population, causing a risk of inflation and property bubble drawing the whole banking sector into bankruptcy;[21] or the government does not interfere in the property market. The growth of the critical construction industry may be adversely hit, affecting the whole economy as a result. In any event, besides the government subsidies and bank credit, the central authorities have taken measures to tighten the purchase of housing (increased interest rates, increased down-payments at the expense of buyers, forbidden acquisition of a second home) with the aim of maintaining control of the nascent property bubble without threatening the overall growth rate.

Women's rights

According to Mao (as the old quotation goes), women are 'half of men's heaven'. But Mao did not recognize gender, only class categories. One remembers pictures of asexual women dressed in Mao's garb participating in massive demonstrations during the Cultural Revolution; women officials – again, in Mao's dress – wearing thick-framed glasses warmly applauding the 'Great Helmsman', smiling tensely alongside their male colleagues.[22]

Women's rights in China are both a legacy of the past and a blessing of the future. During the Old Regime, women were always dependent on a dominant male – their father, brother or husband. As a widow, a woman could not leave her husband's household to live alone without any means of supporting herself and to enjoy a free life at last (unless she was the mother and the new head of the family). Women did not have anything of their own. Baby girl infanticide and abortion were common practice. Some very young girls were married to boys their age and moved to the bridal house to be used as a servant, if not a concubine of the father or the elder brother. They typically did not know their husband before they got married.

In this regard, the Communist regime did many favours for women. Compulsory education up to the age of 16 was legalized for both girls and boys. The 1950 law on marriage (revised in 1980) cancelled the notion of the 'head of the family'. A woman can transfer her name to her son and keep her income. To prevent premature weddings, the minimum age of marriage is 20 for girls and 22 for boys. It is quite often due to the lack of housing or jobs that a married women stays at her parents' house instead of moving in with her parents-in-laws, so as to avoid the tense coexistence with the mother-in-law. Today, matchmakers still act as brokers.[23] Usually, a girl moves to the next city to support her parents and to earn some money of her own before she gets married.

Though women are relatively scarce in power circles and there are no women among the seven members of the State Council (however, the Minister of Health is female), women are more frequently seen in private businesses. Half of managers are women (7 per cent in Japan, 20 per cent in the USA). Until recently, the richest person in China was a woman. In spite of several setbacks, Zhang Ying, owner of Nine Dragons Paper Holding, in partnership with the American Chung Nam, has a wealth profile of up to US$3 billion. She built up her wealth on the collection of used papers and cardboard before diversifying into real estate and banking. The smoking and sputtering tricycle carrying a load of old used cardboard boxes is a very familiar scene in China's countryside. Her success is remarkable, in the sense that this business is not a strategic business from the government's point of view. She built up her empire not through government connections but, rather, through a network of family and friends. In addition, she built her wealth on an environmental protection business. In contrast, Mrs Zhang Xin, CEO of a property development group (Soho China) listed on the Stock Exchange (US$3 billion), graduated from Cambridge and trained at Goldman Sachs; Mrs Wang Fengying, CEO of Great Walls, a car manufacturer which makes one million vehicles a year (SUVs) of which 30 per cent are sold overseas. In accordance with social 'rules', a man is supposed to marry a woman less 'brilliant' or 'successful' than he, a social group of single women (*shengnu* or spinsters, literally 'too many women') has emerged who have succeeded in business and who are not prepared to sacrifice their career for the sake of a husband.

On the other hand, a number of shops and restaurants – which fill a critical role in socialization – are owned by energetic and smiling young women. But there are also millions of young or very unqualified young women working in huge factories for 12 hours per day for US$1 per hour, living in dormitories, sharing a kitchen and a bathroom per floor with other girls. They are working hard to assist their family pending their return to get married to an unknown man chosen by their parents. Though they paid an unbearable price through suicide and labour accidents, women did not attend the 2012 strikes. They did not show up on the TV screen. A feminist movement conflicts with both social behaviour and the Party doctrine.

Graduates

Each year, 8 million young graduates leave China's universities. Increasing from 1.8 million in 1998 to 6.8 million in 2010, their number is growing fast. One third of them (27 per cent in 2010) will not find employment. Graduates from the most reputed universities, such as Fujian (Shanghai) or Beida (Beijing), will find a job easily in state-owned companies or government offices. However, others will be forced either to accept a much lower-level job at a much lower wage, or to move to the interior provinces. Most of them are forced into 'hotels of job seekers' in the suburbs (*yizu*: ants' nests). Fearing troubles similar to the 1989 Tien An Men events, the government encourages unemployed graduates to accept a position as a school teacher in the countryside, pending their finding a permanent job. Young graduates have been hit the hardest by the global financial crisis and the subsequent shrinking of business.

On the other hand, most Chinese and, above all, foreign companies complained about the high turnover of young managers, up to 30 per cent per annum in some industries. Sometimes, a whole team may move to a competitor (as is often the case in banks). To cope with this situation, some foreign companies formed their own training institution (Carrefour China Institute), others entered into an agreement with a business school or university (CEIBS: China Europe International Business School of Shanghai) to offer the opportunity of an MBA degree to their employees, and some offer a career plan in the same group (Areva).

Most Chinese students feel more concerned about their finding a job rather than the emergence of democracy. This is not to say that they are less concerned about such issues. Rather, they are more pragmatic (some say more realistic). They have never known the reality of the 1989 Tien An Men incidents, which are not mentioned in history textbooks used in schools. As far as they are concerned, they know that the system will not be changed from the outside.

Ethnic minorities

All Chinese citizens are recorded according to their ethnic group. In the 1982 Constitution Preamble, the People's Republic of China (PRC) is defined as 'a unitarily multinational State' (*yige tonghide duominzu guojia*). A nation (*minzu*) is 'an historic and stable community of peoples having a common language, a common territory, a common economic life and a common psychological entity which is expressed in a common culture'. Based on the 2010 census, the Han community accounts for 92 per cent of the total population, the rest (100 million) are divided between 55 officially recognized 'minority ethnic groups' (*shaoshu minzu*). Of the Han community, the largest ethnic group is the Zhuang (16 million). Based on these figures, the minority issue sounds marginal; however, all or most of the minority groups are located in sensitive and strategic areas, giving them a disproportionate weight.

In Tibet, Xinxiang, Yunnan and Huizhou (all bordering provinces), ethnic minorities occupy more than 60 per cent of the total territory. Religious movements (Buddhist in Tibet and Sichuan, Muslim in Xinjiang, Shamanic in Mongolia) are entangled with political issues. Tibet borders India, Xinjiang the central Asian countries, Mongolia is stretched over the Russian border. Most of these provinces are raw material producers. Xinxiang and Mongolia have wealthy mining and hydrocarbon resources. The Himalayas are the water towers of all regional hydrologic systems. All the Chinese rivers flow from the Himalayan Mountains. Anyone who controls this area controls the water supply for the whole region. There are violent upsurges between Tibetan and Han (and Hui) settlers who have monopolized government offices and business opportunities. In 2013, a large number of people from Hong Kong joined a demonstration complaining against a newly established 'course of civic education' at school. Cantonese demonstrations opposed the lack of local dialect in government offices and TV programmes (in Mandarin). In Tibet, Mandarin is a compulsory subject in a college degree. Tibetan is unused in government offices and on the many construction and public work developments granted to Chinese construction companies (Beijing–Lhasa railway track). For this reason, Tibetans cannot find a job in a government office or a Chinese company.

There have been recurrent troubles in the 'Autonomous Region of Tibet' (1959, 1989 and 2008) since the Chinese occupation of Tibet in 1950 (followed by the transfer of the Kham and Arndo provinces to neighbouring Sichuan and Yunnan) and the flight of His Holiness the Dalai Lama in 1959. As a gesture of goodwill, HH the Dalai Lama split up the religious and political wings of the Tibetan hierarchy in the hope of resuming talks with the Chinese government. HH the Dalai Lama put forward the idea of 'autonomy' within a united China rather than 'independence' as desired by the most extreme wings of the movement. China's unity is non-negotiable for her leaders. Anyone who dares to give the impression that he is leaning towards this idea will be swept away by his peers and his countrymen.

8
A Foreign Policy which Serves Growth (and Vice Versa)

A Great Country is a downstream place, where everything comes together, the world female.
(Lao seu, *Tao tö king*)

From 1949 onwards, China's foreign policy went through three stages: during Mao's reign, China fought with all her neighbouring countries; during Deng Xiaoping's leadership, China focused on a policy of domestic growth and withdrew from the international stage; in the last period, starting with the twenty-first century, China's foreign policy was more active – some would say more aggressive, although avoiding any direct clashes. China has territorial conflicts with each of her neighbouring countries. In addition to the traditional fighting on the northern and western mainland in Central Asia (India, Russia), China has also opened new border conflicts in the Sea of China and the Pacific gulf (Japan, Vietnam, Indonesia, Philippines), the ultimate aim of which is no longer to defend (often contested) borders but, rather, to recover losses dealt by unequal treaties of the twenty-first century. It is no longer a matter of border conflict but of regional leadership against rival powers (the USA, Japan and India). To a large extent, China's foreign policy is commanded by geopolitics: border defence and regional leadership. Now that China's economy is integrated into the world economy, the defence of borders is extended to the whole world. Moreover, regional leadership is not only contested in each particular region, but also across the world. China is a regional leader which is aiming to become a world leader.

To 'pro-marketers', China's economic growth should lead to a more democratic regime domestically and to more peaceful foreign relations. To 'pro-realists', China remains a provocative foreign power who exercises peaceful policies as long as these fit in with the strategic objectives of economic growth and regional leadership. However, the implementation of a foreign policy conjured up two very different pictures on the western and eastern sides. In Central Asia, the 'Shanghai Club' was formed under a Russian initiative – a joint organization to fight (Islamic) 'terrorism', soon shifting into an organization of peaceful economic cooperation. Three thousand miles of gas pipes carry hydrocarbon resources from Kazakhstan to Beijing. On the opposite side, control over a string of small and deserted islands became a military situation which pushed neighbouring countries into the arms of the USA.

Mao dreamt of building up a IVth International to challenge Soviet influence (IIIrd International or Komintern), but it never extended beyond certain marginal countries (Albania, Nepal) and marginal (Maoist) groups in Western countries. In 1978, Deng Xiaoping emphasized domestic policies of reform and opening-up, quoting an old Chinese saying: 'hide what is shining and maintain the darkness' (*tao guang yan hui*). Jiang Zemin added up the 'Five Principles' of peaceful coexistence and the 'theory of the three representatives' (workers, peasants and business men). Then, Hu Jintao sang the praises of a 'Harmonious Society' even though it is unclear what this old Confucian concept means in today's China. Finally, Xi Jinping put forward the idea of the 'Chinese dream' (*zhong guo meng*).

On the eve of the twenty-first century, Chinese foreign policy became more active, if not to say aggressive. The factors at play from this new standpoint are economic growth involving access to raw materials, free trade, an internationalization of Chinese companies and nationalist rhetoric (nationalistic gestures and slogans as a substitute for communist ideology). China's awakening took place at the very moment the international stage began to shift, when the focus of the USA turned from the Atlantic to the Pacific. The dual-polar international world (USA–USSR) collapsed. There was a brief shift to a uni-polar world (the USA), which then became an even shorter tri-polar game (the USA, the European Union and China) before shifting again to a new dual-polar stage (USA–China).

The tributary system

Under the Old Regime, China was the 'Middle Empire' (*zhong guo*: literally 'central territory'). China's Emperor ruled over 'everything under Heaven'. His power stretched across all that stood 'between the Four Seas'. Foreign relations with neighbouring countries were carried out according to the tributary system. Foreign countries pledged allegiance to the Emperor through the system of '*dons et contre-dons*' (Marcel Mauss). In the early fifteenth century, Zheng He's sea expeditions, which gathered together thousands of highly sophisticated sailing ships (ships with ten masts that were three or more times larger than the Portuguese caravels), were neither aimed at subduing foreign peoples or territories, nor establishing new trade posts. Instead, the aim was to renew the allegiance of foreign countries. It was a mere display of force. As time passed, this tributary system turned to trade. Every year, foreign embassies used to follow the Emperor, his family and the court (30,000 people) to the summer resort of Shengde (on the Mongolian border) beyond the Great Wall. This was done to pay tribute to the Emperor but the present and counter-present system became a trading system. Among the ambassador's retinue were merchants authorized to trade, on this occasion, within the limited quotas set up by the Emperor himself. In those days, 'soft power' was called 'silk diplomacy', as pieces of precious silk were used as rewards and currency.

Within the ideological and geographical framework of a Westernized nation-state, which was characterized by a common people using a common language (and a common faith), defence of borders was essential. In an empire inhabited by a variety of different peoples, speaking a variety of dialects, border challenges are less important than regional leadership as expressed by tributary system. The arrival of Western merchant ships on the south-eastern coasts was an issue of no significance – after all, they were merchants, a necessary evil – delegated to local officials. Challenging problems usually came from the mainland, from the north and the east. When, in 1979, Deng decided to 'teach Vietnam a lesson', a neighbouring country which had been a Chinese province for over 10 centuries and which was showing too much independence, he applied a type of tributary system. When African countries complain about China's plundering of natural resources by corrupt officials, they denounce the policy of 'infrastructures against raw materials' as a new form of colonialism, a modern translation of the former tributary system.

The two major public works of ancient China, the Great Wall and the Great Canal, are both defence lines, a sort of Maginot Line, designed to protect China against Barbarians coming by land or by sea. Self-sufficient and highly civilized, China enjoyed a trade surplus as a highly developed nation: China exported luxury goods (spices, textiles, silk dresses, steel, writing paper, lacquer ware and porcelain) and imported raw materials (slaves, horses, skins, copper and wax). The tributary system worked until the Western countries managed to catch up with Chinese technologies through spying[1], theft[2] or domestic development through home-grown technology. Later on, European countries manufactured products resembling Chinese goods ('Chinas' of the Western Indian Companies) to be resold to China. In the wake of the Industrial Revolution in Great Britain, the flow of exchange shifted back: Mancunian textile factories bought their raw cotton from China only to resell finished products back to the Chinese, thus causing the ruin of the local craft and nascent Chinese industry.

European tradesmen who needed Chinese grown products such as tea and cotton broke into the Chinese market with gunships to sell manufactured goods. By selling opium along the Yangtze basin, Britain worked out a new 'triangular' trade: opium shipped from Bengal to China, tea and cotton shipped from China to England, and textiles shipped from England back to India and China. Following the War of Secession (1861–5), European countries had to find an alternative supplier of cotton (Egypt, India and China). China would go on to take advantage of World War I to develop domestic industries, Shanghai's shipyards becoming the largest in the world.

Basic principles of Chinese foreign policy

In a typical 'Western' government of nation states, foreign affairs are closely related to the country's sovereignty and, consequently, belong to the upper and most prestigious levels of government. In China, Foreign Affairs is a relatively marginal department. A Ministry of Foreign Affairs did not appear until the late nineteenth century in the last years of the Old Regime. Today, the holder of this critical position, Wang Yi, appointed in 2013 in the wake of the renewal of the ruling team, does not hold a high position in hierarchical ranking: he is not a member of the Politburo or the State Council. His career has been occupied by affairs of the Asian department (including being China's Ambassador to Japan), which gives an idea of the government's priorities. Foreign policy is run by the Party's 'Central Group of Management of Foreign Affairs', which reports directly to Xi Jinping and puts together all the top ministers and agencies involved in foreign affairs.

Policy of non-interference

After an alignment policy on the Soviet Union (1949–60), then fighting on two fronts (anti-imperialism and anti-revisionism), then a *de facto* alliance with the USA against a common enemy in a triangular diplomatic system (1972–82), China shifted to a more independent foreign policy. Following the collapse of the Soviet Union and the Eastern European countries, the 'triangular' policy was no longer necessary: neither China nor the USA needed a balance of power against the Soviet Union. In a new multi-polar world system, China enforced a policy of non-interference and non-alignment which befitted a more independent stance. Partnership (*huoban*); but no more formal and compelling alliances as defined by Deng Xiaoping on the occasion of the partnership with the new Russia (the 'Five Principles of Peaceful Coexistence').

From 1949 to 1979, China was at war with all her neighbouring countries: Korea (1950–2),[3] Taiwan (1958: Quemoy and Amoy bombing once the US Fleet interfered to make landing in Taiwan impossible), India (1962 in Arunanchal Pradesh), repeated fighting on the Russian border (1969 on the Oussouri River), Vietnam (1979 in Yunnan followed by resuming fighting in 1986–7), followed a long period of peaceful relations. Once he had reached a position of power (1978), Deng re-established peaceful relationship with the neighbouring countries and travelled to former hostile countries (Russia, USA, Europe, Japan) as a gesture of new peaceful relationships, advocating a foreign policy of 'low profile' to focus on the policy of reform and opening up at home.

On the eve of the twenty-first century, military and economic tensions resumed but in a new form: confronting the US Fleet in the Sea of China (2001 and 2009), conflict with Japan over the Senkaku islands, Vietnam, the Philippines (Nanshan islands) and in Indonesia (Paracel and Spratly islands). Even Turkey was forced to recall its ambassador to China in 2011 in the wake of the repression of the Uyghurs (a Turkic muslim ethnic group). China's inability to the peaceful settlement of regional territorial conflicts in her own backyard is a sign of international weakness and limited regional leadership.

Furthermore, a policy of non-interference allows China to play a pragmatic game of 'infrastructure against a long-term supply of raw materials'. This is very attractive to emerging and developing countries (Africa, South America) in search of a free source of funds upset by political and neo-liberal conditions placed on credit facilities by Western countries and institutions (the 'Washington concensus' of the World Bank and the IMF). This is perceived by them to be an unacceptable breach of national sovereignty. China implements a 'one size fits all' rule when exploiting a full range of global bargaining assets to reach her ultimate goals. To start with, the US$4,000 billion foreign exchange reserves provide substantial and cheap credit facilities to oil diplomatic wheels. As a result, China sometimes finds herself dealing and trading with rogue regimes (Syria, Sudan, North Korea, Cuba, Zimbabwe), usually managing to avoid involvement in regional conflicts. For example, China is now Brazil's largest trading partner following an 'infrastructure against raw material' (oil) deal smoothed over the extension of a US$10 billion 10-year loan to Petrobras. In Europe, China subscribed to substantial amounts of Treasury bonds from troubled countries and made a commitment to contribute to the funding of the new European Stability Mechanism with the expectation of being recognized in the statute of 'market economy' (so far in vain). In Greece, COSCO, the largest shipping company, runs one of the two Pireus terminals (pending the construction of a second) as a bridge-head to the single European market.

The defence policy

With a 2,300,000-strong army and 200,000 reserves, China has the world's largest army (up from 5,500,000 in 1950). Deng Xiaoping, who had a military experience,[4] gave up the traditional revolutionary strategy of 'the people in arms' as theorized by Mao to put emphasis on professionalism. The military budget (as far as we know) is the second largest in the world – far behind the USA[5] (China's military budget is one fifth that of the USA) but twice as much as Russia, the third largest (see Table 8.1).

From the beginning of the twenty-first century), China has resumed the construction of her navy (for the first time since the fifteenth century).[6] This should allow her to 'project' forces up to the Mediterranean Sea (58 submarines, of which eight have a nuclear capacity, and one aircraft carrier[7]). China is already participating in joint naval manoeuvres against 'piracy' in Somalia. In addition, China is a leading country in the cybernetic war[8] (system penetration, industrial spying and data stealing). The aim of this new force is to protect international communication links (Aden, Malaka) and supply sea routes for the raw materials of which she is

Table 8.1 Defence budgets 2011 (US$ billion)

		% PIB	**% total**
Total	1,630.0		
USA	711.0	4.7	41.0
China	143.0	2.0	8.2
Russia	71.9	3.9	4.1
UK	62.7	2.6	3.6
France	62.5	2.3	3.6

most in need. Though an oil producer, China imports two thirds of its oil consumption from overseas.

The CCP maintains close control over the Army. The National Liberation Army (NLA) is a Party department. The Party Military Commission is chaired by the General Secretary himself, while the Vice-Chairman is usually the next prospective General Secretary.

Chinese diplomatic goals

Until now, Chinese foreign policy has been primarily determined by the policy of reform and opening-up. Drawn by foreign investments and exports, the Chinese economy needed market openings, free trade, a managed currency and a peaceful environment. The current shift in economic policy to domestic demand, liberalization of financial markets, upgrading of the range of Chinese products and Chinese overseas investments has drastically changed the type of relationship China has with trade and investment partners.

WTO membership

Following five years of painful bargaining with the USA, China eventually signed a treaty granting it membership to the World Trade Organization (WTO) in December 2001. As China was still 'the world's workshop', she was still highly dependent on export capacity and foreign investment to provide her capital, technology and know-how. As China was exporting labour-intensive products and importing hi-tech products, the 'terms of exchange' were steadily deteriorating. To turn the flow of trade on its head, China needed access to developed markets and advanced technology. As a new member of the WTO, China was prohibited from imposing any discriminatory measures on other members, or imposing price controls with the aim of supporting Chinese products and suppliers; China was also required to redraft Chinese regulations to put China in compliance with WTO rules, and prohibited from granting subsidies to exported agricultural products. China was given three years to remove all obstacles to exporting companies. A period of five years' grace was granted to extend the WTO regulations to service industries – in particular, to financial services.

China took advantage of joining the WTO. From 2002, the export growth rate was always higher than the GDP growth rate. Within the next ten years, Chinese exports increased 6.62 times, imports 6.74 times and the trade surplus 5.42 times (11.4 in 2008, before the global

Table 8.2 Foreign trade/GDP (US$ billion)

	2000	2001	2002	2003	2004	2005	2006	2007	2008	2009	2010	2011
Export	249	266	325	438	593	762	969	1,220	1,430	1,202	1,578	1,898
Import	225	243	295	413	561	660	791	956	1,132	1,006	1,396	1,743
Surplus	24	22	30	25	32	102	177	264	298	196	181	155
Export (%)		6.8	22.1	34.7	35.4	21.7	27.1	25.9	17.2	–15.9	31.2	20.3
Import (%)		8.0	21.0	40.0	35.8	17.6	19.8	20.8	18.4	–11.1	38.7	24.8
PIB (%)		8.3	9.1	10	10.1	11.3	12.7	12.7	14.2	9.6	9.2	9.2

Source: National Bureau of Statistics.

crisis). This was while GDP increased (only) 3.76 times. An increase in exports provided a significant contribution to the GDP growth rate (see Table 8.2).

Squeezed by WTO regulations, China increased her non-tariff barriers. In a country where the government is in a position to interfere at every stage of the manufacturing process, Chinese companies can easily bypass these regulations: direct and indirect subsidies, fiscal exemptions, soft loans and free land all put at the disposal of exporting companies by local authorities and differential power fares, and so on. With fraud[9] commonplace, although not a great deal more so than in other countries.[10] Chinese countervailing duties (CVD) aimed at aligning foreign competition doubled from 2004–7 to 2008–11. In 2012, the USA formed the Emergency Trade Enforcement Centre to support US companies in this field. In the event of disagreement over a product, China will systematically raise issues over disputes on another product (e.g. European wines against Chinese solar panels, American tyres against Chinese auto spare parts).

Foreign direct investors have a Chinese partner owning a majority stake forced on them. Foreign companies are not eligible to partake in government auctions (for public works and infrastructures). China is now an expert in the standards war. China has upgraded Chinese standards to keep foreign companies away.[11] Misappropriation of foreign patents is common practice. Foreign companies are sued for violation of labour regulations (Foxcon), environmental crime (rare earths) and national security (Google). In the financial industry, foreign banks are not permitted to open more than one branch in any city. Licences to trade in domestic securities are capped by the banks and industry, both for each bank and for the banking industry as a whole. A foreign bank may be stripped of its quota, if a Chinese bank has exhausted its quota. Counterfeiting is the largest Chinese industry. In 2011, of the number of fake goods seized by European customs 80.6 per cent (in volume) and 83.6 per cent (in value) were Chinese. The most faked goods are pharmaceutical products (23.9 per cent), packing (21.2 per cent) and cigarettes (17.6 per cent), dresses and mobile phones being marginal (3.5 per cent and 2.8 per cent). As the world's largest consumer of raw material, China is in a position to manipulate commodity markets.

According to an enquiry by the European Chamber of Commerce in China (2010), foreign companies are subject to discriminatory measures: court decisions on government instructions, blatant counterfeiting, backdated tax regulation, unfair government auctions[12] and bureaucratic harassment, and so on. The plight of companies such as Google,

Apple, Carrefour, Danone, Schneider, Volkswagen, Glaxo Smith, Honda in China is well-known. Usually, formal government action is preceded by a strong media campaign from government-owned media.

Supply of raw materials

Today, China is the world's largest energy consumer. Two thirds of the demands for energy resources are supplied by Chinese coal – China is the world's largest producer of coal. Energy consumption increased sixfold from 1980 to 2012. In the meantime, energy consumption in the USA stabilized despite continuous growth due to significant increases in productivity. China consumes three times more energy than the USA to manufacture the same product. In addition to coal consumption, petroleum accounts for 10 per cent of energy consumption, the rest made up by hydropower and renewable energy. A net importer from 1992, China is now the world's largest oil importer, far more than the USA. This gap is expected to continue to widen, as ethanol and shale gas should make USA self-sufficient within a few years. China's imports increased from 13 per cent of total imports in 1990 to 30 per cent at the time of writing. This is while the USA effectively did the reverse: decreasing from 30 per cent in 1990 down to 13 per cent in 2013. China's supply sources are primarily located in the Middle East (Saudi Arabia), Africa (Nigeria) and South America (Venezuela). Imports are made mostly in the form of crude oil. A long-term policy of increasing her stock levels and refining capacity has made China less vulnerable to price fluctuations.

China is implementing a wide range of instruments to guarantee access to raw materials. In developing countries, China has put forward 'infrastructure against raw material' long-term contracts. In developed countries, China is taking equity shares in companies which have mining permits and advanced technology. In both cases, Chinese companies are strongly supported by financing instruments, such as sovereign wealth funds (China Investment Corporation, State Administration of Foreign Exchange, National Social Security Fund), government subsidies, and interest free or soft loans (China Development Bank, Export Import Bank). But China is facing increasing obstacles: protectionist reprisals, protectionist measures, tightened control of foreign investments and the threat of being prohibited from foreign participation. Backed by financial and political support from the government, Chinalco made a bid on the Anglo-Australian Rio Tinto, the largest mining company and iron producer in the world. The Australian government used the well-known 'poisonous pill' which, in the event of a threat to take over the operation, funds will be raised through a massive capital increase subscribed to by other investors (in this particular case, the US competitor BHP Billiton). A World Bank enquiry came to the conclusion that China's investment in Africa contributed up to 50 per cent to the continent's growth. But some local countries are complaining that Chinese investments do not help local employment and that Chinese construction companies do not use local manpower. More generally, some complained that the Chinese investment policy – buying raw material and selling manufactured goods – is colonialist by nature. Pillaging natural resources through corruption sustains existing non-democratic regimes and selling Chinese-made goods kills nascent local industries at their point of take-off.

As the quasi-monopolistic producer (with a 95 per cent market share) in 'rare earths' (indispensable components of some strategic products such as specializd steel, China tried to 'corner' the market by imposing sales quotas under the pretext of environmental spoils. In the form of a reprisal, other potential producers (Vietnam and the USA) reopened closed pits which were no longer profitable at the then current market prices. Ill-advised moves by China drew the attention of foreign governments to these highly vulnerable and sensitive raw materials, and pulled a number of countries back into the market again at the expense of the Chinese monopoly.

In the field of agricultural products, China feeds up to 20 per cent of the world's population while it owns only 10 per cent of the world's arable lands. Thus, China bought 2.1 million Ha of cultivable land in neighbouring countries (Laos, Cambodia), which occasionally caused uprisings among deprived farmers (Burma). According to Chinese authorities, foreign lands bought by China are uncultivated[13] But this does not take purchases by Chinese individuals into account which, again, does not improve China's image with her neighbours.

Internationalization of Chinese companies

The aims of the internationalization process of Chinese companies are severalfold: access to raw materials; control of the production line up- and downstream; and access to advanced technologies, developed markets and components manufacturers. However, the main purpose is to make Chinese companies international (i.e. to transfer modern management methods, funding techniques and accounting practices to China).

Amongst the 100 leading companies in emerging countries, 30 are Chinese (Boston Consulting Group, 2013). From a geographical point of view, Europe is heading the league of target countries with 48 per cent of all Chinese overseas acquisitions (of which 95 per cent are of non-raw material investment). The bulk of overseas Chinese investments are in raw materials. As with foreign companies investing in China, Chinese companies investing overseas were soon disappointed by majority shareholding and turned instead to middle-sized component companies and minority participations. In Europe, the flow of Chinese investment was further induced by the global financial crisis, which pulled down stock prices to very attractive levels (sometimes below the net asset value). Chinese overseas investment accounted for relatively little in percentage terms compared with other countries. High visibility of Chinese overseas investments caused protectionist reprisals from some countries. Following the failed takeover bid attempt by Unocal of CNOOC (2005), the US government formed the Committee on Foreign Investment in the United States (CFIUS). The same year, Lenovo acquired the PC Department of IBM, which made them the world's second largest PC manufacturer, head-to-head with its main competitor the Taiwanese firm Acer.

But market penetration works two ways: China is manufacturing 'Chinese' goods to be sold on Western markets. China's government dispatched a circular to Western car companies in China to design 'Chinese' products according to Chinese tastes to be sold on Western markets. So far this policy of exporting Chinese-made cars has proved unsuccessful as the quality is not yet up to international standards. On the renewal of the joint Airbus venture in Tianjin in 2013, Chinese partners (AVIC) sought to obtain the authorization to sell the A320 built in Tianjin to foreign countries, thus competing with the major shareholder – Airbus itself. The request was turned down – until next time. In contrast, for the first time, a Chinese affiliate of Hermès, Shang Xia, opened a shop in the heart of the Saint-Germain-des-Prés area in Paris, to sell luxury goods initially designed for the Chinese markets.

Internationalization of the Yuan

According to a Senate report, the Chinese policy of weakening the Yuan would have cost a million job losses in the USA from 2005. By holding the official foreign exchange rate below the market rate, China took advantage of currency management (as opposed to the free market) to keep prices of Chinese products in the international market below the market price. But the issue is not that simple and a weak currency policy entails as many minus points as plus points.

1. First, by definition, nobody knows what the 'market price' is and the 'artificial' currency underrating since the central bank intervenes every day to keep the rate within a +/– 2 per cent margin of the 'official' rate. The end-of-day rate used by the banks is fixed by the central bank at the end of the trading day. Underrating ranges from 0 to 30 per cent according to economists and analysts. In addition, the price differential raises the purchasing power parity (PPP) rate compared with the market price. Moreover, the market rate theoretically reflects the bid/offer rate based on the flow of currencies, (provided, of course, that there is no government or central bank market intervention). Some price components distort the currency rate even if the market price does reflect the bid/offer balance. For instance, wage increases are a way to increase the labour costs of exporting companies and, thus, increase the price of Chinese-made products on the international market. As has been noted, the average levels of the Chinese wages have increased substantially over the last couple of years since 2012.
2. Moreover, the rapidly increasing foreign exchange reserves (US$4,000 billion), fed by a regular flow of trade surplus and foreign investments, entail some major drawbacks. As foreign currencies are exchanged against the Yuan for domestic use, the growing foreign exchange reserve becomes highly inflationary by nature on the domestic market. In order to neutralize the inflationary effect of the increasing foreign exchange reserves, China's central bank must take steps (including the mopping up or withdrawing of excess Yuan from the market) which conflict with the domestic monetary policy of low interest rates and high liquidity, designed to support a strong growth rate and a low unemployment rate. It is a vicious circle: the more the central bank buys dollars, the more it feeds the inflationary pressures. If the central bank stops buying dollars, the dollar rate will collapse on the market and the purchasing power of the extensive dollar denominated Chinese foreign reserves which remain will collapse as well. China is forced to reinvest the dollars bought in dollar denominated assets (such as government Treasury bonds), as there is no other feasible alternative (other than euro bonds) in term of risk/return ratio and, above all, liquidity. For instance, this includes the ability to seek out a counterpart (buyer or seller) in the event of need without triggering adverse rate fluctuations.
3. There is no formal evidence that a weakened Yuan would automatically lower exports and increase imports, thus contributing to a more balanced flow of trade. Currency devaluation may (under some

circumstances) boost the trade surplus (or lower the trade deficit). The devaluation process provides a short term 'breathing space' to the country, which is allowed a settling-in period to impose the reforms aimed at increasing their competitiveness (productivity) so as to rectify the trade balance. If the structural reforms are not implemented in time, devaluation is worthless – even counterproductive. Sooner or later, devaluation-driven inflation will more than compensate for the short-term benefit of an artificially low foreign exchange rate.

In the short term, the success of currency devaluation is subject to some well-known general conditions:

1. The devaluating country should be the only one to proceed (otherwise the price effect will be nullified).
2. The devaluation should take place in a rising or recovering trend of growth (exports will not increase if there is no further demand on the international market).
3. The immediate effect of currency devaluation is the increase of import prices and decrease of export prices on the international market if – and only if – the companies are ready and properly equipped to take advantage of this brief price differential opportunity.

If these conditions are not fulfilled, the devaluation will be pointless; the increase in import prices (oil, raw material and components) will trigger nothing but renewed overall inflation.

In the long term, it is far from obvious that a weakened currency is the best way to rebalance the flow of trade. The Yuan foreign exchange rate has increased by 30 per cent against the dollar over the last ten years (2005–14) while the US trade deficit has doubled. In the postwar period, the German Mark and the Japanese Yuan strengthened under the pressure of their trade partner and allies: USA/Japan, EU countries/Germany (all within the European Monetary System exchange rate mechanism). Nonetheless, the trade surplus kept growing after a short adjustment period. The more the exchange rate increased, so too did the surplus. This is due to trade structures. In economic terms, the effect of a rate change depends on the respective elasticity of imports against and exports. If the loss in volume is more than compensated for by the gain in value, the trade surplus increases. The price differential is due to the productivity differential. If the price increase is more than compensated for by the productivity differential, the trade surplus (in value) increases. In the German and Japanese cases, both countries manufactured high-quality and highly praised products such as machine-tools. In the long term, the inflated price of their products is a strong incentive for German and Japanese exporters to compensate for higher export prices through increasing productivity. This, however, is a cumulative effect which makes things 'worse' as times passes. What used to be a handicap has now turned out to be an advantage.

China is in a difficult transition period: on one hand, she must protect her nascent industries until they are strong enough to face evenly distributed world competition; on the other hand, given that growth is nurtured by domestic investments and foreign trade, China must maintain a free trade system for Chinese exporting companies. All developed and developing countries (including the USA, the UK, Germany and Japan) proceeded along the same line: protectionism during the take-off period, free trade once the national industries are strong enough to confront the international market, and take advantage of lower labour costs and increasing productivity. Some large federal countries combine the best of both, managing to use free trade on the domestic market (the USA, Germany) while maintaining trade barriers and tariffs with foreign countries. Thus, China is demanding equal treatment on the international market while implementing all sorts of obstacles to the domestic market. These include not only weakening currency, but also discriminatory measures; no access to government auctions and restrictive access to credit; labour and environmental regulations; and so on. Western countries focus on the wrong target: Chinese manufacturers are not cheaper because they obtain benefits from a weak currency on the foreign market, but because they are more competitive in terms of cost, and – as labour and other costs increase – in terms of overall productivity. Western countries should demand reciprocity in a free trade environment, rather than concentrate on a target which is beyond their reach. Free and even access to credit or government work auctions is more important than a strong currency. China is more vulnerable to free-trade restrictions than other countries: the foreign trade percentage of GDP amounts to 30 per cent in China against 17 per cent in Europe and 4 per cent in the USA.

A weak currency also hinders China's efforts to impose regional leadership. China's trade balance has a huge surplus against the USA and the EU but a significant deficit against all surrounding countries, including Japan and Australia. Such heavyweight emerging countries as South Korea, South Africa and Brazil have been very critical of China's foreign exchange policy. Some countries, such as Japan and South

Korea, managed to manipulate their currency (buying dollars against their own currency, further increasing their dollar denominated foreign exchange reserves) to lower the exchange rate with the expectation of counter-balancing China's 'policy of weak Yuan'. This, however, was never successful for very long, since it is impossible to beat the deep-rooted market trend in the long run.

If and when China resumes currency revaluation against foreign currencies, it should be done on domestic grounds (anti-inflation policy, productivity rise), rather than under the pressure of disgruntled Western countries. If, for example, the Yuan strengthens against the US dollar but the euro becomes stronger against US dollar, *in fine* the Yuan is actually weakened against euro. In other words, the USA and China may come to an agreement at Europe's expense. When the USA coughs, Europe gets pneumonia.

Since 2005, China has managed a slow but steady Yuan revaluation against the dollar. This stopped for a year (June 2009–July 2010) in the aftermath of the global financial crisis, as Chinese exporting companies were severely hit until the recovery plan reached its goals and growth resumed. In 2005, US$1 was worth 8.3 Rmb. Seven years later (2012), US$1 was only worth 6.3 Yuan (a 25 per cent fall) (see Table 8.3).

In order to cope with this situation, China undertook a set of measures to neutralize the domestic inflationary effects of the growing foreign exchange reserves and to further internationalize the Rmb market through the development of an off-shore Yuan market.

One People's Bank of China (PBOC) department, the State Agency of Foreign Exchange (SAFE), buys dollars against Yuan, while another PBOC department (money market management) buys Rmb against government bonds to withdraw Yuan which have been dispatched on the market. On the one hand, the PBOC is selling 3–6 months of 'financial bills' (the maturity of these very short-term treasury bonds is 3 or 6 months) on the market to mop up the excess Yuan inflating the

Table 8.3 Exchange rate: US$ v. Rmb (number of Rmb per US$)

1985	2.93	1992	5.51	1999	8.27	2005	8.19
1986	3.45	1993	5.76	2000	8.27	2006	7.97
1987	3.72	1994	8.61	2001	8.27	2007	7.60
1988	3.72	1995	8.35	2002	8.27	2008	6.94
1989	3.76	1996	8.31	2003	8.27	2009	6.83
1990	4.78	1997	8.29	2004	8.27	2010	6.76
1991	5.32	1998	8.27			2011	6.45

money market. Theoretically, at a national level, this is a mere book-keeping transaction (write on/write off). But, in effect, financial bonds – a very liquid market, since it is fed by the central bank – became the benchmark (reference rate) of the interbank money market.

On the other hand, in order to protect the purchasing power of the dollar denominated foreign exchange reserves, SAFE has two alternatives: either to switch to another currency (e.g. to sell dollars against the euro); or to buy dollar denominated real assets (such as US companies) instead of financial assets (such as Treasury bonds), with the expectation that stocks increase based on real value, rather than offset a decrease in currency. To this end, China is backing the internationalization of Chinese companies investing overseas. In addition, the government formed a several hundred billion sovereign wealth fund (CIC) to invest foreign exchange reserves in foreign companies and real assets (mining, manufacturing units, subcontractors and technology).

Of US$4,000 billion foreign exchange reserves in 2013, SAFE invested US$2,400 billion in dollar assets (of which over US$1,300 billion are US Treasury bonds), the rest being invested in US companies or assets. Investments in Treasury bonds were used as cash, easily negotiable at a stable price, at short notice – whenever needed. Moreover, SAFE diversified the foreign exchange portfolio by investing in third currencies (the euro, the pound sterling, etc). But this policy is not without its limits. If China is selling the US dollar against another currency, the dollar foreign exchange rate decreases rapidly, together with the remaining US denominated reserves as well, in term of purchasing power (e.g. in terms of other convertible currencies). In other words, China has more to lose than to gain in further pursuing this policy of foreign exchange reserve diversification. No other market (other than the euro market) is as liquid as the US dollar market. As far as we know, China's foreign exchange reserve is composed of 60–65 per cent dollar assets, 20–25 per cent euro, 5–7 per cent sterling and 3–5 per cent Japanese yen.

The internationalization of the Rmb market is another avenue towards further convertibility (free trading by residents and non-residents alike). There is no such currency as a fully convertible currency: all currencies are more or less convertible (tradable) but there are different levels of convertibility. For instance, the currency may be fully convertible by non-residents and non-convertible by residents. The currency may be used for financing trade or the purchase of foreign real assets, but not for financial transactions. In addition, a fully convertible currency does not only require appropriate government legislation, but also needs a broad, well-supplied and highly diversified market which is not developed by government decision. It must be followed up by market traders, companies in search of funds and institutional investors in search of rewarding investment opportunities meeting their risk–return targets. Thus, in line with the usual government techniques, China is experimenting with different methods, selecting the best and, step-by-step, broadening the scope and the range of successful avenues.

As mentioned, Rmb undervaluation is said to range between 5 per cent and 30 per cent. Further to the observations made regarding the actual foreign exchange rate, there are some clues which suggest that, over the last few years, the gap has shrunk: lower trade surplus (from 10 per cent of GDP in 2007 before the financial crisis down to 2.8 per cent in 2012), lower volume of foreign direct investments, increased Chinese overseas direct investments, increasing volume of Rmb billings and off-shore payments, authorization of some Chinese companies to hold their foreign exchange income abroad, and so on.

According to a tradition which dates as far back as Aristotle, the functions of a fully-fledged currency are threefold: means of payment, reserve currency and accounting instrument (and some economists add up to the list: lending instrument). It is worth noting that the latter two functions (reserve currency and accounting tool) are nothing but a by-product of the former (means of payment). The means of payment could be used as accounting measure and reserve holdings. It is meaningless to hold gold or other treasures if you cannot sell them in time of need. Step-by-step, the Yuan is expanding its share in the different areas.

After a period of experimentation, the government authorized some Chinese companies (mostly government owned SOEs) to denominate the foreign trade in Rmb (whether exports or imports), if the counterparties agreed to keep the proceeds in a foreign account opened in a foreign bank, usually in Hong Kong. This is the key issue: as Rmb is not a convertible currency freely tradable against another currency, holders of Yuan deposits cannot use them other than by buying Yuan denominated Chinese goods. A holder of Yuan deposits cannot use them if there is no market of Yuan assets available. As a result, the Chinese government allowed Chinese companies to raise funds on the offshore market (Hong Kong) and foreign investors to buy Yuan denominated assets. However, the Yuan billing has been growing so rapidly that it slightly overran the euro in 2013 (7 per cent of overall billing and transactions according to the international interbank settlement system, SWIFT).

Most transactions have been centralized in the Hong Kong hub, which is supplied with the necessary Rmb lines of credit. To widen the Rmb offshore market to the whole world, swap lines of credit between PBOC and foreign central banks (Bank of England and Central European Bank) (Rmb against the US$ or local currency). In the Western hemisphere, the money and exchange market is based in London, while the Rmb bonds and stock market may be developing in continental exchanges as well (Euronext in Paris and Deutshe Börse in Frankfurt).

Subsequently, Rmb deposits have been increasing swiftly on the offshore market, primarily with Hong Kong banks. Most Chinese IPOs or bond issues are placed both on the domestic (Shanghai) and offshore (Hong Kong) markets. As a result, foreign investors holding of idle Yuan deposits in Hong Kong banks can invest their Yuan liquidities in more rewarding investments than in bank saving accounts. After a slow start (due to the global financial crisis), the volume of the offshore Yuan bond market (Hong Kong *dim sum* bonds)[14] has been booming since 2012. Initial borrowers were Chinese state or state-related institutions, which gave initial impetus to the market while the investors were mainly restricted to the foreign central banks (the Bank of Japan subscribed to US$10 billion Chinese Treasury bonds) or AAA institutional borrowers (the IMF, the World Bank). The corporate bond market developed rapidly. An increasing number of Chinese SOEs are exploring new borrowing avenues to diversify their sources of funds and prevent the credit crunch (credit restrictions such as those put in place in 2013). Relatively few foreign companies have been tapping the domestic bond market (Caterpillar, American Express, Samsonite, IFC). Apart from being an alternative source of funds, the Yuan market is unattractive for Western borrowing companies. This is because the Yuan is more expensive and more risky, both in terms of interest rate and revaluation prospects. However, a Western company making a direct investment in China may be attracted by borrowing in Yuan to prevent any unpredictable foreign exchange risk on top of the industrial risk.

On the other hand, Chinese authorities granted so called 'QFII' (Qualified Foreign Institutional Investors) licences to foreign banks and some investment funds. However, the QFII licences are tightly controlled and granted to a limited number of first-class institutions, with the quotas allocated being split between individual quotas and full industry quotas (lower, of course, than the addition of the individual quotas). But the Chinese exchange market is so closely controlled and supervized by government agencies (CBRC and CSRC)[15] that some Western investors (such as Société Générale) gave up and decided not to participate in the issuing and placement of bonds and stocks of Chinese listed companies.

Hundreds of investment companies have been formed over the last few years by foreign investment banks in partnership with Chinese banks and insurance companies. Sometimes, these companies are formed by local authorities anxious to draw in foreign investors and bring financial support to the local Chinese companies in addition to the restricted bank credit (e.g. Sailing Capital International in Shanghai, Highland Capital Management in Yunnan, a joint venture of Beijing city and a foreign investment bank).

Sovereign wealth funds (SWFs)

Among the top 10 sovereign wealth funds (SWFs) identified, four are Chinese: the State Agency for Foreign Exchange (SAFE), the China Investment Corpn (CIC), the Hong Kong Monetary Authority (HKMA) and the National Social Security Fund (NSSF). They represent a strike force amounting to over US$1,000 billion (i.e. one fifth of the world's SWFs).

The most frequent criticism of SWFs relates to the lack of transparency. The volume of managed funds and the investment strategies are not disclosed, which disturbs the smooth working of financial markets and industrial policies. SWFs do not perform the same functions and do not have the same goals in each country. Even within the same country, there are sometimes divisions. Some SWFs are designed to put aside current stocks of raw material resources in order that future generations will have a supply once natural supplies are exhausted (Norway).[16] Other SWFs are looking for the best return or the best risk–return ratio of managed funds (Singapore: GIC and Temasek, Kuwait: KIA). Some are nothing but a financial arm (Saudi Arabia: SAMA) of governmental industrial and/or political goals (Qatari: QIA). Chinese funds typically fall into the last category (see Table 8.4).

Formed in 2007, the CIC is the government's financial and industrial arm. As far as can be known from portfolio management, the CIC is backing government goals: guaranteeing the supply of raw materials, access to advanced technology, purchasing overseas market shares and internationalizing Chinese SOEs. Following a fierce battle between the central bank (PBOC), which had a more financial approach, and the Ministry of Finance, (MOF),CIC finally swallowed Central Huijin Holdings Co., then affiliated to the PBOC, to strengthen the Chinese banking industry. The CIC reports directly to the State Council, but within the CIC, Huijin Holdings retained some degree of autonomy. Originally, Huijin was formed by and supervized by the central bank (PBOC) with the aim of releasing the large state-owned banks from

Table 8.4 Sovereign wealth funds (US$ billion by end 2012)

Abu Dhabi	ADIA Abu Dhabi Investment Authority	627
Norway	Government Pension Fund	611
China	SAFE State Agency for Foreign Exchange	568
Saudi Arabia	SAMA South Arabia Monetary Authority	532
China	CIC China Investment Corp.	439
Kuwait	KIA Kuwait Investment Authority	296
China	HKMA Hong Kong Monetary Authority	293
Singapore	GIS Govt of Singapore Investment Corp.	247
Singapore	Temasek	157
Russia	National Welfare Fund	149
China	NSSF National Social Security Fund	134
Qatar	QIA Qatar Investment Authority	100

Sources: Sovereign Wealth Fund Institute, OECD.

non-performing loans and to increase the bank's net worth before the expected 'privatization' and further listing on the stock exchange. Prior to the 2002–3 banks privatization process, Huijin removed non-performing loans inherited from Mao and transferred them to several defeasance companies, increased the bank's capital, opened the shareholding to foreign investors through reserved capital increases and finally continued with the 'privatization' (i.e. the IPOs and listing on the stock exchange). Following the 2008–9 financial crisis, Huijin was in charge of 'cleaning' the large state bank's balance sheet by removing the non-performing loans once again. This was due to the rapid increase in credit volume (twice as much in 2009 compared with 2008) and the subsequent increase in provisions for credit losses and the, as yet unforeseen, deterioration of bank net worth. According to the 2011 CIC annual report, the government poured another US$550 billion into the CIC's resources while the return was 11.7 per cent of total assets in 2010.[17]

The Party-State, through the CIC, plays a very active role in bank management and other government-owned companies, no matter what the extent of their actual direct or indirect shareholding. The Chinese government uses all possible available means and institutions: the CIC on both the domestic and the international market, where Huijin retains a certain measure of autonomy; SAFE, a central bank department, is in charge of managing the foreign exchange reserves; the NSSF, which is in charge of managing Social Security resources and pension funds; the Hong Kong Monetary Authority (HKMA), which still enjoys a limited form of independence under close scrutiny. The SAFE, which was not supposed to be involved in long-term overseas investment, took a stock share in the exploration affiliate of the French power and oil group GDF-Suez. In contrast, CIC, in charge of the management of overseas industrial investments, bought government bonds on the US and the EU markets as a manner of short-term, risk-free cash management (pending the completion of the investment programme). Also, CIC funds may be used in the financing of domestic investment.

The CIC investment strategy has more or less followed the ups and downs of China's overall policy. Initially, the CIC made some errors of judgement – such as the acquisition of a participation in the American investment bank, Bear Sterns and the European commercial bank Fortis, a joint venture between Belgium, France and Luxembourg in charge of local authority financing. Both of them went bankrupt shortly after China's participation. Later, in the wake of the global financial crisis, the CIC was solicited by Western governments to bail out failing banks (UK: Northern Rock (formerly the Northern Rock Building Society), in the USA: Fannie Mae and Freddy Mac, in Germany: LandersSpaarbanken). Also, the CIC subscribed to substantial amounts of some basically defaulted European government debt (Greece, Spain, Ireland, Portugal). The CIC made a huge profit in between, due to the then unusually high interest rates of the bonds which could be resold later on at a much higher price once the debt markets had recovered and the interest rates had grown back. It was thought that China would participate in the yet to be formed European Monetary Stability Mechanism to bail out distressed European banks. But China was expecting to be granted the statute of 'market economy' and the cancellation of arms suspension sales (following the 1989 Tian An Men events) in return. Failing to achieve what was wished for, China turned down this proposal on the grounds that EU members should first put their own affairs in order.

Challenging the Bretton Woods system

In 2010, China took the opportunity of a World Bank capital increase to raise its shareholding from 2.77 per cent to 4.42 per cent. This made China the third largest shareholder, behind the USA and Japan, but before Germany, the UK and France. In 2012, following IMF bond issues, China subscribed to US$5 billion worth of bonds, which made China the third largest contributor behind the USA and Japan (US$100 billion each) but ahead of European countries (US$25 billion each). As far as the International Monetary System is concerned, China has repeatedly criticized the USA's 'lax and irresponsible' monetary policy, demanding a renewal and amendment of the Bretton Woods agreement

(1944) and criticizing the US dollar's 'exorbitant privilege'. According to the traditional 'benign neglect', the US dollar is managed by the Federal Reserve according to exclusively American domestic interests (growth, unemployment) no matter the consequences abroad. As a result, the USA enjoyed the privilege of an unlimited double deficit (budget deficit and trade deficit) by issuing more dollars.

In order to anticipate a new system, which sounds quite unlikely in today's environment, China took the initiative to form common emergency funding instruments with neighbouring countries under the threat of bankruptcy through international cash shortage. China put together swap transactions (local currencies against the dollar) with other central banks as a substitute for the IMF's soft loans. In addition, China is extending a substantial line of credit to support the take-off process of developing neighbouring countries. As such, she is considering forming a new Development Bank with the BRICS (Brazil, Russia, India, China, and South Africa) strong enough to compete with the World Bank and the local Asian Development Bank, both run by the USA in the interest of its local allies.

But China is increasingly reluctant to be involved ('trapped') in regional or multinational institutions and is shifting towards more bilateral relationships.

From regional to world leadership

Before counting its friends, China is counting its foes: the USA and Japan – the USA because they are perceived to be the world's policeman who constricts China's breathing space and Japan because it is a hereditary enemy, from the disastrous Treaty of Shimonoseki (1895) to the dreadful war and occupation (1931–45). Then, to a lesser degree, neighbouring rivals (including Russia and India) are considered as foes because their respective spheres of influence overlap. Russia is distrusted because there is always the traditional threat of danger from the north; India, because they challenge regional leadership. On the Pacific side, China is the major trade partner with all the countries around the Pacific Ocean but any further prospect of trade and monetary integration conflicts with territorial litigations. China is more inclined to bilateral agreement as opposed to multilateral cooperation or alliances, although this is not in accordance with its traditional policy of independence. Despite this, China reluctantly decided to join some of the existing regional cooperation organizations. Today, China is still either a full member or observer of several regional cooperation organizations: a full member of the 'Shanghai club' in Central Asia, and an observer of

ASEAN in south-east Asia and APEC in the Pacific area. Both countries, the USA and China, are competing to use regional economic organizations as a bridgehead and a means of influence.

Based in Bangkok and formed in 1967 as a means of surveilling Communist China, ASEAN comprises ten countries (Singapore, Brunei, Malaysia, Thailand, Indonesia, the Philippines, Vietnam, Laos, Cambodia and Burma) – which, in today's context, have nothing left in common but economic and trading interests and their defiance toward China's territorial ambitions. This is the reason why a reluctant China, which perceived ASEAN as a regional arm of the USA, joined the organization as an observer. In 2009, ASEAN + 1 (Japan) members agreed to cancel customs duties charged on 7,000 products and services from the 1 January 2010. This accounted for 90 per cent of their overall trade relations. In 2001, China put forward the idea of forming a huge free trade zone including ASEAN and China. By joining ASEAN, China is expecting to facilitate its imports of raw materials (iron ore, gas and rubber) and exports of manufactured goods which had, up to that point, been hit by a 5 per cent customs duty. The new free trade organization can compete on an even basis with the European Union and the North America Free Trade Agreement (NAFTA). As a follow up, members have agreed on common programmes (regarding the environment and tourism), such as a joint development of the Mekong River. But ASEAN is not only a former defensive pact turned economic zone. In 2003, ASEAN members adopted an agreement (the Bali Concord II) which states that democracy is important for peace and stability. Hitherto, the statement has not been followed up with anything more concrete.

Following the 1997–8 payment crisis, Asian countries agreed to put together swap (reciprocal) credit exchange lines (the local currency against the US dollar) to prevent IMF involvement. Set in place in 2000 on a bilateral basis, the agreements were renewed in 2010 on a multilateral basis. The Chang Mai[18] agreements (EAFTA or ASEAN + 3: China, Japan and South Korea) allowed member countries to draw from a common pool of dollar reserves (US$120 billion) if they face an emergency foreign payment crisis. This is similar to the IMF's mechanism but with one important proviso: a line of credit proportionate to the country's quota is unconditionally available immediately. Following the membership of Australia, India and New Zealand, ASEAN + 6 became CEPSEA.

Formed in 1989, the APEC (Pacific Forum) is a rival organization sponsored by the USA which groups 21 neighbouring Pacific countries. The idea is to balance the free trade areas of Europe and North America. The average custom duties fell from 16.9 per cent in 1989 to 6.6 per cent in 2008. At the 2011 Honolulu (Hawaii) summit, followed by the 2012 Vladivostok summit, US President Barack Obama took over the Trans-Pacific Partnership (TPP), the former 2005 initiative of Brunei, Chile, New Zealand and Singapore later to be joined by the USA, Australia, Malaya, Peru, Vietnam, Canada and Mexico. After a period of uncertainty, China declined to join the new venture. TPP aims to build up a free trade zone with Japan and South Korea to compete against the rapidly growing China. Initially, Japan and South Korea were reluctant to join an 'anti-China' organization, but in the wake of the territorial conflicts in the Sea of China, they joined the new TPP organization. It is, therefore, unsurprising that, some months later, President Barack Obama put forward the idea of a similar free trade zone across the Atlantic with the European Union. The whole project is clearly perceived to be a challenge to Chinese economic growth.

At its inception, the 'Shanghai Club', a central Asian organization formed from a Russian initiative based in Shanghai, was primarily aimed at joining forces to combat the threat of 'terrorism' (i.e. Islamic) in this remote area comprising deserts and mountains. The 'Shanghai Club' consists of four central Asian countries: Kazakhstan, Kirghizstan, Turkmenistan and Uzbekistan, with two regional leaders: Russia and China. Its main aim is to keep the growing influence of the USA in Afghanistan at bay. Candidacies from the USA and Japan were turned down. China's other aim is to balance Russia's increasing influence among former members of the Soviet Union which have huge raw material resources: oil and gas. After some limited military manoeuvres and anti-terrorism cooperation, the Shanghai Club turned to economic cooperation. China worked out several oil and gas supply bilateral agreements. Since 2009, 1,000 miles of gas pipes have been constructed to transport gas from Turkmenistan through Uzbekistan and Kazakhstan up to Xinxiang, to be connected to the Chinese network to supply Beijing and Shanghai 3,000 miles away. China is very active in Kazakhstan (though Chinese communities are very limited in this country), granting soft loans and constructing various infrastructures in exchange for gas and oil supplies and exploration permits. At the last meeting (2013), China put forward the idea of forming a common Development Bank.

Finally, created in 2009, the BRICS organization put together emerging countries from each continent: Brazil, Russia, India, China and South Africa. Although these countries, combined, account for huge economic power, they have very little in common. China and Russia are opposed to Brazil's candidacy for a permanent seat on the United Nation's Security Council. Brazil and South Africa are fiercely critical of

China's policy of weak currencies and protectionist measures. To make a gesture of goodwill, at their 2013 Durban meeting BRICS member countries decided to increase the volume of trade denominated in their currencies and to form a common Development Bank.

Soft power policy

It is agreed that China is not a Nation but, rather, a Civilization. However, historical patrimony and intellectual inheritance are poorly managed. The USA is only two centuries old but American culture has spread all over the world (including in China). In the twentieth century, over 1 million Western books had been translated into Chinese while, in the meantime, only 3,000 Chinese books have been translated into Western languages.

Though an heir to a long tradition of scientific achievements and cultural masterpieces, China does not use its 'soft power'; this is partially due to the Chinese government. In his New Year 2012 address, President Hu Jintao once more urged to Chinese citizens to be vigilant of the increased infection of Western culture and way of life. He denounced 'a strategic plot aimed at Westernising and splitting up China'. He continued; 'Western culture on the international stage is strong whereas ours is weak.' In contrast, Chinese students have a poor knowledge of the history of their own country.[19] A network of 320 Confucius Institutes (Confucius, rather than Marx) provide the teaching of Mandarin and cultural initiation similar to the British Council, Alliance Française, Goethe Institutes or the Casa Velasquez. But the Confucius Institutes are under tight Party control.

China is, however, steadily opening up to the outside world. The teaching of Mandarin is spreading rapidly all over the world. In the USA, the number of American students studying Mandarin has increased by 50 per cent in ten years. Though Mandarin is an international language by nature,[20] Chinese culture is relatively unknown in the Western countries. Even though China has developed local institutions – a mix of authoritarian and market-oriented institutions – which may be the most suitable to face the current world uncertainties, China's institutional framework is hard to export and ill-suited to other countries and other contexts.

In the background, the two rivals – the USA and China – are pushing forward their pawns on the Asian chessboard. Though China is, by nature, more inclined to bilateral agreements, the country managed to penetrate and distort some of the regional organizations for its own benefit. One such example is ASEAN, which was initially designed to protect Asian members from China's pervasive Marxist influence. But China is no longer Marxist. On the other hand, the US-sponsored TPP initiative is clearly a way to challenge perceived Chinese threats. In addition, China's relationship is somewhat ambiguous regarding her neighbouring countries. On the one hand, China is developing strong economic and monetary links but, on the other, she is increasing its sea power and encroaching on empty islands. Largely government-owned media coverage of exacerbated nationalist demonstrations nurtured by the Party-State are perceived as a threat by neighbouring countries that are inclined to seek shelter from the USA against growing Chinese neo-Imperialism and aggressive regional leadership.

9
In Search of Civil Society

The notion of one single Party has always existed in China, only it was made of Confucian Literati.
(Cyrille Javary)

Between the Party and the People, civil society – understood as 'the field of civil, organized, social life which is voluntary, self-sufficient and independent from the State'[1] – acts as a dynamic intermediary, data transmission system and shock absorber. China does not operate an authoritarian government system but rather, is totalitarian. Whether the Party-State is more flexible does not change its basic nature. Public freedoms are monitored the same way as the planning system is in the economic field; the more strategic the area, the more controlled it becomes. As long as the Party-State is not directly challenged, the government is largely accommodating but, should it feel its power challenged, it is uncompromising. Elections can be demanded, but not a multi-party system; there are some limited freedoms of speech, but no right of association. Censorship is omnipresent, even though it may be applied in a more flexible and (sometimes) clever way. Books are allowed but confidential essays are not, if the Party doctrine is questioned. Movies critical of the State or Chinese society are forbidden in China but permitted abroad. An artist who uses his reputation to support dissidents will be sued under whatever pretext (corruption, tax fraud) and his passport withdrawn.

Foreign media view any sign of flexibility in the rigid Chinese system as a victory for democracy. The Party-State maintains strict control of information through a tight network of Party-sponsored press agencies, TV channels, newspapers and magazines aimed at covering the full range of social stratums. Any divergence is severely sanctioned.

Hu Shu Li was a manager of a well-known and highly praised independent business news magazine, *Caixin Media*, when she was dismissed without notice and without explanation, because she inadvertently moved to a forbidden area. Foreign media is heavily dependent on government sources, although most are not properly equipped to follow up and make in-depth enquiries about a source's provenance.

Most social unrest is caused by localized incidents which do not affect the government machine as a whole. Such incidents have quite the opposite effect; protests and demonstrations strengthen Party authority, as it gives them the opportunity to become a benevolent referee. The 'Centre' is perceived as a last recourse against a local corrupt official. Therefore, the average citizen may be more tolerant of the wealth obtained by their leaders – after all, they deserve it, but omnipresent

Box 9.1 The Wukan siege

In 2012, Western media reported the siege of a village called Wukan, with a population of just 12,000 people, in the Guangdong province in the south-east of China. In fact, there had been tension and fighting in this region since 2009. As is often the case, the expropriation of farmlands by the local Party secretary (on behalf of a real estate developer who just happened to be one of his closest friends) caused a popular uprising. One of the demonstrators, Xu Jintao, died while in police custody. Villagers attacked Party offices and chased off Party officials. Local officials took the matter seriously: the village was surrounded by police forces; all water, power and food supplies were cut. The villagers were unfazed and relentless. The Party was therefore forced to implement other methods to regain order and control. As demanded by the villagers, 'free' elections were held in April 2012. Li Zuluan, the former mayor and chief opponent, was released from jail and unanimously re-elected. Western media proclaimed 'victory' for democracy and a sign of further progress. In actual fact, the Party only withdrew because 2012 was a sensitive time for them with the renewal of the supreme leaders coming in November 2013. One year later, another Guangdong village (Chengdu) protested against the expropriation of a 33 Ha piece of farmland resold to a business man acquainted with the Party secretary. The village, which was by this time completely surrounded by the police, had all its power cut. In this instance, the Party did not withdraw and this new uprising went unreported.

daily corruption is simply becoming unbearable. So long as Party legitimacy is not challenged, it can be flexible with its courses of action, either repressing or compromising as it sees fit. Whatever the case, the Party is the winner. The failure of the 1989 Tien An Men events, the steady rise of purchasing power and the development of communication means led opponents to believe that external protest is hopeless. Public opinion enquiries demonstrate that the Chinese population feel more concerned by social stability and national unity than democracy and public liberties.

The very achievements of the policy of reform and opening-up led to deep changes in progressively more complex social structures. Within a few years, Chinese society became more diversified – so much so that the Party-State had to rethink the social control system and adjust it to the new expectations of the various social layers. Nascent public opinion and civilian society shed light on the increasing gap between the political system and the growth model. The 'political' market and the 'economic' market are increasingly diverging. The more the market is liberalized, the more the Party tightens its grip. It is the mere logic of the system.

Party and state

The government governs, but its policy is fixed by the Party. Under imperial rule, in accordance with Legalist tenet, the Emperor was invisible ('the power behind the curtain'), ministries and local governors governed on his behalf. The power machine's core does not usually become involved in day-to-day business. If the Emperor had to make an appearance, it meant that something had gone wrong in the government process. In everyday rule, the Party stays in the shadows. As with the Vatican, the Party is ruled by secrets and rituals. But the Party is dependent on local officials to set policy in motion, to make it real. Decisions taken in secret are implemented through directives, promotions and demotions if directives prove to be ineffective. To outside observers, the only way to glean something from the Party is to scrutinize its game of musical chairs. The secretary of a province or the head of a critical agency such as the chairman of the central bank or China's sovereign wealth fund (CIC) is more powerful than a minister of central government. A member of a given faction being promoted, or the member of another being demoted, is a significant event. Some top officials have been sued, charged and sometimes even executed for corruption (the best way to set aside any rival). Observers require an in-depth knowledge of the changing weights of government positions and fluid allegiances; for example, the position of chairman to the central bank (Zu Xiaochuan) has expanded alongside the monetary and exchange policies. A top leader must be backed by a strong network of supporters but must never appear too visible, as this could cost him the support of other Party factions.

Bureaucratic system

Chinese bureaucracy has united the country for over twenty centuries – a country run by a bureaucratic caste united by a common culture, language, thought and way of life. As it used to be for twenty centuries, Chinese bureaucracy is a body of civil servants paid and removable selected for their capabilities instead of their family background, integrated within a hierarchical organization, run by a regulated system within which instructions and information is channelled through written documents. It dates as far back as the 'Fighting Kingdoms' (5th–3rd centuries BC) before taking shape under the Song dynasty (960–1368 AD). The feudal system (*fengjian*) of the last, legendary Zhou dynasty (1122–256 BC) made way for a true bureaucratic system (*junxian*) before the Empire emerged (221 BC). The bureaucratic system was born in the network of 'prefectures' and 'strongholds' set up by Lord Shang Yang, Prime Minister of the Qing Kingdom. The first imperial dynasty's (*Qin*) territorial partition is about the same as today. Following the crushing of the 'Rebellion of the Seven Kingdoms' under the Han dynasty (206 BC–220 AD), a system of direct management was implemented. From the Song dynasty (960–1279), the caste of literati-bureaucrats was united by neo-Confucian ideology which, today, the Party is attempting to use for its own ends.

Confucius dreamed of a prime minister-counsellor, a staunch supporter of the Emperor but free-minded and independent enough to admonish him should he diverge from his duties and risk losing the 'mandate of the Heaven'. This did not, however, stand the test of actual government. The position of prime minister was nullified for the last time under the Ming dynasty (1368–1644). The Emperor assumes complete power and responsibility as the bulwark core of an enormous spider's web. The government is split between six independent 'ministers' (*liubu*): civil service, finance, rites, army, justice and public works. There are no cabinet meetings and there is no foreign office. The Department of State Affairs (*shang shu sheng*) was created by the Mongolian Yuan dynasty, who needed the support of the bureaucratic class to run such a large country. This Department was, however, dispensed with by the following Ming (Chinese) dynasty. Each minister reported straight to the Emperor through the Grand Secretary (*neige*) and through the Grand Council (*jun ji chu*) under the Qing. In the seventeenth century, Emperor Kangxi allowed local officials to send documents and reports called 'Palace memorandum' (*zouzhe*) directly to him, which were returned to the issuer with the Emperor's annotations in red ink. The management of the Empire was hierarchical: each layer depending on the next. The network of provinces, prefectures, counties and villages was about the same as it is today. The number of people per government official was very large, in the range of 100 to 300,000 people (as opposed to a figure of 500 to 1,000 in the first European centralized kingdoms, such as Great Britain and France).

Given the small number of available jobs, half of the young Mandarins were placed on waiting lists. Pending their appointment, young graduates were assigned unofficial positions to learn their profession on the spot. To assist him in the management of his jurisdiction, a newly appointed governor brought with him, as personal staff, relatives or family friends who had graduated with lower-level examination passes, or who had missed the national examination in Pekin. A local bureaucrat, whatever his position in the hierarchy, no matter how large his jurisdiction, could not rely on a permanent bureaucratic network. They had to recruit deputies and assistants at their own expense. As these placements were usually filled by relatives and family clients, it was a hotbed for corruption and nepotism. For day-to-day management, they had to rely on their local leaders, who were in charge of raising taxes, censuses, conscripts, lawsuits and public order. Needless to say, the government official would usually 'forget' to raise taxes or fees for their friends and relatives. In order to fulfil his duties, the local Mandarin had to raise extra (illegal) local taxes (*lijin*: tolls), the proceeds of government taxes being entirely transferred to the Court. By the end of the Empire (Qing dynasty), the Court relied on local governors and prefects in charge of all the management duties: fiscal, judiciary and economic. Even a locally assigned general reported to local governors or prefects. There was no separation of powers at any level.

The imperial administration penetrated all areas of social, political, economic and even personal life. Farmers did not own their farmland. The land owner was, in turn, highly dependent on the government and local administration; local administration was, in turn, entirely dependent on him. Some were financially ruined by their local duties, others became outrageously wealthy. Local communities relied on the leading factions to deal with misuse of power and corrupt officials.

Teaching and education was the same all over the country and religious orthodoxy was defined by the Emperor. The Empire's 'ideology' was Confucian but the Court used 'legalist' principles to govern.

A civil servant is a literate, highly educated person shaped by studying the Great Classics, ruling through his personal qualities (virtue) and collective customs (rites). He was selected through a multilayer system of examinations regional, provincial and imperial. The meritocracy of the imperial system of selection should not be overrated. In spite of the anonymous examination process, preferential treatment was commonplace. Some merchants purchased degrees on the behalf of their sons. Heirs of senior civil servants praised for their achievements or loyalty were exempt from the vigorous examination process. Emperors relied on the bureaucratic class as a government tool and a social group to balance other sources of power (the Emperor's wife, mother and concubines, the Emperor's family and Forbidden City eunuchs). Loyalty is more appreciated than competence. Also, the formal and literary features of exams were progressively opened to new issues. To the traditional tests of poetry and dissertation were added maths and law by the Song dynasty and physical tests by the Ming dynasty: archery and riding.

Future Mandarins were trained on their family estates by private tutors, or in a private 'academy'. Teaching methods and writing techniques were the same. Education and examination were aimed to make an *honnête homme* (honest man), a general practitioner rather than a professional, able to deal with any sort of business, person or situation. Common education and network management provided the bureaucratic class a high degree of homogeneity, and made it easier to spread information and improve common understanding. Senior civil servants spoke the same language and shared the same set of common values. In contrast, the building of a bureaucratic and hereditary caste deepened the gap between senior civil servants and the people they managed, who more often than not did not speak the same language. Senior civil servants were appointed for no more than three years to prevent the creation of local fiefs. They were then asked to move to another position in another area. Local officials who were yet to graduate imperial exams had no chance to further their careers but were, however, indispensable to civil servants as a means of liaising with the common man.

The imperial bureaucratic system was 'totalitarian' long before the term itself even existed. The bureaucratic system has survived up until now with the same merits and the same weaknesses.

Party organization

In China, there is no system of checks-and-balances and no separation of powers. All sources of power are kept tightly under the Party's control and all government functions are split between the Party and the State. The Party has many fingers in many pies: trade unions, business associations, teaching professions, big companies – whether privately or government owned, religious groups, ethnic minorities, and so on. The Party controls the State apparatus through the Party Organization Department, the army through the Party's Central Military Commission, the economy through the National Reform and Development Committee (NRDC), and Party members through the Organization Department and the Department of Discipline. Within an organization which by nature is very hierarchical, coordination is ensured through 'Leading Groups' reporting to the State Council. Not all bureaucrats are Party members, but all leading positions are fulfilled by Party members. Party, state and business leaders are drawn only from Party schools. Lower officials have no such expectations. To implement decisions, the Party relies on government bureaucrats and less senior Party members. The Party's sole instrument of control is the power to appoint, assign, promote, demote, sanction or dismiss (if not worse).

Careers are closely scrutinized by the Organization Department to identify the promising young Party members and to root out deviance. The Organization Department sophisticated staff management techniques. Each Party member is rated every year according to a system of points related to the entire job spectrum and weighted in accordance with the Party's priority. The Party Organization Department is not immune to corruption and nepotism: 2007 saw a Chinese version of Gogol's *Revizor*;[2] a man presenting himself as a member of the Organization Department managed to receive US$63,000 from a local bureaucrat to whom he promised a position in the Beijing Offices.

The head of the Department of Organization (*Zhongzubu*) is the most powerful among Politburo members. He handles personal files, promotes or demotes at will and takes the initiative to fulfil disciplinary enquiries. The Party is opaque even to its own members. In principle, the hierarchy works two ways – up and down – but, in practical terms, information is shared downwards at the mercy of decentralized departments, while information is shared upwards at the mercy of local bias. The tragic outcome (35 million dead in two years) of the 'Great Leap Forward' (1958–60) was due to over-optimistic reports from local officials under Mao's pressure, each statistic outdoing the previous one, sending false reports about food reserves. As the actual food supply did not match the officials' reports, the people starved to death. When a horrified Marshall Yue Che went to visit his family in the countryside, he tried to draw Mao's attention to this atrocity with a deferential private letter; he was dismissed right away on the ground of 'revisionism'.

Theoretically, state bureaucrats and Party officials are appointed through an electoral process. But, in most cases, there is only one candidate – the Party candidate. Other candidates, if any, must be approved by the Party. A Party directive reminds local officials that there should be several candidates for each position. Every bureaucrat is overseen by a Party member who should ensure that the Party's instructions are properly carried out. The supreme government body is the State Council which is composed of the same members as the Party's Politburo. Ministers are in charge of the management of their own administration, but they have no political power. They are merely senior civil servants. The government is chaired by the Prime Minister, who reports back to the Party General Secretary.

After years of deadly insider fighting, the Party worked out a peaceful process of transferring power from one generation of leaders to the next. Chinese citizens used to speak in terms of 'generations' – we are now in the 'fifth' generation (Mao, Deng Xiaoping, Jiang Zemin, Hu Jintao, Xi Jinping) – as former Chinese used to speak in terms of the number of years in the current ruling Emperor's reign. A spoils system allocates key positions to the wining faction and its supporters. The General Secretary and his team are 'elected' after a lengthy and obscure power race within the Party for a five-year term renewable (i.e. ten years, which is long enough to work out a new policy but not so long as to nurture undesirable expectations from the rivals).

In November 2012, Xi Jinping was 'elected' General Secretary, along with the other members of the State Council and Party Politburo (Li Keqiang, Prime Minister, Liu Yunshan, Zang Dejiang, Zhang Gaoli, Yu Zhengsheng, Wang Qishan) and the Chairman of the Party's Central Military Committee. In March 2013, Xi Jinping was 'elected' President of the Republic and Li Keqiang Prime Minister. This is different from Hu Jintao, ten years previously (2002), who took a couple of years to get rid of former Jiang Zemin factions (Jiang Zemin remained Chairman of the Party Military Committee for a further two years). Xi's fast take-off was a sign of his strong hand in the Party. Within three months, Xi had taken over all key positions, Hu Jintao had retired and Xi had got rid of the 88-year-old Jiang Zemin, one of the most influential Party *padrone*. Except for a handful of crucial positions – such as the chairman of the central bank – Zu Xiaochuan, a staunch reformist and pro-marketeer, all the top positions were renewed within days. A very timely 'anti-corruption' campaign was undertaken to keep all potential opponents at bay. It was no surprise (except to Western media outlets) that the inauguration address did not mention any new political initiatives but, rather, the launch of yet another anti-corruption campaign which brought about a fresh purge of the bureaucracy. A November 2013 meeting of the Central Committee, several times postponed, provided the occasion to put together a long list of political measures (62 in total), although they were without concrete agenda or schedule.

On paper, the General Secretary is all-powerful. He is the all-powerful engine but still heavily dependent on the Party and the government machine. He is neither Left nor Right, neither a Reformist nor a Conservative but, instead, the common denominator of all the Party's clans. He is not the supporter of any given policy; rather, he puts forward policies acceptable to the widest proportion of Party leaders. The Party is not made of political wings but rival networks: the 'princelings' (*taizi*) heirs of well-known veterans (Xi Jinping), the 'Shanghai gang' (Jiang Zemin), the 'Youth League' (Hu Jintao), and so on. Political clans are not divided by critical political issues but by networks based on personal adhesion: province, education, language, family links and business connections, and so on. Someone from the provinces who is promoted to Beijing administrative offices is soon betrayed by his accent. Naturally, he gets together with his fellow countrymen. To make sure that the new General Secretary is not going to diverge from what has already been agreed on, the government programme is approved one year before he takes office such as the current 12th Plan, 2011–15). As with the President of the United States of America, the Party's General Secretary uses their first term to implant his supporters and spread his ideas, with the expectation that, if re-elected, they will be free to implement a more ambitious programme during the second term.

If a Party leader is overambitious, all other leaders join forces to make sure that he is expelled from the system. Bo Xilai, ex-Secretary of Chongqing (a south-west metropolis of some 35 million people), supported a new, Maoist stance. His fall was brought on by his chief of police and close associate, who took refuge in Chengdu's US Consulate. After debriefing, the US government was more than happy to release Bo's associate and to hand him over to the Chinese government. Western media recounted in sordid detail Bo Xilai's fall, an erotic tale of sex, dollars and murder. But Bo Xilai had plenty of time to get rich when he was the all-powerful secretary of Dalian, another industrial centre in Manchuria.

Party democracy

Party membership is much more diversified that it originally looks from the outside. The Party is split between various factions of solidarity groups not necessarily based on political issues. Some factions aim to regroup a wide scope of party members stretching across the entire political spectrum. This is the opposite of solidarity groups, which are based on a much narrower provincial or perhaps Party positional powerbase (politicians versus civil servants). When General Secretary Jiang Zemin's power was squeezed between 'Reformists' (along Deng's line) and 'Conservatives' (along Chen's line) in the early 1990s (following the 1989 Tien An Men events and 1992 Deng's trip south, which ignited new momentum for reform), Jiang escaped the situation by picking up an energetic and highly effective prime minister – Zu Rongji, a senior civil servant, former Shanghai Secretary and chairman of the Central Bank – who maintained rigid control over the Party and government machine. Jiang relinquished his economic powers to Zu who, instead, concentrated on administrative issues, thus drawing the faction of senior civil servants primarily concerned with 'effective' management to Jiang's side.

In 1998, the Organic Law on Village Committees, which made local council elections compulsory, was eventually issued after ten years of hot debate. According to the Ministry of Civilian Affairs, there were 610,000 village councils in 2008, including 2.4 million elected members. But other legislation was necessary to remind Party members in charge of election management that there should be more candidates than elected people. In reality, only candidates chosen by the Party are authorized to apply. In the Wukan saga (see Box 9.1), a young school teacher aged 22 who considered running for office was threatened with the sack if she did so. Another candidate was detained in police custody until the application deadline was over.

Similarly, local Party secretaries are, theoretically, elected. The incumbent is selected and confirmed by the upper levels of the Party. Decisions are meant to be collective but, in most cases, the village secretary remains in place for such a long time that he can build up a personal fiefdom. In fact, the secretary's authority depends on the kind of population he manages. As opposed to the image of a nation made of equal citizens united around their leaders, the Chinese population is split by a variety of transverse unofficial social groups and organizations which have stood the test of time, wars, revolutions, natural disasters, droughts, floods and famines. Today, numerous networks of mutual aid, religious sects and charitable associations are tolerated because they have taken over social services tossed aside by the local government and former state companies. Local 'temple' associations are aimed at maintaining the local family temple. It is customary for inhabitants of the same village to bear the same family name. Wealthy members of the family finance schools, medical centres and scholarships not only through an altruistic family spirit, but also through political or social clientelism. If a newly assigned Party member is assigned to a tightly knit community, he is often forced to negotiate. Should he try to impose his authority by force, he risks losing touch with the local population, whose unofficial, flexible and invisible groups are difficult to pin down.

It is widely agreed in Europe and the USA that concentrated towns are more suited to socializing, while village peasants are scattered about. In China, it is the other way round. In the town, people are lost and isolated in the crowd; it is easier to identify informal organizations. Most members of informal organizations are migrants lacking work permits, disconnected from their family roots. In the countryside, informal organizations are less visible but knitted more closely together because it is crucial for the group's survival. This is something which has long been established and has grown stronger over the centuries. Everything depends on a bureaucrat's flexibility and understanding, and the strength of the local association. The main source of conflict is land seizures, a very sensitive issue for farmers who often belong to the same family and share the same fate.

Party legitimacy

Until Mao's death (1976), the Party ideology was a Maoist-type mix of Marxism, a revised blend of 'ruralism' and nationalism – Marxism 'with Chinese characteristics'. According to the history taught in Chinese schools, China before 1949 was 'feudal' – a term more ideological than historical, since 'feudalism' was non-existent in China's history (at least in the Western sense – i.e. a hierarchy of delegated, hereditary and rival powers). The balance of power was not shared between the monarchy and land-owning aristocracy. Since the first dynasty (221 BC), all Emperors struggled to prevent rival powers such as imperial family members, family members of the empress, eunuchs and senior civil servants. Factions were repeatedly and uselessly condemned by the monarch, the only person high enough in the hierarchy to embrace the notion of national interest, as opposed to factions dedicated to private interests. Merchants were scorned by the literati who supposedly disdained money. Merchants became rich but they failed to organize themselves as a political class with common interests (though there were 'guilds' and other business associations). The Chinese 'bourgeois' class in Marxist terms has never been 'revolutionary', no more today than yesterday. The wealth accumulated by merchants through trade, banking (usury) or industry (craftsmen) were usually 'wasted' on the consumption of luxury goods, at best poured into real and land estates.

From the very start of the reform policy (1978), the Party sought a new ideology fit for the new policy. Growth rate, purchasing power, reforming for the only purpose of reforming are not substitute ideologies strong enough to mobilize 1.3 billion Chinese citizens. Deng Xiaoping's 'Four-Way Modernization', Jiang Zemin's 'Three Representatives Theory', Hu Jintao's 'Harmonious Society', Xi Jinping's 'Chinese Dream' all sound more like slogans, rather than political programmes. Based on his first speeches, Xi Jinping is seemingly returning to Deng's pragmatism, far from any ideological rhetoric. In 2014, Deng's 110th birthday anniversary was celebrated with a wide display by the new leaders. 'Pragmatism' may be a programme, but it is not a policy. By definition, pragmatism is more a method than a political goal, even though it is more understandable to the Chinese citizen suspicious of reshaped ideology.

Nationalism has always been part of the Party's statements, based on remembering the unequal treaties of the nineteenth century and the ferocious Japanese wars of the twentieth century. Nationalism can be easily spread but difficult to contain. So far, the Party has managed to stop nationalist demonstrations before it was too late. In addition, nationalism nurtured by territory claims is inconsistent with China's ambition of regional leadership. China's repeated claims to isolated and deserted islands lost in the middle of nowhere drive neighbouring countries looking for a shield against Chinese neo-imperialism into the open arms of the USA.

In addition to its 'nationalist' stance, the Party presents itself as the 'worker's party', given that urban and working class interests have always been supported by the Party. Labour regulations suppressed by Mao in 1955 were re-established by Deng Xiaoping in 1987, followed by numerous other laws and regulations, such as the 1995–2007 National Labour Law contracts. But the various organizations in charge of implementation (Party, trade unions (ACFTU) affiliated to the Party, local authorities, and so on) applied new regulations in accordance with local context and circumstances. The legislation included a provision on 'labour committees' including government representatives (the local labour office), trade unions (ACFTU) and company management. As a result, government representatives always find themselves in a majority position. Union representatives are not expected to defend workers' interests but, instead, to find a solution suitable to all parties, to settle the outstanding claim and to bring the workers back to work.

The Rule of Law

The recognition of a written and objective norm applicable to all, including the government, is indispensable to the proper workings of a market economy as it reduces uncertainties and transaction costs. An entrepreneur about to take a critical decision must be certain that the rules of the game will not be changed in the course of his business, that he can expect to collect the return of his (human and capital) investment and that he can rely on a certain stability in the business environment. To this end, the entrepreneur must benefit from the protection of common law. The more a market is 'free', the more it must be 'regulated' (to protect this freedom) otherwise the market will be regulated by the law of the jungle. The transparency of trades, the protection of contract obligations and registered patents, the subsequent lack of Party interference, all these rules and many more are essential to the working of a price mechanism. A healthy market needs rules and courts to make them operational.

The Roman Empire and the Chinese Empire had a great deal in common, even though the Roman Empire lasted 'only' five centuries, while the Chinese Empire lasted 22 centuries. For example, they both shared the idea of belonging to a common world of language, culture and civilization. But they were divided by the notion of law, the Rule of Law. When, according to Cicero, Publius Gavius was beaten to death and crucified on Verres' instructions, he called not for mercy but cried: '*civis romanus sum*' (I am a Roman citizen).

Before becoming an Empire, Rome was a City; before becoming an empire, China was a kingdom. One was a sea empire (*mare nostrum*) open to the outside world, while the other was a continental, self-sufficient empire (*Zhong guo*). When a slave, a freed man or a foreigner was granted Roman citizenship, he could claim for common law. An unknown tent-maker from Cicilia called Paul of Tarse appealed the decision of the procurator of Judea before Caesar's court. When Octavius reached the Emperor's throne and became 'Augustus' (in Chinese, *di*), he did not risk taking the title of 'king' – which had cost Caesar, his uncle, his life. Imperial institutions slipped under the disguise of Republican institutions. Augustus was only a '*princeps*', the first among his peers. All the Emperor's edicts were endorsed by the Senate and taken in the name of the Roman people (Senatus Populusque Romanum).

Following the Caracalla edict (212), all the free men of the Empire were granted Roman citizenship (even though the final aim of the Caracalla edict was more fiscal than legal). In Rome, the law, taken in accordance with the legal procedures, was applicable to all including the Emperor himself and the magistrates.

When China's first empire was formed (Qin dynasty) in 221 BC, the institutional framework of the Kingdom of Qin was, as such, transferred to the new Empire on a *tabula rasa*. Qin's former king chose not to use the title 'King' but chose, instead, to call himself 'Emperor'. This revived the old but still existent idea of a united empire under a single ruler. The Emperor is a 'Son of Heaven' (*tian zi*), ruling all that stands 'under the Heaven' (*tian xia*) 'between the four seas'. The Roman citizen was subject to common law: the Chinese subject was the Emperor's subject. In Rome, the law was the law because it had been adopted in accordance with the proper procedure. In China, the law was the law because it was the edict of the Emperor. In Rome, the source of law was shared by many institutions: the People's Meetings (plebiscite: *plebs dixit*), the Senate (*senatus-consultum*), the two Consuls (*imperium*) and the two People's Tribunes (veto rights). Magistrates were selected among the citizens duly registered by the 'Censor' in charge of the 'census' of free men who fulfil the conditions. In China, there is only one source of power and authority i.e. the Emperor – today, the Party.

Eventually, Rome also produced its own generation of 'Legalists'. In the Late Empire (third–fourth centuries AD), the Emperor was '*nomos empsychos*', literally the 'living law' – the only source of all laws. According to Paul: 'All power comes from God' (the Bible, *Romans*, 13.1), a sentence which was further used and misused by all supporters of the King's absolute power. In the late thirteenth century, the Legalists – who supported French and British Kings, Philip IV the Fair – laid claims against the Pope's pretention that stated : '*Le Roi est empereur en son royaume*' (The King is Emperor in his Kingdom). Nonetheless, among the ruins of the Late Empire, studies of Roman law continued to improve due to such remarkable thinkers and *retor* (rhetors) as Gaius and Ulpian. The first 'code', as understood above as a recollection of existing rules put together along a set of rational principles, emerged in the Late Empire (the 'Theodosius Code', named after the Emperor Theodosius I) pending the completion of the well-known 'Justinian Code'.

Confucian tradition distinguishes rites (*li*) and the law (*fa*). The 'wise' judge rules through rites and the law, combining the authority of the rites and the power of the law. The judge who has no virtue of humanity (*ren*), rules through the law (*fa*) only. Confucians praised the 'government of men', which relies on humanity, as opposed to the 'Rule of Law' which relies on the formal law. For Legalist thinkers (Han Feizi), who formed their doctrine during the period of the 'Fighting Kingdoms' just before the Empire was born, the law is the law ... because it is the law. The law must be complied with not because it is just or fair and has been established in accordance with the corpus of law, but because it is the edict of the ruling Emperor (or by his duly empowered delegates). Antigone's dilemma, which opposed natural/divine law and common law, is unthinkable in China (in the proper sense of the word: 'not understandable'). The check-and-balance system of power separation is unknown in Chinese history: as a magistrate, a Mandarin is both a judge and a manager. There is no such thing as a 'Code' of rules in China's history, not a collection of scattered laws and rules but, rather, a corpus of rules set up in accordance with a set of principles (often recorded in a Preamble). Following the excesses and violations of the Cultural Revolution, Party leaders felt the need to establish the Rule of Law to prevent the return of chaos and arbitrary law. But, thirty years later, the rules of law engraved in the 1982 Constitution are yet to materialize.

As early as the third Plenum of the 11th Central Committee in December 1978, a Party statement (quoting Deng Xiaoping's speech) stated that the Party was dedicated to building up a 'legal socialist system'. Democracy must be 'institutionalized and legalized' in order to guarantee 'stability, continuity and full authority of the legal system'. The policy of reform should be processed through the law and not through arbitrariness. The 1982 Constitution split the Party and the State. In 1999, the National People's Congress stated that the ultimate goal of the Constitution was to 'build up a socialist country governed in accordance with the law'; in 2004, 'the state must respect human rights' (which includes 'property rights').

Legislative procedures have been reformed to make them more transparent. Legislative power is split between the National People's Congress, which meets each year, and local People's Congresses. Between the annual meetings, permanent committees prepare the workload in close cooperation with the Party. Appointed by the National People's Congress, the supreme ruling body is the State Council (chaired by the Prime Minister) which supervizes members of the cabinet and local authorities. Ministers are nothing but senior civil servants with a technical function under the supervision of a member of the State Council. At each level, a Party Bureau of Legislative Affairs is in charge of preparing drafts and supervizing the implementation of laws and regulations.

The courts are not independent either. Paid by the Party and subject to the rule of the public prosecutor, judges are part of the government. Judges also depend on the Party during the course and at the outcome of trials. The powerful Party Central Commission of Political and Legal Affairs (*zhengfawei*) is supported by a network of local legal committees to ensure the coordination of the public prosecutor's office, the courts and the police. In accordance with the 1989 legislation on administrative claims and the 1994 legislation on indemnities, individuals are empowered to sue government offices before the court and to obtain reparation. As long as the case does not touch the Party, judges may apply the law; however, if they have to deal with a sensitive case, such as land seizures or bureaucratic corruption, the courts declare themselves incompetent. Claims following the collapse of ill-conceived and badly built Sichuan schools incompliant with legal requirements, which collapsed on children during the 2008 earthquake, have been turned down by the courts on this ground. Even lawyers and barristers are supervized by the local Office of Legal Affairs, which reports to the Ministry of Justice.

The Party has its own courts and judiciary system (*shuanggi*). The Party can call on a suspect Party member and detain him as long as necessary before he is released, or brought before a court. The cancellation of the labour camp system (*laogai*) in late 2013 did not affect the Party system of *shanggi*. Because of the lack of the Rule of Law, many Chinese individuals, or even companies, petition Party headquarters (*Zhongnanhai*) in Beijing. The petition system (*xinfang*) is a legacy of the Empire which allows an individual, a group of citizens or a company to bring a court decision to the Party bypassing the government and the courts. In 2008, according to the Ministry of Justice, the Party treated more claims than the judiciary system. Many professionals complain about the petition system, which bypasses the legal system and distorts court decisions.

Corruption

'Li Gang paid 300,000 Yuan to secure his job, but within two years he is expected to collect 5 million Yuan. The return is 1,500 per cent. Is there a more profitable business under Heaven?'[3] The Bo Xilai case drew the attention of the world media but it was the latest in a long line of similar cases: Liu Zhijun, the powerful Minister of Railways (who is said to have collected several billion dollars from public work auctions); Chen Langyu, the Shanghai Party secretary (who tapped into pension funds of city employees to buy real estate companies); Du Shicheng, Party secretary of Qingdao; Chen Tonghai, Chairman of Sinopec (China's second largest oil company); Jin Renqing, Minister of Finance; Xu Zonghong, Shenzen mayor; Chen Xitong, Beijing mayor and member of the State Council; the Chairman of the Bank of China (the bank involved in all foreign transactions); the Manager of the Settlement Department of the Bank of China; the Harbin branch manager of the Bank of China along with 67 of his colleagues; Huang Guangyu, founding Chairman of the Gome group, then the richest man in China (US$6.3 billion), and so on. In 2012, the *New York Times* estimated the wealth of the then Prime Minister, Wen Jiabao, at US$2.7 billion.

According to a central bank study (PBOC, 2011), 18,000 Party members have been involved in corruption cases in the last 20 years accounting for US$124 billion of exit funds. According to the OECD (2005), corruption amounted to 3.5 per cent of GDP. According to a study by the official National Audit Agency, 10 per cent of public funds are embezzled in one form or another; for example, public fund misappropriation, collection of illegal taxes, records of ghost workers, and so on. Some industries are obviously more exposed – such as public works and construction. The misappropriated funds end up in Hong Kong bank accounts. The volume of fund transfers from the mainland recorded by the Hong Kong Custom Office is twice the amount of fund transfers from the mainland registered by the China Customs Office.

Corruption is not unique to totalitarian regimes – not to consider India, the world largest democracy, where the rate of corruption is higher than that of China. But, in China, corruption is part of the system, as it is indispensable to the smooth working of the Chinese growth model. By making transactions easier, corruption is meant to be a sort of commission. Chinese corruption is part of a much larger system benefiting from an institutional context which dates back centuries. Decentralization in such a large country is a further incentive, as it gives local bureaucrats too many opportunities to commit corruption. Under the Empire, corruption was a necessity. Mandarins assigned in remote provinces had to raise illegal taxes to finance local expenditure. In addition, they had to maintain a retinue of family members and friends in search of a rewarding sinecure. After all, the newly appointed Mandarin had to 'redeem' his family, which had spent a fortune to finance his education. Classical Chinese novels are full of ambitious and astute young men in search of a patron to make their living. The great poet of the Tang dynasty Li Bai (701–62) used to be a *protégé* of Emperor Ming Huang (in the then capital city of *Chang'an*), who appointed him as an interpreter of the Hanlin Academy until the Emperor himself got tired of his chronic 'intemperance' and drove him away.

Communist China faced the same dilemma as before: a much too centralized government and a much too decentralized bureaucracy. A totalitarian government which does not comply with its own rules is naturally inclined to arbitrariness. Due to the size of the country, the central government has to delegate its powers to local bureaucrats. Officials sent from the Centre are perceived as strangers by local people. This marks a fundamental misunderstanding and difficult coexistence between the bureaucrat expecting to pursue his career and the local bureaucrat with no such expectations. Instructions are sent down and information is sent up, but reports are sometimes distorted. Even reform policy provides new opportunities for corruption (land expropriation, sale of government owned assets). The 2008–9 Recovery Plan, which emphasized local investments, led to so much waste and misappropriation of funds that the government had to dispatch several missions of enquiry to the provinces the following year.

The Party and society

An efficient democracy requires not only the appropriate institutions, but also a split between private and public spheres, State and Society. The check-and-balance mechanism does not work unless a multi-party system and the separation of powers make it possible. In contrast, a totalitarian government hunts down any civilian organization perceived to be a separate power standing between the government and the individuals. In China, reform policy has always been tied to the Single Party system. Every attempt to breach its power and authority is severely repressed. To a Westerner, punishments sound harsh, unjustified and disproportionate. The Party may be open to social change provided its power and function are unchallenged. But, in face of a single, overwhelming Party, Chinese society is much more fragmented and diversified. This is a legacy of the past and the outcome of social changes triggered by the policy of reform and opening-up.

Chinese society has always been fragmented between a variety of challenging rival powers: factions, clans, regional solidarity groups, powerful families feeding wider and wider circles of clients, high-ranking officials, wealthy merchants, the caste of the literati, local landowners, intellectual societies, informal groups of educated men dedicated to arts and letters, academies, 'temple' associations and families gathering to celebrate a common ancestor, and so on. Such networks were not made to dismantle the country unity or to challenge the central power but, rather, to act as a drive belt between the power and the people. Emperors continued to rebuild China's unity – always disunited, always reunited – against the internal challenging powers and the external threats of Barbarous people. The Court continued to retake lost provinces and recover central power. The pride of a Confucian official was not only to be run by the spirit and the virtue of 'humanity' (*ren*), to be compassionate to disadvantaged orphans, widows, ruined farmers, and so on, but also – and primarily – to be a staunch supporter of the person of the Emperor. Without the support of the Mandarin class, the Qing dynasty could not have repressed the recurrent uprisings and rebellion (Taiping, 1864–71; Boxer Rebellion, 1900). Imperial government background was built on Confucian ideology but, in effect, it follows Legalist government framework. According to the 'Legalists', ruling techniques are based on the 'theory of the two jaws' (i.e. people are squeezed between sentences and rewards). Sentences must be so harsh that nobody dares to infringe the law again. A *good* law is a law which is tough enough to dissuade potential criminals so that the law is no longer useful. What counts is the harshness of the sentence.

When opposition rears its head, the government has two alternatives: to repress or to swallow (one not being exclusive from the other) but, in both cases, the government is always the winner. Dialectics (not to say the dialogue) between the Party and its opponents is rather similar to a judo match. Neither side wishes to revive the chaos and violence of the Cultural Revolution or the Tien An Men events. Each side tries to unbalance his opponent. Opponents use Party vocabulary and rhetoric, merely claiming for the enforcement of existing laws in order to destabilize the government when it is forced to infringe its own rule. On the other hand, the government uses the very strength of its opponent to expose infringement of social order which, in light of past experience, is still a nightmare for most Chinese citizens.

The number of demonstrations has increased ten times in ten years and what used to be tolerated so far is now no longer acceptable. According to government data, the number of demonstrations (over 500 participants) increased from 8,000 in 1993 to 180,000 in 2010. Traditional catalysts for trouble – networks, mafias, religion and ethnic fighting – now have the additional troubles caused by growth – inequalities, the frustrated middle class, entrepreneurs, intellectuals, dissidents and Internet users, and so on.

Networks

Networks (*guanxi*) may be the most obvious alternatives to the governmental sphere and are the background of a civil society. Historically, solidarity groups have emerged as a substitute for the lack of Rule of Law. Personal relationships and occasional conflicts were not settled by magistrates but by networks. *Guanxi* are personal networks which, by nature, escape government and Party control, though they are extensively used in social, economic and political life. Embedded in power structures – companies, government, bureaucracy and even in Party organizations – Chinese networks are ancient institutions. The concept of *guanxi* is associated with the notions of both 'rite' (codified relationships) and 'hierarchy' (dependence relationship).

The *guanxi* character is made of the combination of the two characters: '*guan*' meaning 'to close' but also 'to care for' and '*xi*' meaning 'tied up', 'link' or 'relation'. The character implies the notion of a network which is extended through a set of circles including close relatives, family members, clans, friends, college mates, business relationships and even encounters. *Guanxi* are not 'societies of equals' (Fourier) or 'societies' (Free Masons, Opus Dei, University alumni). *Guanxi* are personal networks based on personal links which last a lifetime: they come from the same province, sometimes even from the same village; they speak the same language or dialect; they often share the same name even though they are not directly related. Joining a network does not mean that you share the same common roots. Many members of the 'Shanghai' group were not born in Shanghai – such as Hu Jintao, who used to be Jiang Zemin's close associate when the latter was the Shanghai secretary. Some networks are based on a common career including an ideological or political adhesion; for example, the Ministry of Finance is said to be more 'pro-statist' while the central bank is said to be more 'free-marketist'.

Religions

Under Mao, Communism had some religious characteristics: the cult of personality, the collective recitation of Mao's mantras summarized in a 'Bible' (the Little Red Book), the omnipresent icons of the Great Helmsman. Due to the spiritual emptiness following Mao's death and Marxism becoming diluted to invasive capitalism, China is experiencing a resurgence of religious sentiment. In new religious practice, it is somewhat difficult to distinguish between what is inherited from ancestral civilization and what has been borrowed from the secular religions of our time. In China, the religious trend is even harder to identify, as it is mixed up with other political, economic, social and ethnic parameters.

In China, there are three traditional religions: Confucianism, Taoism and Buddhism (an imported religion from India, where it has almost disappeared) there is also a fourth religion which is the least-visible as well as the most widely practised – the so-called 'temple' religion. This is a popular local religion which pays tribute to and celebrates rites of ancestors and local deities. Add to these the foreign religions of Islam and Christianity, which is split between Protestantism and Catholicism. If our understanding of 'religion' involves adhesion to a set of common beliefs in common scriptures (the Gospels) and the joining of an organized movement (the Church) split between clerics and laymen (such as defined by Emile Durkheim)[4], we can hardly speak of a Chinese 'religion' without God, Pope, Church or scriptures, which sound more like a wisdom than a faith.

In China, there has never been such a thing as Western 'wars of religion' or Muslim *'jihad'*. Even though the Court may be infatuated by this or that religion (Buddhism in the sixth century, Neo-Confucianism in the tenth century), there has been no official faith other than Neo-Confucianism from the Song dynasty onwards. The Confucian religion acted as the cement of the Heavenly bureaucracy and ideological framework of imperial China. But, rather, the Confucian 'religion' is more a way of life, a common education of the elite, a code of conduct which teaches how to proceed in social circumstances, how to know one's place in the social hierarchy and bureaucratic society, how to cope with unexpected events or encounters.

Under the Empire, there were two kinds of religion, the 'temple religion' and the 'learned religion', the popular and cultivated one (Confucianism, Taoism and Buddhism), which was the vehicle of written education and culture. Young pupils learned to read and write by studying the Four Great Classics (Confucius *Analects*, the Book of Rites, the Odes, and the Book of Mutations). Writing was a means of education, culture, social standing and, eventually, a means of power. In the late nineteenth and the early twentieth centuries, Chinese reformists thought traditional Chinese religion (i.e. Confucianism) was an obstacle to the country's modernization and an instrument of power at the disposal of the foreign (manchu) ruling dynasty (Qing). As such, it has to be broken down. 'Temple money must be allocated to schools'. Reformists were considering a religious system based on the split between state and religion, similar to the 1905 French religious law passed shortly before the Chinese Empire collapsed (1911) and the Chinese Republic was born (1912). Both Sun Yansen and his successor, Chang Kaicheck, were converted to Protestantism, which was meant to be more 'modern'. In contrast, Chinese patriots supported 'national' religions such as Confucianism. As a religion rooted in China's history and tradition, it deals with the personal (virtue), family (cult of the ancestors) and the national (ideology of the bureaucracy) way of life. Foreign religions such as Catholicism were associated with 'imperialism' and 'unequal treaties'. When Chang Kaicheck took over power, he ordered religions (both foreign and Chinese) to better organize themselves and to apply for official recognition. Unofficial religions were sought out and shutdown.

Taking over the legacy of the 'modernists', China's Communist Party is opposed to any sort of religion on the ground of materialism (Marx), modernity (anti-Confucius) and nationalism (anti-foreign religions). In 1949, the CCP expelled foreign ministers and missionaries The CCP resumed the Kuomintang policy – religion must be organized in association duly authorized by the government. After Mao's death (1976), following the start of the reform and opening-up policy, the Party returned to this traditional policy. Following 'Document 19' (1983), which recalled the freedom of faith, 1985 legislation allowed religions to return provided that they were organized, registered and authorized. Four religions are thus authorized: Buddhism, Taoism, Christianity and Islam. Some religions which are not authorized are registered under the umbrella of charitable organizations. Several specialized offices are created: the Department of United Front in the Party, State Bureau of Religious Affairs in the Ministry of Civilian Affairs. Following the Falung Gong events (1999), regulation was tightened but the overall legal framework remained the same. The CCP is even more tolerant than the Kuomintang. The religious field is split between religions that are authorized, or prohibited, or not authorized but tolerated.

Though Buddhism is originally a foreign religion (Northern India), it is the most suited to coexistence with a Communist government. Its members are scattered, each monastery is independent, the faith is tolerant and the Buddhist faithful are active members of charitable associations which took the place of the social benefits cancelled by the state-owned companies. Thus, Buddhism loosely organized within an association was the first religion to be authorized. Moreover, the CCP soon understood that Chinese Buddhism could be a very strong marketing instrument, a soft power backed by many overseas associations. Religious tourism (pilgrimages) is fast growing in such temples as Shaolin (Hainan) – well-known by movie-lovers, Bailin (Hubei) and Famen (Shaanxi). An international conference (Buddhism Forum) was successfully organized in 2007 and 2009. Local 'temple' cults are too scattered to pose any real threat. In addition, they are often sponsored and funded by powerful local officials or businessmen who participate in informal religious activities (cult of the ancestors) behind the screen of a charitable organization devoted to funding schools, medical centres and bachelorship for migrants living in the towns.

Christian churches (50 to 100 million) raise a different problem. Protestantism is more flexible and better-suited to cope with this situation. Each church is independent. There is no common doctrine, no Pope and no discipline. Evangelist churches are said to be making huge progress. In contrast, Catholicism is viewed with suspicion as it reports to a foreign power, the Vatican. Catholics must join an official Party affiliated association, duly registered and authorized.

Confucianism is not supposed to be a 'religion' and therefore is not formally registered or authorized. After Mao ranked Confucianism amongst the old-fashioned and out-of-date entities hindering and crippling China's modernization, CCP leaders put forward the idea that not only was Confucianism compatible with socialism, but it could also aid its cause. For example, Confucianism was used in the anti-corruption campaign. Confucius' temple in his birth place (Shantong) has been restored. Confucian virtues (honesty, loyalty to the existing government and humanity in public service) – as opposed to the Western 'materialism' of democracies – are very much praised by Asian 'Confucian' regimes (Taiwan, Singapore and Shinto in Japan).

The Chinese associate materialism with the Confucian, Hegelian and Marxist versions. The very idea that the world has been created out of nothing by an all-powerful supernatural power (materialized by a tall, white, heavily bearded man with a Greek profile) is incompatible with Chinese materialism, which is based on the idea of the world's endless continuity with no beginning and no end (similar to the ideas of eighteenth-century French materialists such as Helvetius and Holbach). Traditional Chinese thought ignores the debate on intellect versus sensitive, spiritual versus worldly feelings. There is a Chinese 'spirit' (physically located in the heart, rather than in the brain) but there is no 'soul' in the Western sense.

The middle class

The notion of a 'middle class' is unknown in Marxist doctrine, which understands only 'workers' and 'peasants' as members of the proletariat, plus an ill-defined layer of 'intellectuals' or 'intellectual workers' or 'white-hand' workers. Intellectuals may be influential and should be taken up somewhere in the proletarian army against capitalism. From an historical viewpoint, the lack of a 'middle class' is undoubtedly one of the major weaknesses of Marxist doctrine. Based on the working conditions of his time, Marx could not forecast the emergence of a pivotal 'middle class' and insert this new class into his analysis grid. However, China's CCP has recognized this new social layer by granting them access to the Party, along with the other 'Marxist' classes, in the name of Jiang Zemin's 'Theory of Three Legitimacies'.

The middle class regroups consumers who have overtaken bread-winning level. These are people who can afford to save, to allocate some of their income to mass consumption (housing, cars, electrical appliances). The middle class still accounts for a very marginal population share (20–25 per cent – i.e. 200 to 300 million), but the 'marginal' share is growing fast (the car market is growing by an average 20 per cent per year though it slowed down to 7 per cent in 2014). However the estimates range from 100 million to 400 million. According to a consultant firm,[5] 20 per cent of the urban population has joined the middle class (i.e. 110 million). The same enquiry in 2011 came to the conclusion that 23 per cent of urban households supposedly belonged to the 'middle classes' (i.e. 300 million) due to the growth of urban population and purchasing power. McKinsey estimates (2011) are very close to the above: 29 per cent of urban households (i.e. 190 million in 2011, and 75 per cent in 2025 – 372 million). In the coming years, the growth of medium-sized towns (under 1 million) could be higher than that of the large metropolis. (See also Tables 9.1 and 9.2.)

Table 9.1 Consumer expenditures per household (PPP US$ per head), 2009

USA	32,577
China	2,199
India	1,610

Source: World Bank.

Table 9.2 Number of households per income layers (m)

	2010	2020
Wealthy	1	12
Upper-middle class	48	234
Lower-middle class	61	66
Poor	93	62

Source: Boston Consulting Group.

The Chinese middle class has failed to fulfil its historical function. According to Western historical 'logic', capitalism should lead to democracy and vice versa. But the Chinese middle class is too fragmented and too diversified to form a 'class' of its own, not to say a 'revolutionary' class. Tied to government, the new bourgeoisie is not going to take the lead of the *Grand Soir*. Most middle-class members are faithful supporters of the Party. As in China's demographic pyramid, the Chinese middle class is too wide at the top and too thin at the bottom. The CCP has long been open to the most dynamic of company managers. As far as middle-rank managers and government officials are concerned, they enjoy the lifelong employment together with the benefits of stability and prosperity guaranteed by the Communist regime. The political market and the economic market are too tightly intertwined. Most new post-graduates choose to join government offices in order to join or gather a social network before they move to the private sector to reap the benefits of their newly formed '*guanxi*'.

Business people

For a long time, the CCP has opened itself to business people in order to better represent an increasingly diversified Chinese population. A number of company heads – both government and private – are members of legislative organs; the National People's Congress (NPC) which is in charge of approving the bills initiated by the Party; the Political Consultative Conference of Chinese People (PCC) which is often, and incorrectly, called the 'Senate' by Western media. It is a mere consultative body. Originally, the PCC comprised the three basic social and political categories: 'workers, peasants and soldiers'. Today, the PCC includes movie stars, businessmen, senior civil servants, billionaires and the chairmen of state-owned companies. Furthermore, annual meetings of the 2,200 PCC members provide the opportunity to exchange business cards and make new relationships. This is the same with the 2,987 NPC members. The Hurun Global Rich List's annual report (usually called the 'Hurun List') listed 83 billionaires (in dollar terms) in Chinese assemblies: 31 in the NPC and 52 in the PCC. In the USA there are no billionaire members of congress. The richest man in Congress is a Republican from Texas (with 'only' US$500 million). In China, the 83 richest members of the NPC and PCC have an average wealth amounting to US$3.35 billion; the 83 richest members of the US Congress have an average wealth of US$56.4 million.

Given the close relationships between business and government, businessmen and senior civil servants are not going to spark a revolution, but they form a 'lobby', an influential group of technocrats. This 'class' or 'caste' of people who are deeply involved in the decision making process, is much more homogenous than the middle class. Of course, one must distinguish between self-made men and company heads heavily dependent on government officials, and managers of state-owned companies who belong to power circles. In a country where there is no separation between the Party and the civil service, between policy and business, where company managers, senior civil servants and politicians follow the same cursus, and share the same interests and way of life, there is a continuous exchange of men and ideas.

In view of such a close relationship between the political and business elite, it is hard to assess a businessmen's actual power. However, they can be seen during important debates within the Party about critical issues. At a more operational level, their common influence is noticeable in the implementation stage of government decisions. This is the reason why the Party often uses the 'announcement effect' to test the *nomenklatura* feeling about a yet-to-be made decision. In this regard, 'reform' is a source of misunderstanding. What is the common ground between the company head who is attempting to improve his company's competitiveness, and the intellectual who seeks further democracy? 'Reformism' should be interpreted as a very pragmatic behaviour which seeks to improve the existing system, rather than a claim for a free market and a multiparty system.

Intellectuals

In China, the relationship between power and intellectuals has always been one of mutual fascination and distrust. For Confucian intellectuals, educated people were by nature the Prince's advisors, but they neglected their historical duty if they omitted to warn the Emperor that he was on his way to losing his 'Heavenly Mandate'. For the Legalist-minded politicians, Intellectuals are useless people who are all talk – in other words, a source of trouble. Shi Huangdi burned books (except professional textbooks) and buried the literati alive.

The CCP is a 'Marxist' party. Its political doctrine has a scientific background. As with Roman Emperors (following Caesar's 'Gallic Wars'), the prominent figures of the Marxist movement (including the least-educated amongst them, as were Stalin or Ceausescu) have always attempted to make some sort of contribution to Marxist thought; the traditional motto according to which 'knowledge and action are one and the same' (Wang Yangmin, 1472–1529) may be the best Chinese translation of the Marxist notion of 'praxis'. Though they are usually strongly divergent from each other, intellectuals can be a powerful weathervane of public opinion, provided they are kept under tight control. In China, the 'Mandarin' tradition has never disappeared. The relationship between the Party and the intellectuals has been a source of misunderstanding, a long story of support and exorcism, cooperation and condemnation. Under Mao (who considered himself a great thinker), intellectuals were perceived to be the same as the bourgeoisie sold out to the imperialists. They had to be 'eliminated' or 're-educated'. The 'Hundred Flowers' policy (1957) gave Mao an opportunity to get rid of the most prominent intellectuals. The Cultural Revolution (1966–76) was the apex of this policy. When Deng Xiaoping returned from exile to take back power, he needed the backing of reformists and intellectuals. Many of them thought that their time had eventually come. But the Tien An Men massacre (4 June 1989) and the following reaction put an end to this rapprochement.

In February 2008, shortly after the 17th Party Congress which renewed the ruling team (Hu Jintao/Wen Jiabao), a think-tank of the Party School published a document entitled 'Sweep up the Fortress: research on the reform of China's political system following the 17th Party Congress'. To start with, the authors of the document protected themselves by stating that the aim of political reform should not be 'a system of general elections or a Western type multi-party system'. They put forward a set of proposed reforms aimed at 'building a modern civil society' and setting the political system in accordance with an advanced and modern economy – but to no avail.

Dissidents are hunted down by the Party-State because they refuse either to challenge the Party-State from the inside without any reasonable expectations, or to challenge from the outside with subsequent marginalization (not to mention the significant personal risks endured: preventive imprisonment, recurrent trials and condemnations, family harassment, re-education camps, and so on). Western media may be misleading: dissidents are isolated, marginalized, discredited, inaudible. The Chinese media do not report dissident comments but, rather, criticize and condemn them. 'What is the most frightening is not to be silenced or sentenced to jail, but to feel powerless and uncertain about the future. There is no procedure, no standard and no explanation of any sort.'[6]

The Internet

It is widely agreed that the Internet is a new space of freedom, beyond the reach of the government, a sort of bloodless revolution without demonstrations and conflicts. But, ultimately, the Internet is more helpful to the government than harmful. The Internet is one of the most sensitive meeting points between the Party and the People. As Internet users have the freedom to express themselves, the Internet is a major source of information and also one of the most accurate. The network provides information in both ways. On the one hand, the Party can learn a great deal about public opinion, as well as corrupt Party officials reported by the Web. On the other hand, it could be used by the Party to dispatch information of its own. Thousands of people are said to be issuing messages in favour of the Party (the 'one Yuan' message students who are thus making some extra income). 'Patriotic' games take the place of 'foreign' games (South Korean), historical sagas where heroic Chinese soldiers fight hordes of Barbarous soldiers (i.e. Japanese and imperialist troops).

In the early days of the Internet in China (2006), this new means of communication led to the gathering of virtual communities who could communicate freely. Through the web, millenary sects have prospered – such as Falung Gong and Zhong Gong. Since then, the Party has greatly improved its controlling machinery. Any suspect word or character belonging to a pre-established list is automatically deleted and the site blocked.

Initially the Party-State authorized more advanced foreign Internet firms to penetrate the 560 million strong (2013) market (that is more than in the US market) through joint ventures with local Chinese partners. Western companies preferred to put together a joint venture with a local company which tried to replicate their techniques, rather than compete with them. Once technology and marketing techniques had been digested, foreign companies (Google, YouTube, Facebook, Twitter and Golden Shields) were forced to give up, under whatever pretext, after a well-designed and well-managed Party-sponsored public opinion campaign. Google moved to Hong Kong. YouTube sold out its share to its Chinese partner. Thenceforth, the Party has dealt with more accommodating, 100 per cent Chinese companies: Alibaba (onsite sales formerly associated with Google) which control Taobao (onsite payment), Baidu (a search engine), Tencent (a gateway access to Internet services), Renren (Facebook's Chinese clone), Sina (online media) which owns Weibo (Twitter's clone). In every media-related company, a Party cell makes sure that company managers are appointed in accordance with Party wishes, that the company is complying with Party directives and that top positions are assigned to the Party faithful. Once a year, a forum of media managers is summoned by the Party to pass on Party instructions and directives. Hackers penetrate individual sites to resell names, addresses and information to the authorities. Since 2013, it has been forbidden to open an account under a false name or a pseudonym.

In order to control the flow of messages and identify undesirable bloggers, the Party has set in place a huge department which comprises over 100,000 people, of whom 20,000 are fully devoted to Internet oversight. Within the company organization chart, teams of controllers are established to check up and screen any suspect information. According to a Harvard team of students which followed the Chinese web for over two years (2011–12), Chinese censors usually let harmless critical comments go but block any message which may trigger collective action as a threat to the Party. Based in Beijing, the Administrative Bureau of Internet Information dispatches the listing of forbidden words and site addresses to the companies.

Protests are initiated either by professional claims (landless peasants, jobless graduates and official corruption), or from marginalized intellectuals who have a very limited number of followers and bear a bad public image because they threaten law and order. Dissident daily life demands very strong characters. Due to the lack of organization, programmes and leaders, differential claims cannot be raised at a political level. According to its context, the Party may repress an item or withdraw it (for a brief while), but in all cases the Party is the winner. From the beginning of CCP rule, the government has steadily and consistently widened its controlling grip, which is ever-more sophisticated and in line with an ever-moving social and technological environment.

Conclusion

Chacun appelle barbare ce qui n'est pas de son usage.
[One calls barbarous what is not in accordance with his custom]
(Montaigne)

Following the Treaty of Tordesillas (1494), Spain and Portugal divided the world between them along a North–South meridian, 370 leagues (925 miles) west of the Cape Verde Islands (46° 37′ W). All that fell to the west of this meridian was allocated to Spain; to the east, to Portugal. The western route to the mythical lands of Cathay (China) was only for the use of Spain, the Portuguese had to take the eastern route. Once they made it to the Malacca Straits, the Portuguese Crown equipped several fleets with the aim of invading China. China would be to Portugal what America was to Spain: a new worldwide empire. All attempts to land failed. Following the last, in Canton, all crewmen including the ship's chaplain were executed. As opposed to America, China was a united country, ruled by a competent bureaucracy, protected by professional armies and local militias.

On numerous occasions, China has been invaded but she has never been colonized. Whenever China was invaded by a Barbarous tribe, sooner or later the Barbarians became sinicized – more Chinese than the Chinese themselves. Accordingly, China has not inherited a given model (as is the case with India) from a colonizing country, Western or otherwise. In the aftermath of decolonization, such a legacy may have been an advantage (though arguable) but, today, it would surely be seen as a hindrance. China may not (yet) be an authoritarian country, but she is no longer a fully fledged totalitarian one. Similarly, China may not (yet) be a market economy, but she is no longer a command economy. According to our Western understanding, she is somewhere in between. Neither is China a capitalist state, even though this is probably the closest definition. There is a certain amount of freedom in China – including a limited and revocable property right; a limited arena of 'private' companies and free enterprises; and some civil rights are tolerated but they can always be revoked at any time, without notice or explanation. It is natural for Westerners to analyse China through Western eyes, to bring China back into a Eurocentric history. But China remained closed to Western standards and influence until the late nineteenth century, thus nullifying any attempt to reason her history according to Western historical standards. To make matters worse, today, Western models are restructuring; thus, they are subsequently useless to an emerging country. After the fall of the Roman Empire (456), Europe burst out into a myriad of barbaric countries which fought against each other for centuries. As Europe touched the bottom (the dismantling of the Roman Empire), China's civilization reached its climax (Tang dynasty, 618–902). Equipped with one common language (Latin) and the remains of a common culture (Greco-Roman), European intellectuals got through the darkness of the Middle-Ages. In the meantime, China had created one the most refined civilizations in human history. While illiterate Frankish Carolingian Emperors were dictating their edicts to a monk, the Song Emperor Huizong was writing sophisticated and moving poems which are still learned in Chinese schools today. Thanks to this isolation, China had the privilege of twenty centuries during which to consolidate refined cultural and intellectual standards before she was confronted with a rival. As Europe painfully labours away, trying to rebuild united policies, China has returned to the forefront of the world. It is, therefore, natural that the two partners have some difficulty in understanding each other. Given the power of the written word in Chinese culture and 'words' in Communist history (which have killed people more effectively than guns), it would seem reasonable to focus on the 'words' issued from China, what they say and, more importantly, what they hide.

Failing to know what China is, we know what it is not. The Chinese growth model is neither a market economy nor a command economy. The Chinese political model is neither a democracy nor a totalitarian dictatorship. The government will not relinquish economic control. The Party will not give up its monopoly of power. Without property rights, the Rule of Law, non-governmental interference, free prices, China is not a market economy. Without a multi-party system, free elections or the freedom of the press, China is not a democracy. And there is no indication that she is moving in that direction either.

From what we know today, the Chinese development model comprises some form of state capitalism (which was rooted in China centuries ago), a control economy which uses market forces at its margin to improve efficiency, a political system which retains some variety of 'proletarian dictatorship', and a single-party regime including some marginal democratically minded amendments within the Party. In the near future, public opinion may be invited, – to a limited extent, – in tightly controlled channels, in debates on major society issues (the one-child policy, pension scheme). The search for consensus, a unanimous form of democracy and a technocratic government are not incompatible with the single-party system. In spite of its numerous weaknesses, the present Chinese model enjoys a strong legitimacy due to political stability and economic performances. In such a hypothesis, it may be worthwhile reflecting on some sort of technocratic lobby, including senior civil servants or businessmen (both public and private) to work out something similar to the postwar Japanese system.

But is such a development model stable enough to reassure the citizens, and flexible enough to weather inescapable evolution? Either the Party will support the evolution that is yet-to-come, or further developments will be imposed by their own strength 'though iron and blood'. When China was 90 per cent rural, all dynastic changes were due to peasant rebellions (including wandering bandits, deserters, fortune soldiers, unfrocked monks, exiled civil servants and corrupt Mandarins, – such characters as showed in the Chinese classical novel *On the shore* (*Shui hui zhuan*), a picaresque saga by Shi Nai-an (twelfth century) in the style of Sir Walter Scott or Alexandre Dumas. Today, urbanization has turned the revolution on its head. Rapidly expanding cities are not only a strong growth stimulus, but also a source of trouble (migrants). Eventually, the so-called emerging middle class will not be sufficiently consistent to represent a real threat.

China's current mix of Party and Society, State and Market is likely to be the best suited to meet the challenges of our time. Even if the Chinese growth rate may slow further in the coming years, it remains far higher than that of the West, even if the population growth, as expected, slows down and reverses. It fits with the return of the state driven by the global financial crisis. The unusually high US growth rate in late 2013-early 2014 was due to a recovery effect. Even though rapidly growing US productivity continues to expand under the joint impetus of fundamental research and practical innovations, the US market is wholly saturated in comparison with that of China. Imbedded weaknesses which, according to China's leaders, are threatening the Chinese growth model (inflation, inequalities, corruption) are all within government reach. A growth in purchasing power may solve some of these issues unless China squeezes herself into the 'middle income trap', in a 'dual society' model with decreasing growth rate and growing inequalities. In the countryside, poverty and famine have disappeared. Local free enterprise is strongly supported by local authorities and the traditional informal credit system. In the cities, migrants dream about being successful business men and having a middle-class way of life.

Following all imperial dynasties, the red dynasty is the first to have discovered the right solution between centrifugal and centripetal forces (i.e. a centralized single-party network combined with a decentralized state bureaucracy). The unending dialogue between reformists and conservatives may be a source of stimulation similar to that of a two-party system in parliamentary democracies. The government method of trial-and-error, of experiments followed by full implementation, has proved effective. The actual workings of the Communist regime are easier to understand through the prism of *Book of Mutations* (Yi Jing) rather than Marx's *Manifesto*. Last, but not least, the centralized nature of the political system makes China's leaders much more reactive in a fluctuating, unforeseeable context, as shown in the 2008 financial crisis. China was the first to react and the first to recover.

* * *

The Party and Chinese society are facing a triple-edged sword: economic, social and political. The first is difficult to settle but achievable; the second is difficult but achievable under certain conditions; the third is both very difficult and seemingly unattainable in the present situation.

From the economic point of view, running the Chinese economy is like driving a racing car: the speed is such that any minor mistake leads to a catastrophic crash. The Party is now fully conscious of the necessity to move from one growth model to another, from an engine driven by investment and export to an engine driven by domestic demand and, first, the consumption engine. Until now, government investment and local authority expenditures were the strongest management tools. From this point on, the Party must move from investment to demand impulse. The government is barely saving, since its resources are designed to make ends meet. The business investment/savings ratio is almost balanced. The only source of additional purchasing power comes from household consumption expenditure, the only sector where savings grossly outrun investments.

But increasing consumption expenditure is not that easy. So far, government measures in this department (life insurance, pension schemes, minimum wages, and so on) have failed to change the growth model. First, this is because most household savings are made for protecting the family against expected and unexpected hitches: children, school and university, health issues and accidents, housing, old age, and so on. The government undertook the installation of a comprehensive social security system but it will take time until the new system can be operated to its full potential. Second, the growth of consumption expenditures requires a change of mentality, way of life and consumption standards. This is far more difficult. Urbanization has broken down families and traditional solidarity groups. Western companies must change their manufacturing and marketing standards and produce more 'Chinese' goods fitted to 'Chinese' tastes.

From the social perspective, the Party is facing some very difficult issues – such as the demographic policy, the one-child policy, migrants, the *hukou* system, the growing inequalities and widespread corruption. Once again, the Party is fully conscious of the hardship. At first sight it looks easy: what a decree has done, another decree can undo. But, in reality, social issues are affecting deep-rooted political and human feelings. Playing with the 'human factor', as the CCP did like an *apprenti-sorcier* (sorceror's apprentice), has triggered long-term mutations in human and social behaviour. Young couples have internalized the one-child policy. City dwellers are fiercely opposed to a drastic change of the *hukou* system, including former migrants who were lucky enough to obtain free housing and a work permit.

Ultimately, the political situation is frozen under present conditions. It is relatively easy to cancel and repress democratic feelings, but it is difficult to retrieve them. As Tocqueville's quotation states in the Foreword, it is extremely difficult for a highly centralized and undemocratic regime to open its doors – like the closing of the Janus-like 'War Gates' in Pericles' speech at the beginning of Thucydides' *Peloponnesian War*. Some private conversations have made it clear that Chinese leaders are seriously considering how to escape the trap before it is too late. It is obvious that some of the economic and social reforms will not be achievable without the change of the whole system. But how to undertake this, and who is suitable for the job? There are few certainties at the present stage as to whether, first, change – if any – will come from inside the Party and, second, a revolution – if any – will be brought about not by some open-minded, liberal student leaders or brave but isolated opponent artists and dissident lawyers, but, rather, by grey-haired, grey-suited, heavy-rimmed glasses wearing, stern-faced bureaucrats.

From its inception, China's culture and civilization appeared so refined, China's leaders showed such a great deal of flexibility that the Chinese people will find once again the internal strength to face new challenges. So far, the 65-years-young ruling red dynasty is behaving in a very similar way to its predecessors: the Qin, Han, Tang, Sui, Song, Yuan, Ming and Qing dynasties. The worst is never inevitable. 'Now let's talk about the general world situation. What was once divided will certainly, someday find unity again and what has long been united will, inevitably, find itself divided' (Lou Kwantchong, *The Three Kingdoms*).

Notes

Introduction

1. Philip A. Kuhn, *Origins of the Modern Chinese State*, Stanford University Press (2002).

2 The Transition Period

1. PBOC: People's Bank of China (the central bank), CBRC – China Banking Regulatory Commission, CSRC – China Securities Regulatory Commission, CIRC – China Insurance Regulatory Commission, SAFE – State Administration of Foreign Exchange.

3 A Fast but Unbalanced Growth

1. The '72' years law means that doubling the GDP requires 72 years if the growth rate is 1 per cent, 7.2 years if the growth rate is 10 per cent, and 10 years if the growth rate is 7 per cent – as is the case with China.
2. The contract was not successfully completed: the Chinese company disappeared before the work was completed, leaving behind all its equipment. The contract had to be reallocated to a German construction company at a much higher price.

4 An Incomplete Banking and Financial Reform

1. Not to be confused with Bank of China, which is a commercial bank specializing in overseas transactions.
2. Elements of this old practice remain in today's China: most companies use barter transactions or intercompany credits through unofficial networks to obtain raw materials and other commodities on time, in the required quantity and of the required quality.
3. He was appointed in 2002 by Jiang Zemin a few months *before* the new team (led by Hu Jintao) was elected.
4. Financial Leading Group of the Party in charge of 'horizontal' coordination.
5. Industrial & Commercial Bank of China, Bank of China, China Construction Bank, Agricultural Bank of China.
6. Huyjin was later swallowed up by the new sovereign wealth fund China Investment Corpn (CIC) which, in turn, reports straight to the State Council.
7. Hong Kong & Shanghai Banking Corporation is the oldest Western bank and was established in China in 1854). While the registered head office remained in London, the operational head office was repatriated back to Shanghai in 2011.

8. Highly prized by investors, the CDB bond rate became a benchmark for long-term bond issues (ten years).
9. HK Calyon used to be affiliated to the near bankrupt Credit Lyonnais (today, LCL) which was acquired by Crédit Agricole.
10. Everbright acquired United Biscuit (UK) in 2012 as part of its international development programme.
11. Vereenigde Oost-Indische Compagnie, British East India Comapany, Compagnie des Indes Orientales.
12. Lombard Street in London, rue Quincampoix in Paris, Wall Street in New York.
13. Unless Empress Ci Xi used the proceeds to erect a magnificent Summer Palace in northern Beijing.
14. In China, the share of existing capital fund traded (the 'float') does not exceed 5 per cent, as opposed to the Western requirement which demands a minimum 30 per cent.
15. A 'lock out' clause prohibits the resale of stocks within a certain period of time; a 'green shoe' clause authorizes the raising of the volume of securities sold in the event of oversubscription during the subscription period.
16. Convertible bonds are not meant to be a 'derivative' contract, though it is a cover instrument affording protection against adverse trends of interest rates and bankruptcy.
17. A 'leverage' is the ratio between the cash paid (deposit) on the inception of the contract and the overall value of the contract. For instance, if the deposit requirement is 10 per cent and the underlying asset price drops by 3 per cent, the loss is 30 per cent. If the contract traded is a three-month contract, the loss is 120 per cent. If the money used to pay the cash base is borrowed, the profit is the difference between the interest rate paid and the profit from the transaction, but the risk is infinite.
18. A 'float' is the number of shares actually available and traded as a percentage of the overall capital base.
19. Following government instruction, all the listed companies had to merge A and B stocks through a compensation indemnity paid to the holders of B stock.
20. 'Capitalization' is the share price multiplied by the total number of shares *or* the potential overall valuation based on the actual market share price at a given time.
21. QFII: Qualified Foreign Institutional Invests. The total volume was increased in mid-2013 to meet expected capital needs of the large Chinese banks and companies.
22. LGVF: Local Government Financing Vehicles.

5 Investment in Human Capital

1. E. Todd, *L'origine des systèmes familiaux*, Gallimard, 2011.
2. The Chinese media often report the theft of babies to be resold to childless couples.
3. This is the basic theme of the most praised eighteenth-century Chinese novel *The Dream in the Red Pavilion*, which was said to be Mao's favourite.

4. In 2013, film-maker Zhang Zimu (*Spouses and Concubines*) was sued for having seven children from different women. He was charged US$30 million in fines.
5. A woman wishing to have an illegal baby tries to get pregnant during the summertime so that she can wear heavy, army-type coats suitable for the winter, as these hide her pregnancy.
6. This may be a rich field of study for a Western psychoanalyst though: in China, the individual is always submitted to the group (family, State, Party). Oedipus complex, Antigone's dilemma or generation conflict are unthinkable in the Chinese context.
7. However, in 2013 an agreement between life insurance companies allowed employees to keep their accumulated savings when they move from one company to another.
8. Cf. the number of ageing people practising *qigong* (the culture of *qi*: breath) in the Beijing or Shanghai streets. Ancient medicine books such as the *Nei Jing* ascribed to the mythical 'Yellow Emperor' (Huangdi) are older than the Greek Hippocrates and the Roman Gallien. The *Great Treaty of Medical Matters* by Li Shizen (1518–1693), an encyclopedia dealing with a wide range of issues, has been translated the world over.
9. In China, pharmaceutical products are not sold in pharmacies but, instead, in hospitals which gave an opportunity to sue foreign pharmaceutical companies such as Glaxo Smith for corruption.
10. There are 50,000 different characters to be learned, one by one. Classics must be known by heart.
11. Such as the most renowned poet of the Tang dynasty Li Bai.
12. But only one out of three returned to China.

6 The Knowledge Economy

1. *Tian He*: 'Star track' – literally 'Heaven River'.
2. The only 'discoverer' who is honoured, as such, like a 'god' is Cai Lun (at the turn of the first and second centuries), the 'discoverer' of writing paper. But this was more an 'honour' to writing and the literati than a personal honour to the man: 'paper' existed before and continued to improve thereafter.
3. 'The things I have learned, I tied them up through a common principle like a thread.' (Confucius, XV–5).
4. Formerly affiliated to the University of Beijing, BGI sequences half of the world's total sequencing. In partnership with foreign institutions, BGI has already completed the sequencing of 2,000 autistic families. In 2012, BGI acquired the US company Complete Genomics.
5. As a result of accounting regulations, intellectual property enjoys the same status as fixed assets, which means shorter amortization time and full deduction from taxable profit.
6. However, Google has been permitted to relocate to Hong Kong.
7. As Donfeng was taking a dominant position in Peugeot's capital (2014), the Chinese company signed a cooperation agreement with Renault, Peugeot's main competitor.

7 Growing Inequalities

1. This is named after the Italian economist Corrado Gini. The index is based on a level from 0 to 1: should all citizens share the same income, the index would be 0; should one person earn all the income, the index would be 1. In Sweden, the Gini Index is 0.2 while in South Africa, the index is 0.6.
2. China Development Research Foundation (2012).
3. UNDP: United Nations Development Programme (2006).
4. Simon Kuznets, Professor at the Harvard University, a Nobel Prize winner of Russian descent.
5. According to the Heckscher–Ohlin–Samuelson law, a refined version of Ricardo's Law of Comparative Advantage, countries involved in the world market become specialized in the industry where they have the greatest comparative advantage (i.e. in labour-intensive industries, in developing countries). Here, the demand for poorly qualified people is narrowing the gap between high and low salaries. In contrast, in developed countries where the demand for highly qualified workers is strong, the gap between skilled and unskilled workers is widening.
6. Actually, 28.4 per cent in China's case.
7. China Statistical Yearbook (2012).
8. Chinese rivers change their names as they cross from one region to another. The Yellow River is 'yellow' because of the alluvium it carries all along its course.
9. Peking or Beijing (the large northern 'bei' city) and Nanking or Nanjing (the large southern 'nan' city).
10. This is the place where the last Ming Emperor, Si Zong, hung himself in 1644 on a tree branch when riders of General Li Zheng penetrated the Forbidden City through the 'north' gate where the Emperor lived.
11. Actually, the 'Great' Canal is not a canal but a ring of north–south canals connecting China's hydraulic systems running west–east.
12. Japanese and Chinese pirates, not to mention Portuguese, Dutch and English, who soon understood that intercontinental trade (Europe–China) was too risky and turned to the far more profitable interregional trade.
13. Nurhaci (?–1626) is the founding father of the Manchu kingdom of Jürchan, Qing ancestors.
14. In China, the bride is dressed not in white but in red.
15. Deng Xiaoping was of Hakka ascent.
16. Landesa Rural Development Institute.
17. Xiao Lin Guo, 'Land expropriation and rural conflicts in China'.
18. Raoul Jacob, 'Drop in China's land sales poses threat to growth', *Financial Times*, 7 December 2011.
19. In China, the minimum legal wage is established by the province or city.
20. Some of them are living in the former atomic bomb shelter labyrinth erected on Mao's instructions.
21. The Central Bank has carried out 'stress tests' of the commercial banks to check what would happen in the event of a 60 per cent drop in property prices.
22. When young Chinese women students join a Western university classroom, the Professor compares their dress and make-up at the beginning and the end of the school year.

23. 'Free marriage' between two young lovers against their parents' wishes is still a common fictional feature. In today's China, they can flee to the city among migrants but they cannot expect to return to their parents' homes until they have earned enough money to buy or rent private accommodation.

8 A Foreign Policy which Serves Growth (and Vice Versa)

1. It is ironic that, today, the Chinese are suspected of spying on and stealing Western technology.
2. Silkworm cocoons were said to have been taken back to Europe inside the linings of priest cloths.
3. Historians still wonder why Mao involved a ruined and devastated country in a new war of attrition following thirteen years of continuous foreign and civil wars. Today, North Korea is a burden and an unpredictable ally, playing with atomic bombs and long-range missiles. In 2013, during the shelling of South Korean islands, all payments to and from Korea were frozen by China.
4. During the civil war, Deng was the political commissar of the second 'army on the march' headed by Lin Biao.
5. US military doctrine states that the US army should be as large as the total of all other countries to make it possible to intervene in all different areas simultaneously.
6. From 1405 to 1433, Zheng He led several oceanic expeditions which took him as far as the Eastern African coast. Some experts believe that he may have circumnavigated the world a century before Magellan.
7. The threat of this old unarmed submarine is more symbolic than real, since it has been bought from the Ukraine.
8. US secret services managed to identify the source of a cyber attack against US companies to a building in Pudong, a top-secret army zone called 'Unit 61398' sheltering a number of experts using several thousand servers. The Madian Report (2013) numbered hostile system penetration since 2006: 141 companies plus a number of government offices.
9. After the massive bail-out of GM by the federal government, the USA staked a claim against Chinese companies manufacturing auto-part spares.
10. Between 1995 and 2009, the WTO received 400 claims, of which 93 derived from the USA and 107 were lodged against the USA, 81/66 against EU and 6/17 against China (CNUCED 2009.) But, from 2010 onwards, China was the largest target of claims.
11. In 2013, the 'anti-trust' Department of the Ministry of Commerce authorized the US$63 billion acquisition of Xstrata by Glencore (two foreign companies). Glencore is the world's largest raw materials brokerage firm with a 17.8 per cent market share in China. This was done on the condition that the latter commits itself to supply a given volume of copper, which, at first glance has nothing to do with 'anti-trust' violation.
12. To keep foreign companies away from a public auction, the auction is brought forward at the last minute so that only the Chinese company can attend.
13. Japan and Korea are following the same policy of buying huge estates of foreign lands.
14. After the name given to a local food recipe by foreigners.

15. China Banking Regulatory Commission, China Securities Regulatory Commission.
16. In light of disappointing returns over the last couple of years, Norway's Government Pension Fund – which is subject to liquidity and ethical standards – has formed an affiliated investment company aimed at increasing the return of the overall sovereign fund while isolating more risky ventures which demand different management techniques, standards and supervision.
17. Only a small portion of the resources are invested, the rest being kept in low-interest monetary and bond investments to make funds available in the event of investment opportunities.
18. Very conveniently, Chang Mai is a sleepy resort at the meeting point of China, Thailand, Burma, Laos borders.
19. According to Chinese textbooks, the 35 million who died during the 1960 Great Leap Forward were killed due to climatic conditions. The Cultural Revolution was due to a handful of factionists who misled Mao. Everything before 1949 is said to have been 'feudal' even though, technically speaking, feudalism has never developed in a highly centralized Empire such as China.
20. As early as the late seventeenth century, Leibnitz expected Chinese to become the universal language. He was deeply impressed by the specificities of Mandarin, a language based on ideograms and alphabetical signs understandable to everybody no matter their native tongue.

9 In Search of Civil Society

1. Larry Diamond.
2. Known in the West as *The Government Inspector.*
3. Statement of a member of the Party Discipline Commission quoted by the weekly *China News Week.*
4. *Les Formes élémentaires de la vie religieuse* (1912).
5. Dragonomics (2006).
6. Murong Xuecun, a Chinese writer, in an interview in *The Guardian* of May 2013.

Bibliography

Acemoglu, Daron and Robinson, James A. (2012) *Why Nations Fail: The Origins of Power, Prosperity and Poverty*, Crown.

Arrighi, Giovanni (2007) *Adam Smith in Beijing, Lineages of the Twenty-First Century*, Verso.

Baumol, William, Lidan, Robert L. and Shramm, Carl J. (2007) *Good Capitalism, Bad Capitalism, and Economic of Growth and Prosperity*, Yale University Press.

Brandt, Loren and Rawski, Thomas (eds) (2008) *China's Great Transformation*, Cambridge University Press.

Barth, R. James, Tatom, John A., Yago, Gleenn (eds), (2009) *China's Emerging Financial Markets, Challenges and Opportunities*, Springer, Milken Institute Series on Financial Innovations and Economic Growth.

Chow, C. Gregory (2007) *China's Economic Transformation*, Blackwell Publishing.

Cipolla, C.M. (1969) *Literacy and Development in the West*, Pelican.

Clegg, Jenny (2009) *China's Global Strategy, Toward a Multipolar World*, Pluto Press.

Cousin, Violaine (2007) *Banking in China*, Palgrave Macmillan.

Damm, Jens and Thomas, Simona (eds) (2010) *Chinese Cyberspaces*, Routledge.

Elvin, Mark (1973) *The Pattern of the Chinese Past*, Stanford University Press.

Economist, The (2013) 'A Giant Cage, China and the Internet', 6 April.

Fairbank, John K. and Goldman, Merle (2006) *China: A New History*, Harvard College.

Fewsmith, Joseph (ed.) (2010) *China Today, China Tomorrow: Domestic Politics, Economy and Society*, Rowman & Littlefield.

Fraser, J.T. (dir.) (1986) *Time, Science and Society in China and the West*, Amherst, University of Massachusetts Press.

Gang Yi (1994) *Money, Banking and Financial Markets in China*, Westview Press.

Gao, Jian, (2007) *Debt Capital Markets in China*.

Goossaert, Vincent, and Palmer, David A., (2011) *The Religious Question in Modern China*, University of Chicago Press.

Gries, Peter Hays and ROSEN, Stanley (eds) (2010) *State and Society in 21st Century China*, Routledge.

Gu, George Zhibin, (2006a) *China's Global Reach: Markets, Multinationals and Globalization*, Fultus Books.

Gu, George Zhibin (2006b) *China and the New World Order: How Entrepreneurship, Globalization and Borderless Business are Reshaping China and the World*, Fultus Books.

Guo, Yong (2002) *Banking Reforms and Monetary Policy in the People's Republic of China: Is the Chinese Central Banking System Ready for Joining the WTO?*, Palgrave Macmillan.

Halper, Stefan (2010) *The Beijing Concensus: How China's Authoritarian Model Will Dominate the Twenty-First Century*, Basic Books.

Huang, Yasheng (2008) *Capitalism with Chinese Characteristics: Entrepreneurship and the State*, Cambridge University Press.

IMF Working Papers:
Aziz, Jahangir and Duenwald, Christoph (2002) *Growth–Financial Intermediation Nexus in China.*
Dunaway, Steven and Xiang Ming li (2005) *Estimating China's 'Equilibrium' Real Exchange Rate.*
Sector-Level Productivity, Structural Change, and Rebalancing in China, Nabar, Malhar and Kai Yan (2013) WP/13/240.
Tao Wang (2004) *China: Sources of Real Exchange Rate Fluctuations.*
Yingqiu Lua and Tao Sun (2013) *Local Government Financing Platforms in China: A Fortune or a Misfortune?*, WP/13/243.
Zhongn Xia jin (2003) *The Dynamics of Real Interest Rates, Real Exchange Rates and the Balance of Payments in China.*
Islam, Nazrul (2009) *Resurgent China: Issues for the Future*, Palgrave Macmillan.
Jacques, Martin (2009 [1978]) *When China Rules The World: The End of The Western World and The Birth of A New Global Order*, Penguin Press [Paris, Collège de France, IHEC].
Jenner, W.J.F. (1992) *The Tyranny of History: The Roots of China's Crisis*, Allen Lane.
Kang, David C. (2007) *China Rising: Peace, Power and Order in East Asia*, Columbia University Press.
Kroeber, Arthur (2011) *China's Next Decade*, Gravekal Dragonomics Research.
Kuznets, S. (1966) *Modern Economic Growth*, Yale.
Kuznets, S. (1971) *Economic Growth of Nations*, Yale.
Kuznets, S. (1979) *Growth Population and Income Distribution*, Norton.
Lardy, Nicholas (2012) Sustaining *China's Economic Growth After the Global Financial Crisis*, Peterson Institute for International Economics.
Li, Jianjun, HSU, Sara (2009) *Informal Finance in China*, Oxford University Press.
Li, Minqui (2008) *The Rise of China and the Demise of the Capitalist World Economy*, Pluto Press.
McKinnon, Ronald (1993) *The Order of Economic Liberalization: Financial Control in the Transition to a Market Economy*, Johns Hopkins University Press.
Maddison, A. (2007a) *Contours of the World Economy, 1–2030*, Oxford University Press.
Maddison, A. (2007b) *Chinese Economic Performance in the Long Run*, OECD.
Min, Zhu, Jinqing, Cai, Avery, Martha (eds) (2009) *China's Emerging Financial Markets, Challenges and Global Impact*, John Wiley & Sons.
Moore, Thomas G. (2002) *China in the World Market: Chinese Industry and International Sources of Reform in the Post Mao Era*, Cambridge University Press.
Morris, Ian (2010) *Why The West Rules – For Now, The Patterns of History, and What They Reveal About the Future*, Farrar, Strauss & Giroux.
National Bureau of Statistics of China (2014) *China Statistical Yearbook.*
Naughton, Barry (2007) *The Chinese Economy, Transitions and Growth*, MIT Press.
Needham, Joseph (1978) *The Shorter Science and Civilisation in China*, Cambridge University Press.
Nefti, Salih N. and Yuan Menager-Xu, Michelle (2007) *China's Financial Markets, An Insider Guide to How the Markets Work*, Elsevier Inc.
Ocampo, José Antonio and Stiglitz, Joseph E. (eds) (2008) *Capital Market Liberalization and Development*, Oxford University Press.
OECD
(2003) *China in the World Economy.*
(2004) *Rural Finance and Credit Infrastructure in China.*

(2005) *Governance in China.*
(2007) *Chinese Economic Performance in the Long Run*, Angus Maddison.
(2013) *OECD Economic Survey, China.*
Peebles, Gavin (1991) *Money in the People's Republic of China*, Allen & Unwin.
Pei, Minxi (2006) *China's Trapped Transition, The Limits of Developmental Autocracy*, Harvard University Press.
Perry, Elisabeth J., & SELDEN, Mark (eds) (2010) *Chinese Society Change, Conflict and Resistance*, Routledge.
Pettis, Michael (2013) *Avoiding the Fall China's Economic Restructuring*, Carnegie Endowment for International Peace.
Pommeranz, Kenneth (2000) *The Great Divergence*, Princeton University Press.
Prem Shankar Jha (2009) *Managed Chaos: The Fragility of the Chinese Miracle*, Observer Research Foundation.
Purcell, V. (1965) *The Chinese in Southeast Asia*, Oxford University Press.
Pye, Lucian (1988) *The Mandarin and the Cadre: China Political Cultures*, Center of Asian Studies of the University of Michigan.
Ramo, Joshua Cooper (2004) *The Beijing Consensus*, London, Foreign Center.
Riedel, James, Jin, Jing, Gao, Jian (2007) *How China Grows, Investment, Finance and Reform*, Princeton University Press.
Rogoff, K. S. (2004) *Evolution and Performance of Exchange Rate Regime*, FMI.
Shambaugh, David (2000) *The Modern Chinese State*, Cambridge University Press.
Shambaugh, David (2008) *China's Communist Party: Atrophy and Adaptation*, Oxford University Press.
Shambaugh, David (2011) *Charting China's Future: Domestic and International Challenges*, Routledge.
Shambaugh, David (2013) *China Goes Global: The Partial Power*, Oxford University Press.
Shen, Simon and Blanchard, Jean-Marc (2010) (eds), *Multidimensional Diplomacy of Contemporary China*, Rowman & Littlefield.
Shi, Victor C. (2008) *Factions and Finance in China: Elite Conflict and Inflation*, Cambridge University Press.
Tsai, Kellee S. (2007) *Capitalism without Democracy: The Private Sector in Contemporary China*, Cornell University Press.
Tse, Edward (2010) *China Strategy*, Basic Books.
Walter, Carl E., Fraser, G. and Howie, J.T. (2003) *Privatizing China, The Stock Markets and Their Role in Corporate Reform*, John Wiley & Sons.
Walter, Carl E., Howie and Fraser J.T. (2011) *Red Capitalism, The Fragile Financial Foundation of China's Extraordinary Rise*, John Wiley & Sons.
Wang, Yue and Ramburuth, Prem, (eds) (2010) *Thirty Years of China's Economic Reform, Institutions, Management Organisations and Foreign Investment*, Nova Science.
Wang Hui (2009) *The End of the Revolution: China and the Limits of Modernity*, Verso.
Wedeman, Andrew (2012) *Double Paradox: Rapid Growth and Rising Corruption in China*, Cornell University Press.
Willis, John E. (2010) *Past and Present in China's Foreign Policy: From 'Tribute System' to 'Peaceful Rise'*, MerwinAsia.
Wright, Teresa (2010) *Accepting Authoritarianism, State–Society Relations in China's Reform Era*, Stanford University Press.
Wu, Fulong (2006) *Globalization and the Chinese City*, Routledge.

Wu, Jinglian (2005) *Understanding and Interpreting Chinese Economic Reform*, Thomson.
Yang, Dali (2004) *Remaking the Chinese Leviathan: Market Transition and the Politics of Governance in China*, Stanford University Press.
Yang, Li and Kuhn, Robert Lawrence (2007) *China's Banking and Financial Markets: The Internal Research Report of the Chinese Government*, John Wiley & Sons.
Yusuf, Sharif, Nabeshima, Kaoru and Perkins, Dwight H. (2006) *Under New Ownership: Privatizing China's State-Owned Enterprises*, World Bank, Stanford University Press.
Zhang, Peter G. (2011) *The Chinese Yuan: Internationalization & Financial Products in China*, KPMG/ Wiley.
Zheng, Shiping (1997) *Party vs. State in Post-1949 China: The Institutional Dilemma*, Cambridge University Press.
Zheng, Yongnian, and Tong, Sarah Y. (2010) *China and the Global Economic Crisis*.

Index

GPSR Compliance
The European Union's (EU) General Product Safety Regulation (GPSR) is a set of rules that requires consumer products to be safe and our obligations to ensure this.

If you have any concerns about our products, you can contact us on

ProductSafety@springernature.com

In case Publisher is established outside the EU, the EU authorized representative is:

Springer Nature Customer Service Center GmbH
Europaplatz 3
69115 Heidelberg, Germany

www.ingramcontent.com/pod-product-compliance
Ingram Content Group UK Ltd.
Pitfield, Milton Keynes, MK11 3LW, UK
UKHW041906040925
462611UK00003B/129
* 9 7 8 1 3 4 9 4 9 9 5 5 7 *